T0339864

# Partners in Gatekeeping

# Partners in Gatekeeping

HOW ITALY SHAPED U.S. IMMIGRATION POLICY
OVER TEN PIVOTAL YEARS, 1891–1901

**Lauren Braun-Strumfels**

The University of Georgia Press

ATHENS

Published by the University of Georgia Press
Athens, Georgia 30602
www.ugapress.org
© 2023 by Lauren Braun-Strumfels
All rights reserved
Set in 10.25/13.5 Minion Pro by Kaelin Chappell Broaddus

Most University of Georgia Press titles are
available from popular e-book vendors.

Printed digitally

Library of Congress Cataloging-in-Publication Data

Names: Braun-Strumfels, Lauren, 1979– author.
Title: Partners in gatekeeping : how Italy shaped U.S. immigration
    policy over ten pivotal years, 1891–1901 / Lauren Braun-Strumfels.
Description: Athens : The University of Georgia Press, 2023. | Series:
    Politics and culture in the twentieth-century South | Includes
    bibliographical references and index.
Identifiers: LCCN 2023006017 | ISBN 9780820365411 (hardback) |
    ISBN 9780820365404 (paperback) | ISBN 9780820365428 (epub) |
    ISBN 9780820365435 (pdf)
Subjects: LCSH: United States—Emigration and immigration—
    Government policy—History. | Italy—Emigration and
    immigration—Government policy—History. | Office of Labor
    Information and Protection for Italians—History. | Sunnyside
    Plantation (Ark.)—History. | Italians—United States—History. |
    Italians—Southern States—History.
Classification: LCC JV6483 .B698 2023 | DDC 325.73—dc23/
    eng/20230315
LC record available at https://lccn.loc.gov/2023006017

For Dahlia and Fielding,
who will probably remember the gelato best

# CONTENTS

# PREFACE

The research for what would become this book first began in September 2004, over a series of gloriously sunny days that, like many stories of life in Rome, included getting lost and eating gelato. For several days I wandered fruitlessly searching for the location of the Archivio Storico Diplomatico dell'Ministero degli Affari Esteri (ASDMAE), tempering my frustration with afternoon stops for *zabaglione* gelato. After one morning spent at the American embassy to obtain an official letter, and followed by several phone calls that yielded no useful information, one in-person exchange with a carabiniere officer somewhere in the *centro storico*, and a lengthy report of the results of his phone call, I took a very long bus ride to the other side of the Tiber River to wander around the streets bordering the Fascist-era Olympic stadium. The officer had promised the ministry archive building was there, but I saw no sign of it. I stopped to ask the lone pedestrian out that day, an older man on his morning *passeggiata*, for directions. He offered to show me to the door and asked if he could give me a kiss. After refusing both offers I finally managed to find the side entrance to the Ministry of Foreign Affairs hidden behind a line of parked cars and eventually made my way to the historical archives held inside. Over the next nineteen years I would return again—now with much more confidence about the location—in 2005–6, 2014, 2018, and 2022. Set in an unassuming corner of the busy ministry building, the ASDMAE holds the records of Italian diplomatic activity from its posts all over the world. The associated library collects and maintains historical and contemporary publications of interest to diplomats and officials in the Italian government who continue to make and carry out foreign policy.

Even after you find the entrance, working at the ASDMAE can be challenging to Anglophone scholars, which has kept the riches of this archive too well hidden. The cataloging system in the ASDMAE's Ambasciata Washington collection is consistent with the way a busy but small network of ambassadors and consuls carried out their work at the turn of the twentieth century. Most documents from the period examined in this book are handwritten. Newspaper stories appear in the same state as when they were first clipped out of that day's paper. Dark staining on the folio behind indicates that no one has disturbed their final resting place in more than 125 years. Clippings might be gathered together into envelopes repurposed by the ambassador, with the original address still visible. In the endnotes I have provided the level of detail available to me to locate materials within the archive. Some boxes have little internal organization; others have extensive subfolders. Where subfolders exist, that information has been noted. I have preserved the original Italian where I think it helpful to locate items but translated the word *busta*—"box" for clarity to an English-speaking reader. *Pacco*, or "folder," and *posizione*, "position," remain in the notes.

The following pages are the result of almost two decades of blood, sweat, tears, and, yes, quite a lot of gelato. My journey from graduate student researcher to PhD and from dissertation to book followed, in a sense, the serendipitous trip I first took to find the ASDMAE back in 2004. It began with a growing curiosity about Italians sent to farm cotton in Arkansas in the 1890s sparked by a conversation with the late Peter D'Agostino at a departmental happy hour. This was the first official gathering for the inaugural cohort of students in the Program in Work, Race, and Gender in the Urban World (WRGUW) at the University of Illinois in Chicago. On that night professors outnumbered us grad students at least by three to one inside a dark, old bar on Taylor Street where the UIC crowd just served to annoy the Italian American proprietor (the university's construction did result in the bulldozing of his neighborhood, after all, so who could blame him?). Peter's offhand comment about what he recalled seeing in the archives a decade earlier piqued my curiosity at a time when I thought I was training to become a historian of Hispanic migration to the American South. Over the next few years I focused on what I could uncover from my home in Chicago about attempts to colonize the South with immigrant farmers in the decades after the Civil War. Through interlibrary loan I found an almost completely forgotten record of meetings, organizations, and speeches. Over time I could see how these men talked about recruiting Italians, but who actually came to the American South in the 1890s? I had to go to Rome to find out.

By the time I landed at Rome's Fiumicino Airport alone in September 2004, I had spent a grand total of three days in the city and less than a week in the country in my entire life. But in between my first trip in 1993 and the second in 2004, I had devoted three years in college and three more in graduate school to studying Italian, and I'd found a mystery that I believed needed to be solved: how and why did Italian migrants end up in Arkansas at the beginning of the Jim Crow era, at a time when cotton plantations were awash in tractable labor? The seeming paradox at the heart of my research question—why imported labor, and why Italians?—took me five more years of research and writing to explain. I spent four additional years after graduating with my PhD grappling with the next question: how to turn my dissertation into a book. In 2014 I had a breakthrough: the Community College Humanities Association awarded me the first ever American Academy in Rome–CCHA affiliated fellowship. After eight years away I would return to Rome, to the archives, and find myself discussing research, art, and history over jasmine-scented al fresco dinners at the imitable academy high on the Janiculum Hill. My return to the ASDMAE made it clear that the history I was writing wasn't just about a labor experiment that imported Italians to farm cotton in the 1890s. It was about the way the United States managed migration, and the role that Italy played in shaping gatekeeping policy and practice. For the first time I could see this book taking shape.

Flash forward another six years: I had just landed back at Fiumicino with my family of four to begin what seemed only a short time ago like a dream: four months of living in Rome as a Fulbright scholar. I posed the family and our jumbled pile of luggage in front of our new apartment building among the vibrant chaos of viale Trastevere. The happy photo was meant to announce our arrival, which coincided with my son's fourth birthday: February 27, 2020. COVID-19 had ravaged China and the region of Lombardy in the north was in full-blown crisis, but life in Rome seemed normal. I had spent eleven exciting but exhausting months preparing to move my family to Rome. In the final crazed month before our departure, as I scrambled to produce exactly the right paperwork for my husband's and children's visas, I kept thinking, "Just let me in the country and we will be okay." Yet two weeks to the day after we arrived full of optimism and dreams, we boarded another plane, this time heading right back to JFK. Fulbright had been suspended in Italy and within seven days the program would be essentially canceled worldwide. We had lived through a harrowing week of lockdowns and now would repeat the same experience, but this time made more painful by the loss of what could have been, by having been so close to a lifelong dream before I lost it all.

On the afternoon of the day I enrolled my children in Italian public school, I rode the bus to the campus of the University of Roma Tre to introduce myself to the European "Erasmus" exchange students there to study in the Department of Political Science for the year. Only a few moments after I arrived at the meeting we heard the announcement: schools and universities were closing, effective the next day, for at least six weeks. I had held one class session with graduate students enrolled in my seminar in American foreign policy. I had just gotten a key to my new, temporary office, logged onto the computer system, and tried out the closest takeaway *pizza al taglio*. I had just started to imagine what I would contribute to and learn from this vibrant university that felt a world away from my home institution at the time where I taught introductory history survey courses. I had the most optimal teaching load of my professional life and meetings on the schedule to launch research collaborations and plan public events. I dreamed of who I might meet (like how I might parlay my Fulbright term into an invitation to meet the NPR correspondent and the *New York Times* reporter whose dispatches I had long admired from afar). In the space of less than a week this optimism turned to uncertainty in the face of a wrenching decision: to stay in Rome and wait out the lockdown alone, or to return to the United States with my family. At least I did not have to decide when, on March 10, the State Department ordered all Italy Fulbrighters to leave the country within forty-eight hours.

Back home in New Jersey I pivoted from in-person teaching to seminar discussions over Zoom. Now I rose at 7:00 a.m. to begin teaching at the equivalent of 1:30 p.m. in Rome. My kids interrupted me during class. I was a mess. But in between it all my students became an anchor. I drilled down into the core of our studies in the history of American diplomacy, and really emphasized the qualities that are particularly American in my teaching and mentoring. As I completed this course and began my second seminar, this time in U.S. immigration history, I made magic happen: I formed deeply rewarding bonds with my students in Italy, and once again this book came into bright, beautiful focus.

# Partners in Gatekeeping

# INTRODUCTION

In the summer of 1881 Baron Saverio Fava received disappointing news. After less than a year in Buenos Aires, he would be sent to a minor post: Washington, D.C. From the time he entered diplomatic service in 1851, Fava had struggled to prove himself. He faced suspicions that men like him, who had begun their careers in service to the kingdoms that Garibaldi had knitted together into a unified Italy in 1861, retained secret loyalties to their now-deposed kings.[1] Born in 1832 in Salerno on the Amalfi Coast, Fava joined the diplomatic service of what was then the Kingdom of Two Sicilies at the age of nineteen. Two years later, in 1853, he received his first post abroad to Algeria, and in the late summer of 1860 he earned another promotion in the service of King Francesco II just as Garibaldi's army descended on Naples and took control of the city in the war for unification. Fava spent only one month with the title of secretary of the delegation to the Bourbon Kingdom before the king fled his former capital. One month later Fava was put on administrative leave along with other diplomats who had worked on behalf of kings other than unified Italy's first monarch, Vittorio Emmanuele II. This leave would last two long years that felt, to him, like exile.[2]

Officers in the Italian diplomatic corps saw Washington as a backwater, as they believed the U.S. government cared little for European affairs and even less for Italy. By 1881, the year Fava arrived in Washington, the Italian government viewed the city as a "new world" capital, a place "certainly not of brilliant prestige" where they could exile diplomats like him who they believed were insufficiently loyal to the newly unified country.[3] This posting left him feeling unheard and ignored by the Ministry of Foreign Affairs (MAE), and what he found in Washington only seemed to justify his suspicions. He was greeted by only one representative, the consul of New York, G. B. Raffo, who had traveled down to the capital to meet him. The Italian legation in Washington had sat empty for a few weeks, and Fava would remain alone there for the next nine months.[4]

Over the twenty years that Saverio Fava spent in Washington, D.C., he brought about a fundamental shift in U.S.–Italian relations. He presided over the transformation of the United States from a backwater to Italy's most important diplomatic relationship. Today, Washington is the largest diplomatic operation in the MAE. Its embassy employs the most Italian foreign service officers in the world outside of Rome. Between 1881 and his retirement in 1901, Fava managed a steep increase in migration between the two countries that began to crest in the 1890s. He negotiated the defining diplomatic conflict between the two nations before World War I: the aftermath of the gruesome lynching in March 1891 of eleven Italians in front of a mob of thousands in retaliation for the murder of the New Orleans police chief. It was during this dark time that relations were at their lowest point and the countries briefly suspended formal relations and recalled their ambassadors. From this nadir he returned to Washington in 1893 to assume a new title: ambassador of Italy to United States, as the legation became an embassy.[5] By the time he vacated his post and retired from diplomatic service in the spring of 1901 at the age of sixty-nine, Fava had elevated the status of Italian–U.S. relations and established a mission focused on protecting Italian migrants in America, bringing the two nations together in a relationship I define as "partners in gatekeeping."

The records of the Italian diplomatic mission in Washington led by Fava and the institutions he helped create and manage (notably the Office of Labor Information and Protection for Italians at Ellis Island and Sunnyside Plantation in Arkansas), as well as the Italian and U.S. migration policies he helped enact, reconstruct the foundations of U.S. gatekeeping as it expanded from Chinese exclusion to target European migrants. Italian diplomatic records show how American officials created their early system of exclusion and how messy this process was. While scholars have unearthed the roots of the U.S. immigration bureaucracy in Chinese exclusion and resistance to it, less is known about how laws and tactics designed to exclude Asian migrants were applied to Europeans in the earliest years of unified federal border controls following the enactment of the Immigration Act of 1891.[6]

As new requirements for entering the United States emerged in the 1890s, the Italian government sought to understand what those requirements entailed, even as they shifted under hundreds of thousands of migrants' feet each year in this critical decade. In the ten years from 1891 to 1901, an asymmetric partnership to manage migration formed between Italy and the United States. Its records reveal the messy origins of what political scientist Aristide Zolberg called "remote control," illuminating the historical development of the United States as a gatekeeping nation. Widely understood by scholars as emerging in the 1920s, "remote control" refers to specific requirements for entry such as medical inspections and visa and passport requirements performed in sending or transit countries to the standards of U.S. law. According to Zolberg, "the implementation of restrictionism entailed a vast expansion of the American state's capacity to regulate movement across its borders, and the deployment of this capacity within the territory of other sovereign states so as to achieve the elusive 'remote control' to which regulators had long aspired."[7] In addition to establishing an immigration bureau, the border patrol, and immigration stations like Ellis Island (opened 1892) and Angel Island (opened 1910), the U.S. government sought to introduce measures of "remote control"—gatekeeping enforcement outside the receiving nation's borders—that required the collaboration and assistance of border and sending countries and became commonplace after the 1920s.[8] Italian interactions with the emerging U.S. immigration system between 1891 and 1901 show how the United States became a gatekeeping nation.

*Partners in Gatekeeping* expands the concepts and time lines of gatekeeping and remote control. Gatekeeping, largely understood to mean restrictive policies to keep migrants out, expands in scope when one considers the experiences of Italian migrants at the turn of the twentieth century. The expensive, time-consuming work it took to enforce the Chinese Exclusion Act after 1882 grew the immigration bureaucracy in its first two decades.[9] Italian encounters and their government's response to immigration agents at Ellis Island fill out the early history of enforcement. Italians were the first group to encounter en masse new gatekeeping laws established by Congress to limit the entry of "undesirable immigrants."

During his twenty years in office, Fava's efforts were part of a powerful shift that elevated migration to a much more significant and visible role within the governments of both Italy and the United States. The experiences of Italian migrants arriving in the United States fundamentally transformed the kingdom's approach to managing migration, and by 1901 Italy had become a partner in American gatekeeping. Yet the power in this partnership was not evenly shared. An asymmetric partnership took shape between 1891 and 1901 that would continue to influence the practice of border controls in both nations long after. Encounters with Italian migrants also shaped the developing immigration bureaucracy in the United States as it was established by a quick succession of new laws and Supreme Court decisions. Within a relationship tested to the breaking point by the New Orleans lynching, the Italian government questioned the new American enforcement system as it emerged in its first decade.

The explosion of deadly violence and the racist vitriol that flowed from the lynching amplified calls to limit the number of Italians who could enter the country. In response, Italy was the first country of mass migration to take on American gatekeeping beyond its borders. This enabled the transnational enforcement of immigration restriction through measures like visas, passports, and medical inspections and thus set the course for everything from punitive "remote control" policies like "Remain in Mexico" or Haitian detention at Guantanamo Bay, Cuba, to rejected visa applications that meant, after 1924, "the new system of screening immigrants before their arrival was working more efficiently and effectively than ever before."[10] While Italy and the United States emerged as partners in gatekeeping during a uniquely challenging time in the wake of the 1891 lynching, their relationship would influence the conduct of border control for many decades to come.

The United States could not control its borders alone. Rapidly expanding transatlantic migration at the close of the nineteenth century brought the two states together as both the Italian and U.S. governments forged new bureaucracies to manage migration. *Partners in Gatekeeping* decenters the United States by showing how critical foreign partners were to the creation of an effective gatekeeping regime. Italian encounters with U.S. immigration officials fill out the otherwise limited picture of early enforcement in the gatekeeping apparatus. This book examines the first ten years of federal immigration management in the decade following the passage of the 1891 Immigration Act that created the Bureau of Immigration, a new office and a new role within the growing Washington bureaucracy, and ending with Italy's omnibus Emigration Law of 1901, passed partly in response to migrants' experiences at American borders.[11]

These ten years were critical to the creation of the modern gatekeeping system by establishing the antecedents for "remote control" beyond the well-studied Chinese and Mexican cases, taking what we know about the structure, rationale, and results of Asian exclusion and bringing it into conversation with European exclusion. The power of Europeans to negotiate entry in the 1890s fills in a critical gap in immigration control historiography. At the same time when Japan was also using diplomacy to negotiate migration policy for its citizens, Italy—a nation with a comparatively weaker international standing but which enjoyed the benefits as an exporter of nominally "white" laborers—exercised diplomatic power carefully and had different outcomes.[12] The sources detailing this early, seminal phase of diplomatic asymmetric partnership of "immigration as foreign relations" in the 1890s provide a new angle from which to look at both the Italian case and the general history of migrations to the United States.[13]

From 1891 to 1901, Italians were in a unique position to observe, question, and shape the enforcement of U.S. immigration policy. The language of two vague clauses embedded in the federal statute—"likely to become a public charge" in the 1891 Immigration Act (commonly known as the LPC clause) and "clearly and beyond doubt entitled to admission" in the language of the 1893 act—empowered the administrative state to carry out the work of exclusion shadowed by the banality of bureaucratic decision-making in day-to-day inspections. But the fuzziness of American law did not go unnoticed. Despite expanded legal and administrative authority to control immigration, U.S. legislators and government officials soon realized that they could not enforce immigration laws entirely on their own. To the Americans, the Italian government seemed to offer a helping hand to carry out their work.

The Italian migratory diaspora exploded in size and scope at the turn of the twentieth century as millions of people fled poverty, political persecution, and natural disaster.[14] The number of Italian-born persons in the United States grew from 44,230 in 1880 to 182,580 in 1890, swelled to 484,020 in 1900, and then surged to 1,343,125 a decade later.[15] Initially, the population of Italians and Chinese in the United States were similar, but by 1930 Italians surpassed all others to become easily the largest group of foreign-born for the next forty years.[16] More than 2.8 million Italians left Italy between 1891 and 1900. Eighteen percent came to the United States, making it the largest single overseas destination, a status that has held over time. Italians in this period also migrated to Canada, Argentina, Brazil, and Australia, although the United States was by far the most common terminus. (Close to four million left for countries in Europe between 1891 and 1910.)[17] As migration scholar Maddalena Tirabassi summarized, "The United States has always been the first choice in transoceanic migrations and even today it is the country of choice for Italian migrants going overseas." Between 1901 and 1910 six million Italians left with almost 39 percent arriving at U.S. ports, increasing to 41 percent between 1911 and 1920.[18]

Italians spread out across the United States to find employment in almost every major American industry. The Italian-born dominated in needlework and textiles (especially silk), canning, and mining, and they lent their manual labor to build railroads, subways, roads, and bridges. At the turn of the twentieth century Italians formed the backbone of the skilled trades of bricklaying, stonemasonry, and plaster and stucco work, particularly in the northeastern states and fast-growing cities such as New York, Philadelphia, Chicago, and San Francisco, where, while they found their skills frequently in demand, they were often isolated into ethnic enclaves.[19] As the single largest ethnic group to be processed at Ellis Island over its sixty-two-year history and the primary target of inspectors in the station's first decade, Italians' experiences with bureaucratic exclusion illuminate how the United States moved to systematically control working-class migration.[20]

Yet the scholarship on transnational migration suffers from certain geographic and temporal limitations that have marginalized the history of Italians. Building on the solid foundation of research on Chinese exclusion, much recent scholarship has focused on movement within the Americas to understand restrictionism and immigration politics, effectively moving Europe out of the frame. While the influence of the "transnational turn" has brought historians into the space in between and across borders, much of this work continues to separate Italian migration from movement between the United States and Asian nations, and across Mexico, North America, Central America, and Caribbean states. How Italians encountered and responded to early U.S. immigration law adds context and comparison to the better-known Chinese and Mexican cases of gatekeeping as well as to Caribbean histories, countering this geographic silo effect while still emphasizing the significance of sending countries.[21] Through its close examination of the lesser-known history of Italian asymmetric partnership with the United States in the first decade of federal border controls, *Partners in Gatekeeping* illustrates a more complex, distinctly transnational story in the development of U.S. immigration policies and institutions.

## Gatekeeping, Anticipatory Remote Control, and the Asymmetric Partnership

At the same time when the United States was establishing itself as a global empire, the federal government turned its attention to policing the nation's borders. Beginning in 1891, Congress created an immigration system focused on gatekeeping that would become the foundation for the policy and the practice of restriction to the present day. This book makes a new argument about the periodization of immigration restriction and the rise of "remote control" as a key U.S. gatekeeping strategy by expanding the time line on which we typically define this practice. It tells the story of how Italy, proportionally the largest sending state at the turn of the twentieth century, acted to extend the power of American gatekeeping, setting the stage for later periods of immigration restriction and criminalization. The ongoing struggle between Italy and the United States to accept Italian migrants is revealed through diplomatic correspondence, internal government reports, congressional debates, and press coverage in both countries. This record shows how the first decade of federal immigration management was a period of what I call anticipatory remote control. Italy tracked restrictionist moves in Congress at the same time as officers of its diplomatic service watched, and shaped, the application of the law in practice.

This close oversight informed the relationship between the two nations in the ten years following the horrific 1891 New Orleans lynching. In the immediate aftermath of the murders, Italian diplomats failed to force the courts to bring to justice the perpetrators, who were known; victims' families waited for more than two years before a final decision precluded any further legal action.[22] This experience conditioned the Italian government to anticipate American attacks on its citizens, not in the form of state-sanctioned mob violence, but in the halls of Congress and at the inspection station on Ellis Island.

A framework for a federal system of immigration restriction emerged through a series of laws and court cases in the last two decades of the nineteenth century. The apparatus of exclusion began in 1882 when American (and Australian) law barred Chinese laborers.[23] The exclusionary goals of this new federal law could not be carried out by the existing patchwork of state-level border control agents whose main duty was to enumerate immigrants at the port of arrival. A national system of immigration enforcement formed in 1891, the year that Congress created the Office of Immigration, and expanded in 1892 with the opening of Ellis Island, which became home to 119 out of 180 total officers in the year-old inspection officer corps following the closure of Castle Garden station, formerly managed by New York State.[24] Another major piece of federal legislation, the 1893 Immigration Act, created Boards of Special Inquiry to decide questionable cases.

Spurred by challenges to the Chinese Exclusion Act, the Supreme Court handed down several decisions that by 1893 firmly established the power of the federal government to regulate who could enter the country. Taken together, as legal historians Lucy Salyer and Torrie Hester have demonstrated, three cases enabled immigration agents to "sift" persons arriving at American ports, and to detain and deport those found in violation of the law's essentially vague and changing standards.[25] These legal precedents placed immigration enforcement on what Hester has called a "parallel track," removing immigrants' rights to appeal the decisions regarding their status through the federal courts and instead placing their cases under the jurisdiction of administrative law.[26] This expansion of federal power helped birth what political scientists call the "administrative state."[27] As the reach of the federal government only continued to expand over the course of the twentieth century, gatekeeping began to reach deep into the interior of the country.[28]

Gatekeeping is not just about exclusion and the drive toward more exclusionary policy. *Partners in Gatekeeping* deepens our definition of diplomacy as a tool for making immigration policy by offering a powerful case study in Italy that complements existing work on Japanese–U.S. and Chinese relations in the era of Asian exclusion.[29] While historians and scholars of migration have placed the selective admission policies that sought to "sift" European migrants outside of strict exclusionary goals of gatekeeping applied to Asian migrants, the history of Italian encounters with border control and the response of the Italian government to U.S. policy challenges this narrow definition.[30] The history of Italian–U.S. relations, and what these records reveal about border controls in the 1890s, expands the definitions of gatekeeping and remote control beyond what scholars currently think. This redefinition is by its nature surprising and hard to conceptualize, especially as it emerges from a documentary record obscured in a difficult-to-access foreign archive, the Archivio Storico Diplomatico dell'Ministero degli Affari Esteri (ASDMAE), the historical archive of diplomacy of the Ministry of Foreign Affairs. Throughout this book my definitions of gatekeeping and remote control will push against established boundaries, encouraging readers to consider a longer time line for remote control and a broader definition of gatekeeping.

Italians' experiences with exclusion at the border and their government's response to American gatekeeping show how governments worked transnationally to shape the movement of people across borders. Historian Erika Lee has defined gatekeeping as an ideology first applied to the Chinese that used "racializing" as a basis for inferiority, then moved to "containing the danger [immigrants] represented," which wielded "protecting the nation" as a rationale for state action against targeted ethnic groups.[31] After Chinese exclusion laws in the United States established the legal precedents that shaped Italians' experiences with immigration enforcement, Italian migration tested the new laws on the ground at the same time as the Italian government attempted to "control the social phenomenon of migration" through its own tools.[32] The history of Italian migration to the United States in the 1890s shines a new light on immigration policy and interactions with border controls before, during, and after this critical decade when the rules of gatekeeping were being written.

*Partners in Gatekeeping* challenges existing ideas about the origins of remote control by looking closely at the decade 1891–1901. By 1894, the royal government's direct management of migration to the United States had expanded. The chapters that follow examine two particular programs the Italian government supported in the 1890s: a government outpost on Ellis Island it called the Office of Labor Information and Protection for Italians, staffed by officers appointed by the Ministry of Foreign Affairs and managed by the ambassador directly, and sponsored rural immigrant settlement in the American South, called colonization at the time. These efforts to respond to the shifting landscape of American gatekeeping policy presaged activity by other nations in the twentieth century.

The nature of U.S.–Italian cooperation—uneven, relationship-driven, predictive, and also reactive—is the subject of this book and defines what I call the asymmetric partnership between the nations. This book opens with a look through Ambassador Fava's eyes to see his government's reaction to the lynching of eleven Italians in front of a mob of thousands in New Orleans less than one day after some of the men were acquitted for the murder of the police chief. Perpetrated eleven days after the passage of the 1891 Immigration Act, the lynching forced the royal Italian government to change the way it interacted with the United States; at the same time, the United States was changing the way it managed migration by placing the responsibility for its borders under federal control. At this intersection the two nations became partners, managing the style and scope of gatekeeping, testing new solutions and establishing durable precedents for the remote control of American borders that would become standard practice in the twentieth century.[33]

What I call anticipatory remote control emerged out of the specific dynamics of Italy–U.S. relations over this ten-year period at the end of a long debate in Rome over the politics of state power to regulate emigration.[34] After a decade of tracking, questioning, and acquiescing to American policy, in 1901 Italy enacted a comprehensive emigration law that assumed many of the duties of American border control through an extensive new emigration bureaucracy. As the first partner in gatekeeping, Italy's attempts to manage migration in cooperation with the United States profoundly influenced the actions of sending states decades later. The officers of the MAE learned to work with lower-level bureaucrats on the ground instead of in high-profile diplomatic channels, an approach that the foreign service would soon put to use to oversee the processing of tens, and after 1901, hundreds of thousands of Italians arriving annually through Ellis Island.[35] The partnership between Italy and the United States documents the foundations of qualitative restriction before the move to quantitative exclusion culminating in the Quota Act of 1924.[36] This history helps us see, through Italian eyes, the origins of American gatekeeping.

The history of Italian responses to border control illustrates the function of anticipatory remote control. Exclusionary gatekeeping provided the tools that Congress and the Bureau of Immigration then used to selectively reduce the admission of undesirable European migrants.[37] Italian archives illuminate what in U.S. records is an otherwise obscured period but is essential to understanding the transition from Chinese exclusion to European restriction and later to the restriction of other groups.[38] The interplay between Chinese exclusion law and its successful evasion through multiple methods, both clandestine and in the courtroom, propelled the growth of the immigration bureaucracy.[39] Chinese migrants smuggled through "backdoor" countries of Canada, Mexico, and the Caribbean, especially Cuba, in the early twentieth century further shaped immigration policy and its enforcement.[40] In this way, the ineffectiveness of the country's first gatekeeping law influenced the shape of everything that came after. The careful records collected by the MAE of migrants' experiences with exclusion answer questions about how immigration regulation functioned as U.S. immigration officers navigated the transition from counting to "sifting" arrivals, and how the leaders at Ellis Island interpreted the mandate of new laws that expanded the scope of federal power to exclude the undesirable.

U.S. immigration policy did not develop in a vacuum but was fed by the transnational flow of ideas and policies. Speaking to domestic politics in both nations but emerging in a distinctly transnational conversation, ideas about race and criminality influenced the emerging gatekeeping system and shaped how the Italian government and its diplomats responded to the problems, including rampant discrimination and violence, that migrants encountered. In the same decade that the flow of migration to the United States rapidly increased, a group of Italian intellectuals scholars refer to as the Lombrosians, named for the founder of modern criminology, Cesare Lombroso, began publishing in Italy and United States their theories about the innate inferiority of southern Italians. Part of a powerful intellectual school of "nineteenth century science [that] racialized these deeply rooted stereotypes," Italian anthropologists influenced American immigration restrictionists later in the twentieth century, beginning most visibly with the Dillingham Commission's *Dictionary of Races or Peoples* and culminating in the highly restrictive 1921 and 1924 Quota Acts.[41] Lombrosian ideas influenced efforts to restrict immigration to the United States just as these atavistic arguments based on anthropometric features had fallen out of favor in Italy following a period of intense criticism.[42] The reach of Lombrosianism went much deeper into American legislation than it did in Italian law, even though the goal of Lombroso and his followers had been to reform the new Italian state and apply scientific strategies to its social and economic problems discussed at the time as the Southern Question.[43]

The debate over Italian migrants' desirability—as persons prone to criminality and "unfit for self-government," a phrase President William McKinley used to describe Filipinos in 1899 to Americans as a rationale for seizing their islands during the Spanish-American War—unfolded alongside American debates over the fitness of African Americans and colonial subjects for the rights of citizenship.[44] Jim Crow laws began to take shape in the handful of years that the Italian Office of Information and Protection for Italians operated at Ellis Island. The United States emerged as an imperial power at the same time that Congress was debating a literacy test requirement for immigrants. Less than a decade later, the Dillingham Commission, created by Congress to study the "immigration problem," drew its professional staff from the ranks of colonial administration and included elected members who had sat on oversight committees for the federal management of foreign territories, bringing a particularly international/colonial lens to their work.[45]

Where the commission's white southern members brought their views on race to their government service, the Lombrosians also theorized the roots of social problems in southern Italy laid in the people themselves. They were barbaric, "undisciplined and often unable of being educated," with a "savage tendency" confirmed by the criminal, violent behavior of emigrants from the *mezzogiorno* observed in the United States.[46] These stereotypes reverberated around the United States in different ways, from the debates over immigration restriction in the halls of Congress down to the docks at New Orleans where, in 1905, a knife maker was detained for more than a week, accused of being too dangerous to admit because he had a hidden compartment in his trunk full of blades he used in his trade.[47]

The transnational tensions inherent in debates over desirability, citizenship, and migration controls (what in 1888 Italian priest Giuseppe Scalabrini, who later went on to found a Catholic order that ministers to migrants, argued was the state's duty to legislate the freedom to emigrate without compelling people to leave, the literal translation of "libertà di emigrare ma non di far emigrare") manifested through the asymmetric partnership, demonstrating both the strength and the limits of U.S. power.[48] U.S. border controls are a product of both restrictionist and anti-restrictionist ideas and foreign policy priorities. Migration has long flowed from foreign policy, and the asymmetric partnership that formed between Italy and the United States adds an important degree of complexity to this history.[49] An examination of the 1890s shows how diplomacy has long had an influence over migration policy.[50] By emphasizing the United States as the power broker in the gatekeeping relationship but telling this history through the eyes of Ambassador Fava and the royal Italian government, I have written a history of migration that challenges a power the United States likes to present as absolute.[51]

## 1891–1901: Ten Critical Years

The year 1891 introduced the elements of the transnational and sometimes competing forces of immigration regulation that would mark the first ten years of the United States' new federal system. Just two weeks after the passage of the act that authorized a new federal immigration control system, a mob of thousands avenged the murder of the police chief David Hennessy by lynching eleven Italians in New Orleans. This book begins in chapter 1 with these two events that until now have not been examined together. I argue that they are deeply connected. The lynching shaped the relationship between the two nations in ways that profoundly influenced the management of migration.

The chapters that follow traverse the path of immigration restriction over ten years that I argue are critical in the history of American gatekeeping. Beginning in the 1890s Italian arrivals to the federal station broke records, serving as the impetus to policy changes in both countries. However, since a fire at Ellis Island in the summer of 1897 decimated the station's buildings and destroyed much of the documentary record of day-to-day operations, the development of a system of immigration enforcement becomes much clearer as Italian diplomatic sources fill in the gap in the record of early border control. The letters, reports, telegrams, and meetings of the Italian ambassador in this period, Saverio Fava, reconstruct a window into Ellis Island. The Office of Labor Information and Protection for Italians, or simply the Office—a special bureau created by Fava and authorized by Congress on the recommendation of the superintendent of immigration, Herman Stump, in the summer of 1894—was the only outpost of a foreign government permitted to operate in the Ellis Island station. From 1894 until the Bureau of Immigration in Washington revoked its privileges in 1899, the Office mediated the gatekeeping process for arriving Italians. Fava "appreciate[d] the prudent but constant affirmation of the practical authority that the Office was able to assume in the different cases [of exclusion] that take place here every day," wrote his chief agent, Alessandro Oldrini, in a comprehensive report dated December 1, 1894.[52]

The ambassador saw the Office as a sign of preferential treatment by the immigration authorities, and he and his government used it as a conduit to form relationships with and lobby officers at Ellis Island.[53] Indeed, the Office's second chief agent, Egisto Rossi, concluded that the presence of the Office forced the immigration service to become "more rigorous" in its inspection process and more robust in the facilities it offered to the detained.[54] The Italian government worked to protect migrants primarily through the unique Office. Despite its essential contributions to the development of American immigration enforcement, the Office is completely missing from the historiography on immigration policy and its enforcement, Italian American history, or Ellis Island. This book will remedy that gap in chapters that explain the origins and function of the Office, the struggle to keep it open, and the impact that it had even after it closed its doors for good on January 1, 1900.

The sometimes paternalistic impulse to protect migrants—what the officers of the Italian government referred to as the duty of *tutela* or "protection"— propelled the major players in this story: the actions of the ambassador, the two men who served as chief officers of the Office of Labor Information and Protection, numerous Italian consuls stationed in the United States, and the minister of foreign affairs and minister of the interior in Rome.[55] These men tracked the frequently shifting landscape of gatekeeping legislation in Congress while the Office challenged the decisions of immigration agents to exclude poor Italians from admission to the United States. The relationship between the United States and Italy evolved over the course of the 1890s as Italians overwhelmed the inspection system at Ellis Island. At the same time, Italians challenged the exclusionary aspects of the new gatekeeping system in and around what *Harper's Weekly* called the "cage of the rejected" that immigration officers enacted at the Ellis Island immigration station.[56] When American agents moved to exclude Italians from entering the United States, the Office challenged the basis for their decisions. Their interventions did little to alter the bureau's application of the law, and actually strengthened enforcement by encouraging the commissioner to add additional agents and detention infrastructure to Ellis Island, influencing the conduct of border enforcement over the long term. This is the subject of the second chapter.

By 1896 Italians had become the primary target of restrictionists like the Immigration Restriction League and served as a case study for the IRL's support for the introduction of a literacy test to enter the country, a requirement that expanded the scope of gatekeeping power to exclude the poor.[57] At around the same time, the Office and Ambassador Fava were also facilitating the movement of Italian families to an Arkansas cotton plantation called Sunnyside, as the third chapter details, onto land owned by a Long Island railroad magnate named Austin Corbin. The history of this planned Italian colony in the Arkansas delta intersects with the work of Fava and Chief Agent Oldrini to protect migrants by directing them away from crowded and dangerous cities and onto small farm plots. Placed into the historical context of migration politics, Italian agricultural colonization in the South in the 1890s can be seen as a real-world example of how a foreign government tried to find a solution in a new and rapidly evolving world of gatekeeping regulations. The ambassador and the leader of the Office also tapped into growing interest for Italians to solve the post-emancipation "labor problem" in the American South. The longer history of schemes to create immigrant agricultural colonies in the region, which began after 1865 but reached their zenith in the 1880s and 1890s, takes the narrative of Italians in America into new territory.[58]

The history of Italian colonization in the South at the turn of the twentieth century also illuminates the construction of a modern migration control bureaucracy. It demonstrates how a sending and a receiving nation approached the project of state building through migration control and used the structures of border control to add to the power of their governments. The nation-state assumed profound control over migrants' lives in the twentieth century through these border control systems.[59] Colonization in the American South deserves greater attention as it shows how a transnational and regional lens is essential to understanding the trajectory of U.S. immigration policy. "Because the South never succeeded in attracting mass immigration," immigration historian Katherine Benton-Cohen has written, "it has barely figured into histories of the 'immigration problem' of the early twentieth century."[60] The history of distribution policy—which I refer to as agricultural colonization to reflect how progressive reformers most commonly discussed it—offers a window into "the link between emigration and nation-state building," a connection sociologist David Fitzgerald called "neglected."[61] Because colonization required the coordination of local, state, and national officials and private citizens, it offers an unusually clear view onto the formation of border controls as they intersected lines of national sovereignty because, as Nancy Green and François Weil have argued, "emigration, like immigration, needs to be understood at the intersection of structural and individual agency."[62]

The dynamics of the emerging system of gatekeeping can be seen in particular in the year 1896. That spring Egisto Rossi described witnessing "those days of exceptional invasion" as the number of migrants in three months surpassed the amount who had passed through Ellis Island in the entire year previous.[63] A succession of seemingly unrelated events put pressure on the immigration system. In June the founder of the Sunnyside, Arkansas, colony died suddenly, which threw the experiment into disarray. By October, when Ambassador Fava facilitated a special visit to Rome by Commissioner of Immigration Herman Stump to clarify gatekeeping rules, the IRL also launched a very public campaign for a literacy test. Chapter 4 demonstrates how by 1896 Ambassador Fava, the commissioners of the Bureau of Immigration, and the members of the IRL all felt that gatekeeping law was being inconsistently applied. Congressional testimony of Stump and the second commissioner of immigration, Terence Powderly, as well as an 1896 IRL investigation where Ellis Island officials granted access to the most intimate aspects of the inspection process, focused on the inconsistent application of the "likely to become a public charge" or LPC clause, which was the most common tool an inspector could wield at that time to deny entry. This, in the eyes of the IRL and the immigration service's leaders, left the gates ajar and allowed admission of tens of thousands of undesirable Italians. What American leaders observed at Ellis Island became an argument for more strict gatekeeping. The limited reach of Italian law combined with increasing reports of rejections by U.S. officials led in part to a radical reenvisioning of their own management of emigration, the subject of chapter 5.[64]

This book traces the arc of immigration restriction from 1891 to the passage of Italy's omnibus Emigration Law of 1901, an update of an 1888 emigration statute that significantly restructured the country's management of migration by creating a new emigration bureaucracy. Chapter 5 places U.S. and Italian policy within the context of the forces shaping Italian migration law more broadly, explaining why and how U.S.-bound migrants and their experiences influenced policy in Italy.[65] The little-known history of the overlapping formation of governmental institutions to manage migration offers a way to reconsider the importance of the relationship between Italy and the United States. The chapters that follow examine the critical yet largely understudied period of relations between the two countries at the turn of the twentieth century, a time when both were "finding their place among nations."[66] The dynamic between Italy and the United States fundamentally shaped the development of border controls, one of the most pressing international and domestic issues of the last hundred years. *Partners in Gatekeeping* broadens and internationalizes the frame and extends the time line of remote control by looking closely at its origins.[67] This history connects two of the most significant developments of the twentieth-century state: the rise of legal immigration restriction and the attendant growth of bureaucracy to regulate migration. This book establishes how critical the historical interaction of Italian migrants and their government was to the development of contemporary systems of migration control. The history of gatekeeping and the politics of restriction illuminate both countries' responses to migration and the construction of border controls from the late nineteenth into the twenty-first century, controversial topics that continue to play a massive role in contemporary politics in Italy, the United States, and countries around the world.

# CHAPTER 1

# The Murder of David Hennessy and Its Aftermath

As he lay dying, New Orleans chief of police David Hennessy said, "The Dagoes did it." That a man who rose to power by capturing a Sicilian murderer on the loose in the United States might meet his demise ten years later at the hands of Italians was morbidly ironic, an example of the kind of deadly retribution they were believed to naturally exercise.[1] The official death notice read before the mayor and city council warned that as "the victim of Sicilian vengeance," Hennessy's murder on a rainy night in October 1890 must be avenged. The notice hinted at more violence yet to come. "We must teach these people a lesson that they will not forget for all time."[2]

The local press scrubbed clean the chief's record of duplicitous political activity after twenty-one men—most had naturalized but some were Italian citizens, including two businessmen prominent in the rapidly expanding shipping and fruit trade—were initially arrested in the fall of 1890 and nine put on trial for murder in February 1891. The exact circumstances of the chief's murder remain mysterious to this day. Members of the Italian community reported to the consul of New Orleans that the police, who also denied some of the accused their right to consular representation, had used coercive tactics to secure false confessions.[3] At trial defense attorneys discredited key witnesses to the murder as drunks or liars, or as simply having been too far away to make an accurate identification.[4] On March 13 a jury rendered a not guilty verdict for six defendants and the judge declared a mistrial for the remaining three. In contrast to the predictions of the city's leaders who presumed the Italians' guilt, it appeared that justice had prevailed. U.S. Attorney William Grant later told the Justice Department that "the evidence in the case against . . . [the defendants] . . . is voluminous . . . [but] as a whole is exceedingly unsatisfactory, and is not, in my mind, conclusive one way or the other."[5] But the judge made a decision with catastrophic consequences when he sent all nine men, six of whom had been exonerated, back to the prison on Congo Square.[6] Despite assurances from the state of Louisiana that New Orleans's Italian community of thirty thousand was safe, less than forty-eight hours later an armed mob stormed the prison gates and lynched eleven Italians held there. The victims included three men who had just been acquitted, three whose cases had been declared a mistrial, and five still awaiting trial.[7]

Five months after Hennessy's murder, on the morning of March 14, the Italian consul stationed in New Orleans, now fearing for his own life, sent a desperate message to the ambassador in Washington. "Mob led by members of committee of fifty took possession of jail; killed eleven prisoners; three Italians, others naturalized," Pasquale Corte dictated to Western Union with directions to cable the ambassador without delay. "I hold mayor responsible. Fear further murders. I am also in great danger. Reports follow."[8] After Hennessy's murder, Corte and Ambassador Baron Saverio Fava had objected to the mass arrests and interrogations that they believed violated the rights of Italian citizens, but on that day the consul's hands were tied. He could only watch as the violence continued to unfold, even threatening, at one point, his own secretary.[9] Throughout the morning of March 14, 1891, as gangs of men banged at his door, Corte waited for instruction. Soon messages flooded in from Washington and Rome. The prime minister of Italy, Antonio Starabba, Marquis di Rudinì, ordered his legation to act to protect themselves and their citizens. Meanwhile, Ambassador Fava cabled the secretary of state, James G. Blaine, confident that the perpetrators of the brutal lynching would be swiftly and justly punished. His assumption quickly proved wrong. The relationship between Italy and the United States, shaken to its very core on that day, would soon be radically remade in the aftermath of Chief David Hennessy's murder.

The lynching of eleven Italians dragged from inside the stone walls of the Orleans parish prison by a mob led by some of the city's most prominent leaders wielding clubs, sticks, and revolvers was not the problem, the *Washington Post* argued in April 1891. The newspaper dismissed the murder of Chief Hennessy and the lynching that followed as consequences of the presence of a large and naturally dangerous population of Italians: "Referring to the New Orleans lynching, many papers discuss the question why Italian murder returns exceed those of every other nation on earth."[10] Soon Congressman Henry Cabot Lodge of Massachusetts proposed a permanent solution to the problem of too many dangerous Italians: legislative restriction of immigration.[11] Writing for a national audience in the *North American Review* in May 1891, Lodge drew a direct line between the lynching and immigration policy. "I believe that, whatever the proximate causes of the shocking event at New Orleans may have been, the underlying cause, and the one with which alone the people of the United States can deal, is to be found in the utter carelessness with which we treat immigration to this country."[12]

Less than three weeks separated the lynching from the passage of legislation designed, in the words of its drafters, "not to restrict immigration, but to sift it, to separate the desirable from the undesirable immigrants, and to permit only those to land on our shores who have certain physical and moral qualities."[13] Viewed through the lens of immigration and Italian American history, 1891 was a particularly critical year in the development of a gatekeeping apparatus designed to keep Italians out of the United States. The lynching and its aftermath propelled Italy into an asymmetric partnership with the United States, the largest receiving country of its migrants, in the first decade of unified federal immigration enforcement.

The largest mass lynching of foreign-born people in U.S. history overlapped with the expansion of the authority of the government in Washington to enact, and federal officers to interpret, immigration policy. March 1891 marked the beginning of a trend in U.S. legal history toward increasing administrative discretion over the management of immigration. Passed into law on March 3, only eleven days before the lynching, the comprehensive Immigration Act of 1891 is a less examined landmark in immigration history that contributed greatly to the construction of a gatekeeping regime. The act contained thirteen sections that strengthened the exclusion of classes prohibited since 1882, namely, Chinese immigrants, contract laborers, and those deemed "likely to become public charge." The most wide-reaching provision of the 1891 law, section 7, created the office of the superintendent of immigration housed within the Department of the Treasury. The superintendent would report to the secretary of the Treasury and receive a salary of $4,000 per year for his work managing the entry and detention of immigrants arriving at official ports of entry.

The 1891 act marked the transfer of all gatekeeping power to determine who could enter the country from the states (where it had formerly rested) to the federal government. This insulated the power to make such determinations from the oversight of the judicial branch, a process historians such as Hidetaka Hirota, Torrie Hester, and Lucy Salyer have described.[14] Section 8 declared, "All decisions made by inspection officers or their assistants touching the right of any alien to land . . . shall be final unless appeal taken to the Superintendent of Immigration, whose action shall be subject to review by the Secretary of the Treasury."[15] What became known as the "Finality Clause," Salyer writes, "provided the foundation for the unprecedented power of the Bureau of Immigration" and set the immigration agency on a path to largely unchecked administrative authority.[16] Italian migrants would be the first to encounter en masse this new regulatory world as the mechanisms of gatekeeping emerged around them.

The rift in U.S.–Italian relations that followed the lynching marked the importance of the interplay between Italian emigration law and U.S. immigration and naturalization law that Italy's diplomats sought to manage.[17] American authorities questioned the citizenship of the men initially arrested in October 1890 as a way to challenge the Italian government's authority to intervene. The New Orleans lynching tested the ability of the Italian government to use diplomacy to protect its migrants abroad and drew Rome into the reactionary forces shaping immigration policy at the turn of the twentieth century. At the same time Italian–U.S. relations were most strained, Italian diplomats, humiliated and horrified by the mob violence in New Orleans, failed to get local, state, or federal authorities to adequately respond and saw their power sink to its nadir. In the spring of 1891 people across the United States were encouraged to view Italians in their own cities as a greater danger to Americans than Americans were to Italians, despite some Americans having killed eleven people in the course of an hour.

The stark contrast between how Italians experienced the lynching and how American newspapers depicted it helps explain in part why the Italian legation could never force state or federal courts to bring the perpetrators to account for their crimes. Instead of seeing the lynching as an outrage perpetrated on innocent Italians, the coverage depicted the victims—and the larger Italian community of New Orleans—as dangerous murderers unfit to hold American citizenship. The pages of the *Washington Post* declared straightforwardly, "The Italian has murder in his blood."[18] Henry Cabot Lodge described the "unrestricted immigration" of Italians as a growing menace. "The existence of such a society [as the Mafia] no reasonable man can, I think, have any doubt. But," the senator warned, "there is nothing to keep it necessarily within such bounds" and away from respectable American communities.[19]

The lynching opened the door for Americans to denigrate Italians of all classes with racist imagery. For weeks newspapers disparaged the victims and blamed them for their own murders. Adopting similarly racialized language as coverage defending the lynching of Black men, these newspapers also denigrated Italians' fitness for citizenship in a democracy.[20] "Our own rattlesnakes are as good citizens as they," declared an editorial in the *New York Times*. In Chicago the *Daily Tribune* announced, "Mafia murderers slain: eleven Sicilian butchers lynched at New Orleans."[21] These articles sought to isolate naturalized Italians from any protections their former government could offer at a time when diplomats were pushing Washington to punish the known perpetrators of the lynching.

Some newspapers questioned the authority of the Italian government itself. A two-part cartoon published on the front page of the *Philadelphia Inquirer* on April 12, 1891, brought every anti-Italian stereotype to the fore and reduced Rome's concerns with a demeaning metaphor. The first panel depicted the minister of foreign affairs, the Marquis di Rudinì, as an organ grinder, King Umberto I as a peanut vendor with a monkey on his shoulder, and Ambassador Fava as a beggar shaking a tin can. Secretary of State James Blaine stood next to the overturned peanut cart, having tossed it over in anger and knocked the king to the ground in the process. The second panel depicted King Umberto and the marquis grabbing stilettos to avenge the slight.[22]

The lynching exacerbated an imbalance of power between the United States and Italy that would come to affect the enforcement of emerging immigration law. Washington evaded Italian pressure to punish those responsible for organizing and carrying out the lynching by claiming it was a state matter in which the federal government could not intervene. When Consul Corte complained about the slow pace of investigations largely due to the uncooperative city of New Orleans, at various times officials in New Orleans, Baton Rouge, and Washington all pointed fingers at each other in response to diplomats' questioning.[23] When it was convenient to do so, the U.S. government claimed the victims were all American citizens in order to deflect Italy's valid demands for justice regardless of citizenship status. The effect was to carve out a zone devoid of responsibility for victims who occupied a gray space between Italian emigration statute and U.S. immigration and naturalization law.[24] The rules of diplomacy placed responsibility for ensuring the safety of Italian citizens on American soil squarely in Washington's hands. Despite this fact, the State Department, Congress, and the federal courts left the victims without an advocate.

In the early 1890s, as both nations were emerging onto the world stage and "finding their place among nations," Washington's refusal to support the victims' families' calls to prosecute the perpetrators paralleled a strengthening of federal authority to regulate immigration and exercise gatekeeping authority over U.S. borders.[25] Seventeen days after the murders, as Washington argued it lacked jurisdiction to punish the mob's leaders and initially refused to secure indemnity for the victims' families, a clearly frustrated di Rudinì recalled his ambassador to Rome. As Secretary of State James Blaine argued with the prime minister whether the victims were due protection under treaty law, Americans from New Orleans to the halls of Congress began to use the lynching as a rationale for restricting Italians from legally entering the country. The largest mass lynching perpetrated against foreign-born people in this country injected the Italian diplomatic service into domestic debates over immigration restriction.

More than a year later, in the spring of 1892, a piece of legislation introduced by Republican senator Joseph Dolph of Oregon attempted to resolve the legal barrier to federal prosecution of a state-level crime against foreigners. Senator Dolph had long been a supporter of a strong gatekeeping apparatus. He proposed an earlier version of the finality clause adopted, but never actually enforced, in the amended Chinese Exclusion Act he sponsored in 1888.[26]

Dolph's 1892 bill stalled in committee over constitutional questions the lynching had raised, namely, the division between state and federal authority in prosecuting the murder of foreigners on U.S. soil.

The ultimate failure of the Dolph legislation had an impact. In an unstable political climate, in the wake of an economic panic and with a presidential election looming, the collapse of what the Ministry of Foreign Affairs called the "Dolph bill" ultimately strengthened Washington's ability to regulate immigration and confirmed the asymmetric nature of the emerging Italian–U.S. relationship. The failure of this bill to pass focused the ambassador's attention away from traditional diplomatic channels and onto Congress, where he saw new attempts to pass restrictive legislation.[27] Officers in the MAE looked to Washington at a time when federal rather than state law became the primary tool to manage immigration into the United States.[28] Beginning in 1891, the government in Rome (and the Roman and Italian American press) would keep a watchful eye on the progress of gatekeeping laws at the same time as diplomats began working through a series of ultimately unsuccessful interventions intended to spare Italians from restriction.

In 1891 and 1892 both national political parties agreed on the need for but not on the parameters of new immigration limits. The Democratic and Republican Parties each adopted restrictionist planks in their June 1892 conventions. That summer Democrats declared, "We heartily approve all legitimate efforts to prevent the United States from being used as the dumping ground for the known criminals and professional paupers of Europe."[29] Republicans agreed that as a party "we favor the enactment of more stringent laws and regulations for the restriction of criminal, pauper, and contract immigration."

While a rich literature exists that documents the push for immigration restriction in the United States and the targeted groups' mobilization against draconian and discriminatory immigration laws, little has been said about how sending governments responded. The 1891 New Orleans lynching generated a transnational political response to the movement to restrict immigration to the United States. For the United States, as for many other receiving countries at the time, immigration laws became a tool to shape U.S. society.[30] They also established the government's right to determine who could (or could not) enter the country and who could naturalize. By concentrating anti-Italian vitriol and anti-immigrant hysteria at the same time as the implementation of full federal control of the gatekeeping apparatus, and, most consequently, drawing the Italian government into domestic policy debates over immigration limits, the 1891 lynching must be examined as a pivotal moment on the path toward mass immigration restriction.[31]

## The Lynching

In a city that blurred the lines between American-born and immigrant, European and African, and northern and southern sensibilities, the rapid and visible entry of Italians primarily from Sicily into New Orleans unsettled a city that Chief of Police Hennessy and his faction of the Democratic Party had attempted to control. Accounts in Hennessy's time took the guilt of the accused for granted, and the acquittals of March 13, 1891, stirred up the kind of suspicion that had first pointed toward Italians as Hennessy's murderers.[32] That day, a notice appeared calling for a mob to assemble at 10:00 a.m. the next morning at the base of the city's Henry Clay statue "to take steps to remedy the failure of justice in the Hennessy case. Come prepared for action," it read, ominously.[33] New Orleans's Italian consul, Pasquale Corte, tried desperately to prevent the violent outcome of such a clear threat. He spent the morning searching for Mayor Shakspeare to implore him to issue an order to disperse a gathering crowd. Unable to locate him (likely because he made himself hard to find), Corte sought out the governor of Louisiana, who refused to issue any orders except at the request of the missing Mayor Shakspeare.[34] Chief Hennessy's defenders soon turned to an unspeakably brutal form of vigilante justice, lynching, that between 1882 and 1968 took the lives of 4,743 people across the South.[35]

While Corte tried in vain to convince elected officials to maintain order, the mob commenced its bloody work to avenge Chief Hennessy's murder. Estimates of the crowd size vary. In a city with a total population at the time of 242,000, likely between five and eight thousand gathered under Henry Clay's statue on the morning of March 14.[36] Some sources described the mob being as large as twenty thousand, but contemporary illustrations appeared to exaggerate the size.[37] The mood was surprisingly light as "the men, armed with rifles, most of whom were young, went smiling [to the parish prison] as though they were on a picnic."[38] Brandishing rifles and revolvers, clubs, and other makeshift weapons, the lynch mob broke down the doors of the parish prison and indiscriminately began to attack any Italians they could find. One account claimed that William Parkerson, mob leader, lawyer, and campaign chairman who helped elect Mayor Shakspeare in 1889, discouraged the terrorizing mob from killing those who had been acquitted only the day before.[39]

Inside the prison walls seven men were shot in the back, or the head, or both, while the crowd of men, women, and children gathered outside clamored for more action. By 11:00 a.m., one hour after the mass meeting had commenced at the statue of the statesman known as the Great Compromiser, prisoners were forced to exit the prison gates onto Congo Square where "willing hands" applied a noose to four more victims. The crowd raised Emanuele Polizzi, whom the *Illustrated American* described as "the half-crazed Sicilian who offered to turn state's evidence," high enough to see his body clearly above the frenzy. Still alive, he appeared "aghast with terror" facing his imminent death. Soon twelve bullets tore through his face. Onlookers thronged nearby balconies, some using opera glasses to get a closer look. The whole sordid scene outside the prison unfolded in forty-five minutes. Their work now done, the mob's leaders quite literally washed their hands clean of Italian blood and returned to their lives and workplaces.[40] The mob had taken the lives of eleven men that morning.

While indiscriminate ethnic hatred had initially appeared to spur the killings, on closer examination the terrorism respected existing political lines. Long-standing tension around Italians' rapid entry into the city's lucrative fruit and vegetable trade, and the fight to secure Italian votes for the two warring factions of the Democratic Party then dominating local politics, hung in the air around the lynching like a heavy cloud that would not dissipate. One of the businessmen aligned with Hennessy and Mayor Shakspeare's Young Men's Democratic Association (or YMDA) escaped with his life, while another Italian shipping magnate tied to the rival Democratic organization known as "the Ring" was murdered with the others.[41] While three of the victims had a record of murder or other violent crime, five had no such criminal history.[42]

Gallons of ink ran as fast as blood had in New Orleans as newspapers across the country rushed to cover the story as a scandalous Mafia tale. The majority of English-language coverage framed the lynching as a necessary action to counter Mafia influence over the trial of Hennessy's accused killers. Every day for almost a week after the lynching the *New York Times* put a story from New Orleans on the front page. On March 18 the newspaper wrote that the "Black Hand" was behind Hennessy's murder; the accused were clearly guilty and were only acquitted because of a Mafia-issued threat of bodily harm to the jury. Only the lynch mob was free from the influence of the Mafia as "members of the mob had not been and could not be 'got at' or 'fixed' by the mafia," the *Times* explained, a convoluted way of assuaging the mob of guilt for murdering eleven people by emphasizing the moral fortitude of its thousands of members.[43] On March 25 *Puck* magazine published a Louis Dalrymple cartoon declaring "At the Bottom of it All: cowardly juries are the first cause of mob rule." A menacing, masked female figure holding a gun in one hand and a knife in the other, wearing traditional southern Italian peasant clothing, looks through an open window at a seated jury. She lurks over the entire right side of the illustration, as if she could act on her threat at any moment. Her target, the cartoon suggests, is none other than the constitutional principle of

**FIGURE 1.1.** Louis Dalyrimple, "At The Bottom of It All: Cowardly Juries Are the First Cause of Mob Rule." *Puck*, March 25, 1891.

a trial by jury, a bedrock American freedom. Even John Higham, respected scholar and author of the twentieth century's most influential monograph on American nativism, assumed the jury had been bribed.[44] Historian Patrizia Salvetti repeated this claim several times in her 2003 history of Italian lynchings in the United States, yet she gave no evidence clearly demonstrating such interference.[45]

Press coverage repeated the Mafia connection, reflecting and influencing the larger debate over immigration restriction. In April 1891 the *Illustrated American* issued "a solemn warning" directly to its readers. "Men of America, we said, do not be misled by those who pretend that these murder-societies have ceased to exist. Although they have been almost destroyed in Italy, they come to life again on this free soil of ours." The threat was immediate and real: "Strenuous measures must be taken to suppress them, or our cities will sink to the level of bandit-ridden Palermo." Furthermore, the *New York Times* warned, if Italians did not denounce the Mafia, then Americans will come to believe that all Italians condone criminal activity, and then Americans, feeling angry and distrustful, would have a rationale "founded on facts and sustained by reason" for their "hostile feeling against Italians as Italians."[46] To prevent further discrimination and violence, changes would have to come from Congress: tightened procedures, in the words of first federal superintendent of immigration Herman Stump in his annual report to Congress in July 1892, designed "to secure more searching and scrutinizing inspections" that would better enforce new laws to exclude migrants who posed a potential danger.

Stump began his report with a set of statistics intended to frighten the Committee on Immigration and Naturalization: in the period from April 1, 1891, to January 31, 1892, inspectors rejected only one-third of 1 percent of all migrants arriving to the Port of New York, then still located at Castle Garden.[47] "There have been many undesirable immigrants permitted to land, who, under a reasonable and proper construction of the laws now in force, should have been refused admission," he argued, "thereby dumping thousands of the worst classes of European population upon our shores, to become a burden upon our country, a source of menace to honest labor, and an incubus upon society." Stump's testimony acknowledged the need for more effective enforcement to begin with an inspection before a migrant departed for the United States. "This committee can not be unmindful of the tone of public opinion, voiced by the press of our country, as to the turning loose in the midst of our honest laborers and intelligent and religious people the hordes of vicious, depraved, criminal, and pauper elements of humanity now permitted to invade our land."[48]

Beginning in the 1890s, southern Italians seeking to escape poverty and political persecution in the regions of Campania (where Naples is located), Calabria, and Sicily migrated in increasing numbers to the United States. While Italians who arrived in the United States benefited from what Thomas Guglielmo called a "color privilege," they were denied race privilege, a condition they carried over with them from Italy.[49] Italian and American ideas about race attached fixed characteristics to southern Italian migrants. In Italy these ideas circulated in debates over how to solve the so-called Southern Question, as a part of the several-decades-long, violent process of making the united Kingdom of Italy.[50] Early prime ministers sent the army to subdue radical peasant protests in what became known as a Brigand War, the name reflecting the low regard leaders from northern and central Italy held for rural southern workers. Members of Parliament considered the problems of poverty and violence that marked the regions of the *mezzogiorno* as caused by the "inferior civilization" and its "criminality of blood," to use the words of the founder of the Italian school of criminal anthropology, Cesare Lombroso, at the same time as they discussed reforming Italian emigration law.[51]

Basing his academic theories on study of anthropometric features, the work of Italian criminologist Alfredo Niceforo helped define racial ideas that would influence parliamentary debates in Rome and go on to shape U.S. immigration policy for more than two decades, from the 1890s to the era of the Dillingham Commission.[52] "Italy is formed by two dissimilar races," Niceforo explained, with northern and southern Italians making up "two Italies standing in stark contrast, with complete distinct moral and social characters."[53] The *Illustrated*

*American* differentiated between northern and southern Italians when it explained how Sicilians "have, besides, much Arab blood in their veins. This is presumed to account for their lawlessness."[54]

While Italian anthropologists and politicians made a clear distinction, the rhetoric of the 1891 lynching collapsed differences between and among Italians. Distinct geographic, cultural, and linguistic variation between regions in this newly united country disappeared in the headlines in the spring of 1891. The *Washington Post* declared Italy "A Nation of Murderers" in a front-page article that described a people whose "radical excitability is heightened by a warm climate and the national habit of the use of the knife."[55] These articles failed to mention that a united Italy, barely a generation old in 1891, had few if any shared "national habits." An analysis of the coverage over time reveals how newspapers ascribed Italians of all classes with violent, clannish, and politically dangerous characteristics. (Recall how the *Philadelphia Inquirer* had denigrated the ambassador and prime minister, a baron and a marquis, respectively, on its front page as men ready and willing to wield the stiletto knife when wronged.)[56] Notably, the coverage of the lynching temporarily collapsed the northern/southern Italian divide otherwise becoming a standard element of American media treatments of this ethnic group.[57]

This pattern manifested over the next two decades in two very different ways. In Italian American papers, as Peter Vellon has shown, "the Italian mainstream press's defense of Italians and Italian civilization would prove critical to establishing a collective identity as Italians" that had not existed in Italy.[58] Jessica Barbata Jackson found a similar phenomenon in her study of lynchings in Louisiana across the entire decade, noting how the New Orleans lynching spurred the development of fraternal organizations that offered membership based on a much broader sense of Italianness.[59] At the same time, racial ideas about the differences between northern and southern Italians borne out of the difficult process of making Italy shaped how Italians were treated and categorized in the United States.[60] While Hennessy's murder and the retaliatory lynching fueled fears of the wave of Italian migration then building in Louisiana and the United States at large, it also revealed that the racialization of Italians was constantly in flux and situation-dependent, and could be exploited in the service of domestic politics.

Race politics in Louisiana encouraged strange alliances, and the participation of Black men in the anti-Italian lynch mob points to the effectiveness of the "divide and conquer" strategy of white supremacy. Italian race consciousness also challenged southern ideas of social propriety and stoked fears of miscegenation. "One of the reasons why the Italian race was considered inferior was its familiarity with black people," historian Patrizia Salvetti has written.[61]

The African American paper the *New York Sun* noted in 1899 how Italians "are willing to live in the same quarters with the Negroes and work side by side with them, and seem wholly destitute of that anti-negro prejudice which is one of the distinguishing features of all the white races in the South."[62] A 1911 report by consular agent Luigi Scala on Italian emigrants in Louisiana observed how "Italians treat black people with more familiarity than the natives. Indeed, sometimes they live like husband and wife, sometimes publicly. This is taken as an insult against the white race and leads to threats against their lives, and intimations to leave town."[63] It is not surprising that patterns of violence used against African Americans to enforce the color line would also be used to intimidate members of New Orleans's Italian community who crossed it.

At the turn of the twentieth century lynching was a form of extralegal justice meted out in public against victims seen as dangerous to the racial, political, social, and economic order of the South, and in New Orleans in March 1891, politics and money also entered into it. Lynching in the Jim Crow era targeted "uppity" Black southerners who challenged white hegemony. Italians also challenged two major categories of white control: economic and political. Italian fruit and vegetable merchants, who traded freely with Black customers, were serious competitors to native-born business owners.[64] On March 17, 1891, the owner of the biggest dry-goods house in New Orleans, John P. Richardson, told the *New York Times*, "The lynching in New Orleans Saturday is just the thing that should have occurred."[65] Chief Hennessy had taken part in a Democratic Party purge the year before his murder that had consolidated local power in the hands of one machine, the YMDA, by trying to break the power of the "Ring," the faction supported by the city's ethnic minorities, particularly Italians. A fight to secure the increasing number of votes in the Italian quarter animated the YMDA–Ring struggle and may very well have been a reason for Italians to take out the first papers of naturalization, which the state later used to try to deny consular aid to the men arrested for Hennessy's murder.[66]

While political and economic competition underlay the specific racial violence in New Orleans, explanations that quickly followed the mob's actions focused on the language of justice, a pattern common to the practice of lynching.[67] The use of lynch mobs to impose order and intimidate political and economic rivals combined easily with racialized stereotypes of Italians. The New Orleans hometown newspaper, the *Daily Picayune* declared two days after the killings, "It is a method that is to be deplored as lawless and uncivilized, but law and civilization failed at the trial and the community promptly resorted to its own rude but terribly effective method of inspiring a wholesome dread in those who had boldly made a trade of murder."[68] The *San Francisco*

*Chronicle* declared, "Citizens say the defeat of justice made the killings justifiable," one of many newspapers outside the South that reproduced the region's violent logic of white supremacy without question.[69]

The lynching had palpable, and permanent, effects on relations between Italy and the United States. As a direct result of the killings, three weeks later the Italian government suspended official diplomatic relations between the countries when the prime minister recalled Ambassador Fava to Rome, frustrated over the lack of indictments for the known perpetrators in local, state, or federal courts. While the chargé d'affaires, the Marquis Guglielmo Imperiali di Francavilla, remained at his post in Washington and continued to conduct diplomatic affairs, confidential official correspondence tells a clear story of resentment and humiliation.[70] Diplomatic pressure exerted in the lynching's aftermath laid the groundwork for an asymmetric relationship between the two countries to emerge, a pattern seen clearly in the dialogue over expanding immigration restriction and Italy's reaction to the evolving practice of American gatekeeping.

### Creating a Gatekeeping Nation

Coverage of the lynching quickly turned from lurid details and commentary about the murders to calls for new gatekeeping legislation. Newspapers devoured every detail of the crime and its aftermath. These articles amplified fears of Mafia infiltration as an invisible threat. Against the backdrop of the lynching, newspapers from across the country stoked fear, portraying Italians as a dangerous social element to be contained. Reporting to an audience more than twelve hundred miles away, the *Philadelphia Inquirer* suggested that the entire Italian community of New Orleans was like an infection threatening the city's health when it placed an illustration on the front page of a magnified bacterium in the column opposite its drawing of "The Italian Quarter."[71] Painting the victims with a broad brush, the *New York Times* emphasized the threat Italian migration posed when it described "these sneaking and cowardly Sicilians, the descendants of bandits and assassins, who have transported to this country the lawless passions, the cut-throat practices, and the oath-bound societies of their native country." Challenging both their character and their humanity, the *Times* concluded, "Our own rattlesnakes are as good citizens as they. Our own murderers are men of feeling and nobility compared to them."[72] The broader public reaction to the lynching collapsed regional differences that amplified preexisting broadly anti-Italian racism to accelerate the drive toward restriction.

Federal immigration restriction built in intensity throughout the late nineteenth and early twentieth centuries as nativism, scientific racism, and legal and structural changes spurred by the mass migration of Chinese laborers built interlocking support for the prohibition of specific groups and classes. Xenophobia played an essential role in the process.[73] Chinese laborers, in the "yellow peril" campaign, were the first target. After establishing the legal justification to exclude classes of migrants with the 1882 Chinese Exclusion Act, Congress began in the 1890s to add more categories that could be used to deny entry into the United States as it gave shape to the federal gatekeeping apparatus. Intensifying economic turmoil in the 1890s gave an additional push that kept calls for more restriction in motion.[74]

The mechanisms of immigration enforcement connected Asia and Europe as Italians, the "Chinese of Europe," became the new targets for exclusion strategies created to limit entry of Chinese laborers.[75] The Chinese Exclusion Act initially established the legal basis to regulate foreigners arriving in the United States, and over time the law became, in the words of Roger Daniels, "the pivot on which all immigration policy turned."[76] While a series of three Supreme Court cases tested and confirmed the constitutionality of exclusion, the enforcement of exclusionary gatekeeping laws required bureaucratic machinery to issue and check migrants against the law's standards.[77] When Ellis Island opened on January 1, 1892, employees of the new federal Office of Immigration performed the inspections, having been brought over from their former position as "registry clerks" for the state of New York at the Castle Garden station, which had been located at the Battery on the southern tip of Manhattan. Congress's 1891 Immigration Act gave these minor bureaucrats vast discretionary powers to exclude. Inspectors judged through a quick interview the financial, physical, and moral health of the person standing before them.

Soon enough, in July 1892, Stump begged Congress to strengthen the authority of his officers to detain and reject. Only six months after the massive inspection station opened, Stump was in front of Congress, lobbying for a revised statute that would strengthen the ability of federal agents to identify and exclude people he described as "the hordes of vicious, depraved, criminal, and pauper elements of humanity now permitted to invade our land."[78] While he emphasized the value of having invested in a large and well-staffed inspection station and detention and medical quarantine facility at Ellis Island, he argued that existing law was inadequate to stop the entry of "many who should be excluded."[79] His recommendations included three specific changes. The first would limit the discretionary ability of a head commissioner stationed at any port to be the "sole arbiter" to decide admissibility (a leftover from the era when states performed limited examinations at the docks). Stump's concern was that "the present law places in the hands of one person too much power and responsibility," leaving the port commissioner open to persuasion from bribes, patronage-influenced politics, or "generous impulses from within."[80] Stump would have Congress establish a panel of four inspectors to adjudicate cases where any single inspector could not decide whether an immigrant qualified for entry. Third, Stump would extend the jurisdiction to inspect immigrants before departure in foreign ports to ensure compliance with American laws regarding admissibility, thus proposing an early version of "remote control" gatekeeping. In his report Stump asked the assembled representatives to answer calls from the press and the public for a tough new application of immigration law with increased gatekeeping measures designed, in his view, to resist the growing threat.[81]

Stump's proposals outlined new tools of enforcement that would come to define the gatekeeping apparatus. His proposal for a panel of inspectors is the origin of what would become the Board of Special Inquiry, later created in the 1893 Immigration Act, a body made up of four inspectors who had an outsized impact on Italian migrants' cases.[82] To regulate immigration at the turn of the twentieth century meant to systematically categorize and judge men, women, and children to determine if they, in the words of the 1893 act, were "clearly and beyond doubt entitled to admission."[83] He then focused explicitly on the inspection process as the necessary force behind the law.

> All these classes gain admittance in some way and it is the object and purpose of this committee, as far as it is possible, to secure more searching and scrutinizing inspections, made with a view to a more faithful and stricter enforcement of the laws. What seems to have been heretofore called an examination appears from practical results more of a farce than a reality, and the pruning knife must be used with just discrimination, but fearlessly and effectually for the welfare of our countrymen. We might fill the statute book with laws; but without faithful, competent, impartial, and intelligent interpretation and administration of them, they are worthless paper.[84]

All three of Stump's proposed amendments to existing immigration law, when considered with his justifications, show how anti-Italian sentiment that exploded in New Orleans only a year earlier became intimately tied up with a push for increased federal control over the borders. The superintendent concluded, "The examination of from two to four thousand immigrants a day between the hours of 8:30 and 3 o'clock must be of the most superficial character, unreliable, and of little value." Stump questioned whether or not it even fulfilled the expectation of the statute: "It is not much more than a listing and enumeration and does not constitute such an examination as is contemplated by law." In the superintendent's exhortation for "a more faithful and stricter enforcement of the laws," his fears that policies are weak gatekeepers without enforcement, his focus on the inspectors in the new Office of Immigration and that they be competent to perform the task before them, and his conditional faith in the system he was helping shape—all of these responses from the nation's most powerful immigration officer reveal the tensions surrounding the establishment of a broader gatekeeping regime in the United States in the early 1890s. At the same time, the lynching drew the MAE deeper into U.S. domestic politics as the Italian government began tracking closely the progress of congressional debate over immigration restriction, marking this as a distinctly transnational story.

Over time, as the Italian government took an interventionist approach to American gatekeeping policy, the legal questions around punishment and indemnity after the lynching set the tone for a distinctively uneven relationship.[85] Historian Patrizia Salvetti described the imbalance of power between the United States and Italy as "the epitome of the paradox: the nation that suffered the offense had to endure the arrogance of the government that should have made reparation for the injury."[86] In a report to his superiors in Rome written a week after the lynching, Imperiali, Fava's second-in-command, described the lack of action by U.S. authorities as reflective of "contempt or at a minimum callous indifference" to the needs of Italian migrants.[87] Secretary of State James Blaine reportedly told the ambassador before his recall that he cared not at all what Italians thought; Imperiali recalled Blaine's words as "I am perfectly indifferent to the opinions about our institutions abroad; I cannot change the Constitution and even less violate it." Three months later a frustrated Imperiali told the minister of foreign affairs that this outcome "unfortunately reflect[s] the exact way of thinking of the overwhelming majority of American citizens and the legal stand of the government."[88] The aftermath of the lynching set the two countries on a course toward an increasingly asymmetrical partnership where cautious Italian officials, rather than directly pressure American immigration authorities to defend their exclusionary policy, sought explanation and cultivated soft power relationships the Italians believed would protect their migrants and their right to freely enter the country. Diplomacy failed to bring any Americans to account for the lynching, and ordinary Americans, conditioned by the salacious press coverage and racial attitudes, seemed not to care.

The relationship between the two countries was further strained as newspapers and magazines on both sides of the Atlantic questioned the rule of law in Louisiana and challenged Italy's diplomatic power.[89] The influential Black paper the *New York Age* asked, "Is the White South Civilized?" as one of a number of African American and Italian American papers that "sarcastically assailed the alleged civilization of the South, noting the hypocrisy of the 'best citizens' who engaged in murder while upholding the racial superiority of whites."[90] At the same time, American newspapers far from the epicenter of the lynching used their pages to undermine the authority of the Italian legation. The *Weekly Nebraska State Journal*—published more than a thousand miles from New Orleans in Lincoln—questioned the public's faith in the ambassador by suggesting that Prime Minister di Rudinì wanted him out. The front page taunted "Not the Right Man—Is Fava's Removal a Personal Matter?" in the same week the *New York Times* asked if Italy was trying to "get rid of its Minister" to replace him with a better one.[91] In Rome the influential magazine *Nuova Antologia* published an article on "lynch law" by a member of Parliament that laid bare the imbalance of power. "Now it remains to be known what Italy has done and what it could do for the protection of its citizens and the dignity of its government. It remains to know what [the Kingdom of Italy] has given and what the Federal Government of America can give," Pietro Nocito asked. "It remains to be seen whether in the light of civilization and with so much talk of American democracy, the law of the people must be a farce." Lest readers think that only Italians suffered these existential threats, Nocito emphasized, "The question is not only Italian, but for all the states of Europe."[92]

A former congressman expressed the point of view of many Americans when he declared the lynching an entirely reasonable occurrence, not an international incident. The *New Orleans Daily Picayune* published details of an interview by the *Washington Post* that denigrated the victims and minimized the lynching. "'I cannot see,' said ex-Representative Morrow to a Post reporter, 'how this affair at New Orleans can become an international issue. You must remember that the vengeance of the mob was not directed against the Italians as a race, but as a band of supposed murderers, who had escaped their just deserts by the miscarriage of justice . . . It was not a race riot in any sense of the word."[93] Despite the efforts of Italian American newspapers such as the influential *Il Progresso Italo-Americano* to "defend the Italian race," the executive branch gave few signals it was taking the problem of violence against Italian immigrants seriously.[94] Seven days after the lynching, Theodore Roosevelt, at that time a member of the U.S. Civil Service Commission, wrote a letter to his sister. "Monday we dined at the Camerons; various dago diplomats were present, all much wrought up by the lynching of the Italians in New Orleans. Personally I think it rather a good thing, and said so."[95] His dismissal of the Italians' concerns—combined with his casual use of the epithet "dago"—reflects an ambivalent anti-Italianism at the highest levels of the U.S. government at the time.[96] (By 1900 Roosevelt would be elected to his first of two terms as president.)

The representatives of his majesty's royal government were trapped. If diplomats forcefully pursued the traditional course of diplomacy to protect their subjects murdered abroad and pushed for an official inquiry, they ran the risk of backlash in Washington and in American public opinion, which could threaten the free movement of a migrant stream whose remittances were increasing year over year as a percentage of Italy's national economy.[97] Both Italy and the United States were at this time emerging powers trying to establish a role on the world stage, but leaders in Rome knew they could not force the United States to comply with their demands for a thorough investigation of the lynching that might punish the perpetrators and exonerate their dead countrymen.[98] The *Chicago Daily Tribune* highlighted this on its front page on May 22, 1891, with the headline, "Baron Fava's tale of woe—he was told that Uncle Sam would conduct his own affairs." Still facing pressure to resolve the murders, the chargé d'affaires began to advocate for an indemnity for victims' families in negotiations with President Benjamin Harrison. President Harrison first proposed a payment in April 1892 of $125,000. Immediately the American and Italian press decried the offer as degrading, but for different reasons. One American headline declared "Italy Now Appeased" as if the year-long campaign for justice was of little import, easily dismissed with a cash payment.[99]

Internal diplomatic correspondence revealed a prime minister so hesitant to confront the Americans that he actively undermined his own consul as he worked to expose those responsible for the murders. New Orleans consul Pasquale Corte directly challenged elected city and state officials he knew had led the lynch mob as a part of the "Committee of Fifty." The consul even accused the mayor of leading the call to arms, and for this he told Rome, "I am now threatened by a request for my recall by the United States government," although no evidence has emerged indicating he was in actual peril.[100] Instead of protecting him, Corte's own government rebuked the consul. In a letter to Fava, Prime Minister di Rudinì expressed his fear that Corte "may not have displayed a totally conciliatory behavior" in calling out Louisiana and New Orleans authorities publicly for their complicity in the murders.[101] The conflict played out in the press as another embarrassing challenge to Italian sovereignty.

With the Italian legation in conflict over what to do and hobbled by Fava's absence in Washington, inconsistent pressure coming from Italian diplomats obstructed the path to justice. The indemnity payment had to pass through the MAE instead of going directly to the victims' families, and the royal government's attempt to force the courts to apportion payment based on what the *avvocato generale erariale* representing the Italian state, Giacomo Giuseppe Costa, called a "real assessment of damages" was refused.[102] A few years later Costa confided in the minister of foreign affairs in a private report. "It seems quite clear," he wrote in 1893,

> that despite our government's efforts to persuade the United States to be obliged by virtue of treaties and for the same federal laws to rehabilitate the families of the lynched in New Orleans of the damage caused to them by the enormous violence that was the killing of their leaders; yet this debt never wanted to be acknowledged. In fact, the federal government—that challenged the Italian nationality of the majority of those killed—did not want to know who the damaged family members were—refused to pay them directly the agreed sum, handing it to our government instead to distribute it at will—and finally, it did not accept the reserve, which our government wanted to include in the agreement, that is to say that it was without prejudice to the rights of the injured, to be asserted, for the real assessment of damages, before the competent magistrates.[103]

Costa questioned the true purpose of the payment. Was the money offered to extinguish "a civil debt to the families of the lynched" who lost their heads of household, "or is it not a mere diplomatic satisfaction, however necessary, that one government has given to the other to maintain the existence of friendships between them, cemented by formal treaties?" Costa confirmed later in the same letter that he believed the payment confirmed the U.S. government would continue to deny victims' families access to federal courts to pursue civil cases. The MAE drew up a lengthy document explaining the rationale for dividing the $125,000 indemnity among the victims' families that included mathematical equations as well as legal and ethical arguments, signaling an acceptance in Rome of the terminal status of negotiations.[104]

In the aftermath of New Orleans the official restoration of diplomatic relations between the two countries was predicated on the acceptance of what San Francisco's *Voce del Popolo* newspaper, referencing the New Orleans case following another lynching in Colorado perpetrated in 1895, dismissed as "indemnity-charity."[105] Patrizia Salvetti characterized the Italian government's acquiescence to the Americans as "disheartening" for its focus on negotiating indemnity paid to families of the dead—what the Italian American press derided as the "blood price"—instead of legislative changes that would have given statutory authority to punish the perpetrators and recognize the dignity of the murdered men.[106] This followed a pattern set by the racially motivated murder of Italians in Eureka, Nevada, in 1879, apparently to suppress labor unrest led by striking charcoal makers. According to Salvetti, the consul in San Francisco, Diego Barrilis, "suggested a solution that in a few years would become standard operating procedure, albeit a humiliating one: close the case asking for an indemnification for the victims' families in exchange for the predictable acquittal of the police officers responsible for the killings."[107] In New Orleans, the ministry's internal documents reveal that by approving an indemnity without demanding the Americans punish the culprits behind the murders, the Italians acquiesced to the limits of diplomacy to force the United States to act. In this way, the long aftermath of the lynching cemented the rules of an asymmetric partnership that would in turn shape relations over migration issues.

Meanwhile, Italian diplomats watched with trepidation in 1892 as Congress debated additional gatekeeping legislation that tightened the regulation of Chinese migrants. Again, Senator Joseph Dolph of Oregon played a critical role. Dolph had been a sponsor of the bill extending the Chinese Exclusion Act in 1888. In 1892 Dolph introduced the renewal of the Chinese Exclusion Act to the Senate. Later known as the Geary Act for its sponsor in the House, this update of Chinese exclusion required all Chinese persons to carry and immediately produce on request papers certifying their legal residency in the United States, or face deportation. Initially the law specified that "one credible white witness" must certify a Chinese person's papers; this was later amended in 1893 to "one credible witness other than Chinese." The law included a provision for violators to receive one year of hard labor before the Supreme Court declared this punishment unconstitutional. The justices upheld the paperwork requirement, with deportation as the consequence.[108]

Chinese plaintiffs who used the courts to resist exclusion "are always litigating," in the words of one congressman in 1893, with writs of habeas corpus to challenge migrants' detention. This strategy initially worked to blunt the power of exclusionary law and free the detained, Lucy Salyer argues.[109] While the Chinese used federal courts and diplomacy to resist restriction's legal basis, Italians would act through their diplomatic network to challenge inspectors' power to admit or refuse to land an immigrant in individual cases.[110] In the 1890s the traditional avenue of using diplomacy to negotiate migration policy between nations had less impact. By 1894 the Chinese government requested a new treaty to negotiate the provisions of what were now several exclusionary laws. This treaty upheld the registration requirement but reversed a policy that had temporarily prohibited Chinese laborers from reentering the United States. In all, the treaty did little to alter the most stringent aspects of Chinese exclusion or contain the growing gatekeeping apparatus.[111]

In the same month that Senator Dolph also introduced the revised Chinese

Exclusion Act, March 1892, he brought forward legislation to protect foreigners in the United States. In May the Senate held hearings on bill S.2409: Violations of the Treaty Rights of Foreigners, which would guarantee the rights of foreigners to be protected while on U.S. soil.[112] Initially optimistic about the impact of the Dolph bill, the MAE reported "satisfaction that proposals were made by the United States for the purpose of providing punishment for crimes against the person or property of foreigner whose rights are guaranteed by international treaties."[113] The newly reinstated Ambassador Fava and the chargé d'affaires, Marquis Imperiali, who had been left in charge of the legation in Washington until Fava returned to his post on May 16, followed the debate very closely, corresponding with the sergeant at arms for daily updates of the bill's progress.[114] (When Italy and the United States reestablished relations, both countries elevated their legations to embassies.) Much to the surprise of its author but not to the Italian observers, the Dolph bill drew immediate criticism from senators who pointed out how the bill contradicted the constitutional division of power. Most of the debate focused on the legal implications of passing federal law that said that violations of state law committed against foreigners could be tried in the federal courts.[115] In its internal correspondence the Italian legation dissected the bill's weak position. Given that the Republican Party, then in the minority in Congress, was in support, Marquis Imperiali predicted that "Americanism would revolt" if the Republican president pushed for what he argued the Democrats saw as "a proposal that goes against all the most fundamental traditions and principles of the party, and, on top of it, directed against Louisiana, which is its core."[116]

On August 20, 1892, predicting the fate of the Dolph bill, Ambassador Fava wrote a report to headquarters in Rome on the fate of S.2409. Fava's report confirmed that the lynching led the Italian government to agitate for this bill.[117] A reading of the diplomatic letters shows "Fava was legitimately proud" of a small victory in pushing the Senate to acknowledge, in debate over the bill, that it lacked the power to enforce treaty protections.[118] Buffeted by domestic political pressure in a presidential election year, the legislative session expired before the Dolph bill could come to a vote.[119] The only remaining avenue was a constitutional amendment, and diplomats knew this had no chance of success in the existing political climate.

In May 1894 a federal appeals court judge's decision revealed how vulnerable Italian migrants were in the United States even with the intervention of diplomats.[120] Judge Parlange handed down a final decision declaring no law existed that guaranteed the right of the families of the lynching victims to claim damages from the city or the state of Louisiana. (The Dolph bill, had it passed into law, would have given recourse in federal courts.) The editors of the *Daily Picayune* heartily approved. "The people of this city certainly have no reason to object to this decision. It is money in their pockets," read an article headlined "The People Will Not Have to Pay."[121] Consul Giuseppe Papini, who had been threatened by the lynch mob in his role as secretary of the consulate back in March 1891, penned a three-page report directly to his superiors back in Rome the same day. "With such a decision there is nothing more to do," he despaired.[122] He had tucked a newspaper story into his report clipped from the *New Orleans Times-Democrat*. The editors of the second-most-read paper in the city expressed their support for the mob's deadly action in 1891, describing the lynching as an instance where "the people of a community [had to] rise up to suppress lawlessness and punish assassins."[123] Working through hard and soft pressure, negotiation, and ultimately, acquiescence, the MAE had reached the limits of its power to protect its migrants abroad.

Congress turned its attention back to passing laws to further strengthen the power of immigration officers to exclude undesirable classes from entering the country. Over the next decade the lynching and its aftermath indirectly supported assertions of administrative authority to control immigration into the United States. In the struggle against Chinese restriction, diplomacy had little mitigating effect.[124] Italian diplomats could not negotiate real legal protections for its migrants, not through diplomacy, the courts, or Congress. For its part, Congress, spurred in part by the events of 1891, was sharpening the tools it would use "to sift" those arriving daily at U.S. borders.[125] Italians would be forced to navigate the changing rules of immigration enforcement with the legacy of the lynching coloring their interactions.

Fava publicly acknowledged the limits of diplomatic pressure in the face of the U.S. government's hardening position on gatekeeping. In 1902, one year after leaving his post in Washington, the ambassador reflected on the position of Italians relative to U.S. law. From the pages of the magazine *Nuova Antologia* he addressed the lynching with detached language. He offered a vision for the future where Italians would be respected for their contributions and recognized for their humanity under the law. He did not seem optimistic; eleven years after the crime, he asked if a solution to the lynching would be permanently shelved by Congress. Fava wrote about the relationship between the two countries then actively being reshaped by the presence of millions of Italian migrants. "Fairness and law must prevail and impose themselves on all kinds of international relations," he concluded, especially in light of the hard work being done by his countrymen to "increase the wealth and well-being of the Great Republic and [build] increasingly tight bonds of brotherhood between the United States and Italy."[126] The ambassador watched the power to influence immigration policy shift from diplomatic, treaty-based negotiations to falling more strictly under congressional authority. Back in 1891 and 1892 the State Department had responded to legitimate Italian claims in the case of the lynching by stonewalling while Congress renewed Chinese exclusion and continued to debate further restriction using plenary power that insulated U.S. immigration laws from legal challenges.

Meanwhile, Italy adopted an observational stance. While the 1891 finality clause was motivated by the Chinese strategy to resist exclusion in the courts, its broader application would be shaped by the anti-Italianism stirred up by the New Orleans lynching as the structures created by Asian exclusion law expanded to target European migrants. When in 1898 Congress amended the Chinese exclusion law again, the Italian embassy made sure to obtain a copy of the new legislation. The ambassador kept close watch on the proceedings.[127] But his attention was not limited to legislative activity in Washington.

Attached to the U.S. House report was a newspaper clipping that reported on the revival of a long-dormant effort to update the Italian Emigration Law of 1888, which had proven insufficient to manage emigration and deal with serious problems like the lynching of Italians abroad. The unattributed article criticized the Chamber of Deputies for their inaction. "Among the projects that the Chamber has not discussed and that have been left to decay, there was one series of long studies by the Hon. [Prime Minister] Visconti-Venosta and [Minister Luigi] Luzzatti, to regulate our emigration abroad, now insipidly abandoned to itself." A third representative, Minister Canevaro, hoped that the House of Deputies would overcome its "eternal little partisan wars" to react to American immigration law.[128] Feeling the impact of U.S. moves, Italian leaders were in the midst of a long debate over the scope of state power to regulate emigration.

In the 1890s Italians saw a U.S. government increasingly intent on patrolling its own borders and deciding the fate of those allowed inside. An editorial published one day after lynching denied those eleven murdered men the most basic dignity. Calling them "desperate ruffians and murderers . . . [who] are to us a pest without mitigations," the *New York Times* argued the victims deserved their own violent death. The editorial concluded by stating that the lynching enjoyed widespread approval in New Orleans; indeed, some of the city's most prominent men were among its leaders and took no steps to hide their involvement. Local, state, and federal courts had refused to punish the perpetrators, men the *Philadelphia Inquirer* had celebrated as "avengers."[129]

The failure of the Dolph bill and the refusal of Washington or New Orleans, Louisiana, to prosecute the perpetrators of the lynching established a durable precedent at the same time as new immigration law strengthened the discretionary power of federal officials to use in border control.[130] In the words of Superintendent Stump, "the pruning knife must be used with just discrimination, but fearlessly and effectually for the welfare of our countrymen," to protect the United States from the danger posed by people arriving at the borders.[131]

Chinese exclusion law set in motion a process that increasingly insulated immigration law from international pressure to protect migrants from exclusion and pushed diplomats further away from direct influence over the treatment their citizens received. The tragedy of the lynching set the two nations on a course toward a new kind of relationship as the lynching and its aftermath established the terms of an asymmetric partnership. The events of the early 1890s colored the Italian government's role in the United States over the next decade as Asian exclusion policies and processes expanded to target European migrants.

Nine months after the lynching, in December 1891, arsonists set fire to the home of lawyer and lynch mob leader William S. Parkerson. While no one was formally charged, New Orleans newspapers blamed Italians for this attack on a prominent man with strong political connections. Much as they had in March 1891, local newspapers strategically deployed coverage of the arson to denigrate and intimidate the entire Italian community. A full year after the fire, in December 1892, the *Times-Democrat* published a front-page article identifying the arsonists as "Sicilian mafiosi."[132] Casting blame using the language of a common slur also seen in political cartoons—that of "Italian incendiaries"—the newspaper advised Italians of New Orleans to cooperate with the ongoing investigation lest they find their "future welfare and safety . . . in this city" threatened.[133] The *Times-Democrat* was also the leading voice of the YMDA wing of the Democratic Party connected to Chief Hennessy, a point not lost on the diplomatic corps.

Reflecting the state of fear and confusion in the city almost two years after the lynching, Consul Cavalier Riccardo Motta, Corte's successor in New Orleans, shared two articles with the MAE to illustrate how the fire at Parkerson's house was only now, a year later, being blamed on Italians. This, the consul thought, was a bald attempt to undermine the grand jury at that very moment, after much delay, finally deliberating on the city's culpability in the 1891 murders. "The *Times-Democrat* attributes the fire to the Italians and indirectly threatens new reprisals," Motta reported to the ambassador in Washington. "I do not attach much importance to the alleged revelations of that newspaper because it is notoriously an enemy of the Italians, and because some of its principal co-owners and editors took part in the sad massacre from 14 March 1891." The consul ended the letter on a frustrated note that revealed the state of affairs in the city. His report exposed his own receding power following another round of attacks on the safety and reputation of New Orleans's Italian community: "Excellency, your Lordship can detect the current state of this dispute."[134]

## "If Immigration Was Properly Restricted"

The hysterical tone adopted by the media in the lynching's aftermath left no space for the long history of Italian migration to Louisiana. In the antebellum period, a small but consistent stream of northern Italians had come to New Orleans, settled into a variety of occupations and professions in the city, and largely assimilated into the general population. After the Civil War, paralleling the shift in immigrant origin seen more widely across the entire United States, southern Italians began to arrive in the state, finding work in manual labor or sugarcane fields. This wave of mostly Sicilian migrants stood out as their sheer number and pattern of settlement contrasted with Italians who had arrived before 1865.[135] By the 1880s, New Orleans, long a Latin-Caribbean-Catholic city, was attracting Sicilians in sizable numbers as more migrants arrived in Louisiana. In 1890 alone, Italians made up 67 percent of all incoming migrants to Louisiana out of a total number of fewer than four thousand foreigners arriving in the state that year.[136] Between 1880 and 1920, Italian migration to Louisiana overall outpaced all three of her neighboring states combined by a ratio of two to one.[137]

Regional labor markets and patterns of late nineteenth-century migration amplified the presence of Italians in the South in industry and agriculture. Plantations beyond the city limits sought a seemingly endless supply of cheap and tractable labor to cut sugarcane, while in the neighboring states of Arkansas and Mississippi, Italians tried their hand at growing cotton in a supervised labor experiment coordinated in part by Italian consular agents.[138] In these pockets of the rural South, Italians were purposefully recruited to replace Black labor in the post-emancipation era. In 1890 the census counted approximately 11,000 foreign and native-born Italians in Louisiana, a figure that grew ten years later to 29,000.[139] Yet they would not stay in a subordinate place for long.

By 1910, opportunities in New Orleans to expand into the city's burgeoning fruit and vegetable trade had attracted a population of 18,581 Italian-born people who, while concentrated around the French Market in "Little Italy" in the 1890s, over time spread throughout the city. They "avoided ethnic segregation and established ties and relationships with various parts of the community."[140] As Italians came to occupy a variety of roles in New Orleans, native-born Americans fought for their political attention and the fruits of their

**FIGURE 1.2.** Grant Hamilton, "Where the Blame Lies," *Judge*, April 4, 1891. Representing the voice of the magazine, a man looking out over the crowd pouring from Castle Garden station says to Uncle Sam, "If Immigration was properly Restricted you would no longer be troubled with Anarchy, Socialism, the Mafia and such kindred evils!"

labor. Fruit and vegetable trading allowed some Italians to gain status among white business leaders. But the legacy of the events of 1891 lingered, bringing into stark relief the precarity of their position not just in New Orleans but also the nation at large. According to Jessica Barbara Jackson, "The southern experience of Sicilian and other Italian immigrants, in contrast to their experience in the urban north, was originally characterized by a positive relationship with native-born Southerners, which readily deteriorated over time."[141] Notwithstanding the fluid role that Italians occupied within regional social and economic structures, the upward mobility of a small number of Italians in the economy of this unique southern city could do little to reverse national moves toward more qualitative restriction.

The lynching drew the Italian government, and in particular its diplomatic corps, into domestic affairs in the United States at the exact same time that Congress was fashioning the fundamentals of its gatekeeping apparatus. In April 1891 the satirical political magazine *Judge* explicitly tied the two together when it published a cartoon with the title "Where the Blame Lies." The trial, acquittal, and subsequent lynching of Italians in New Orleans in March 1891, *Judge* suggests, revealed the danger posed by the Mafia, whose presence lurked throughout the city. Taking a clear position on mass immigration restriction, the cartoon shows Uncle Sam standing atop a small precipice alongside a man with a top hat who symbolizes the voice of *Judge*. As both men look out at hordes of vulgarly drawn emigrants pouring out of the Castle Garden station at the base of Manhattan, the man in the top hat says: "If immigration was properly Restricted you would no longer be troubled with Anarchy, Socialism, the Mafia, and such kindred evils!"[142] Individual men in the menacing crowd are labeled "German socialist," "Russian anarchist," "Polish vagabond," "Italian brigand," "English convict," "Irish pauper"; their number overwhelms the picture. At Uncle Sam's feet is a sheet of paper reading "Mafia in New Orleans, Anarchists in Chicago, Socialists in New York." More broadly, the events of the spring of 1891 in New Orleans established the conditions for an asymmetric partnership to grow between Italy and the country that would become, by 1896, the most common destination for its emigrants.[143]

As the century came to a close the power of the federal government to carry out immigration policy was confirmed in the courts and in the court of public opinion to tighten border controls in response to domestic political pressure. A letter to the editors of the *Century* in February 1895 announced the formation of a new group of prominent intellectuals calling itself the Immigration Restriction League. The purpose of the organization was in part "to arouse public opinion to the necessity of a further exclusion of elements undesirable for citizenship or injurious to our national character." When the league clarified: "It is not an object of this league to advocate the exclusion of laborers or other immigrants of such character and standards as fit them to become citizens," Italians, more and more, would be classified as unfit.[144] Writing in the *Atlantic* in June 1896, league founding member Francis Amasa Walker, an academic that the historian of American nativism John Higham called one of the most influential intellectual voices in the movement for restriction, characterized "immigrants from southern Italy, Hungary, Austria, and Russia . . . [as] beaten men from beaten races; representing the worst failures in the struggle for existence."[145]

## Conclusion

The 1891 lynching shifted U.S.–Italian diplomatic relations toward an intense focus on the policies and processes of U.S. gatekeeping. Diplomats tried to shepherd immigrants through the increasingly complex admission process and protect them once inside the country, something that ministers often labeled *tutela*, or protection, in their reports. The lynching (which diplomats kept referring to in their private correspondence for years) called out the precarious position Italian emigrants occupied vis-à-vis American law. While it hardened the Italian government's resolve to protect Italian migrants abroad through the diplomacy conducted by its Ministry of Foreign Affairs, the aftermath of the crime revealed how emigrants are, as sociologist Roger Waldinger writes, "at once *of* the sending state but not *in* it . . . at once *in* the receiving state but not *of* it."[146]

Discovering the limits of direct diplomacy after the New Orleans murders, Italy would significantly revise its own emigration law as hostility toward Italians continued to grow. In the United States federal legislation designed to contain the "yellow peril" provided tools for exclusion in a radically expanded enforcement bureaucracy.[147] At the same time that the lynching confirmed the ability of American citizens to act with impunity toward foreigners in their midst, the authority of the federal government to exclude and deport unwanted migrants was growing. The lynching accelerated profound changes already in motion in how immigrants were classified, regulated, and excluded at the close of the nineteenth century.

Reactions to the 1891 New Orleans lynching reproduced in the press with the rhetoric of Italians as a threat predicted immigration policy debates in the twentieth and twenty-first centuries. Contemporary language of border security, illegality, and the danger of "illegal aliens" reflects how crucial the reaction to the lynching has been to the politics of immigration restriction.[148] Yet the shadows cast on immigration policy by the mass lynching of eleven Italians have been obscured by the discrimination it engendered. The reactionary politics around the lynching informed American immigration policy in subtle but powerful ways that, over time, would confirm the legitimacy of the federal government to police its own borders and the people it allows inside. Diplomats increasingly concerned about efforts to exclude Italian citizens from the United States undertook strategies to resist restrictive immigration policy in the aftermath of the horrific events in New Orleans as anti-Italian rhetoric flowed freely in the American press. The mob violence that led to Chief David Hennessy's death precipitated changes to policy that would in turn affect the structure of the entire population of the United States for decades to come.

# CHAPTER 2

# The Italian Government and
# U.S. Border Enforcement in the 1890s

An evocative piece published in *Harper's Weekly* in August 1893 brought to vivid life the day-to-day enforcement at the Ellis Island immigration station of two new American exclusion laws passed in 1891 and 1893. These laws had given the U.S. government the authority to question and detain anyone "clearly and without a doubt entitled to admission" at the place Italians would come to call *l'isola delle lacrime*, or the island of tears.[1] Here, the drama of individual lives clashed with the processes of a new but otherwise mundane bureaucratic system. On the island in New York's busy harbor the *Harper's* reporter found "a strange, a stirring, and an instructive spectacle which is thus presented almost every day in the year upon the great airy second floor of the Ellis Island building." The second floor had been organized into cages for "a motley crowd of immigrants, eating, walking, sleeping, sitting listlessly with folded hands, or soothing their children's fretfulness; these are awaiting remittances or friends to take them on their journey, or else are suspects to be more closely inquired into by-and-by." Even those not corralled into fenced pens looked pitiful as they sat on rough wooden benches and waited. "The smaller company opposite are no more miserable in appearance, though more wretched in their state. *They are the rejected*, to be sent home again on the next sailing of the steamer which brought them," as the 1891 Immigration Act had dictated.[2] "Only the presence of counters here and there piled high with bread and bottles for those who care to buy, and a curious set of low iron fences forming narrow lanes lengthwise through the lower half of the room, disturb the prisonlike aspect of the place."[3]

In the 1890s agents of the immigration bureaucracy carried out their work with detached reserve day after day while "nervously defiant" immigrants seeking entry lined up before them. The 1891 Immigration Act required transoceanic shipping companies to collect specific passenger information in the ship's manifest for inspectors to use in brief interviews. "If their answers agree with those recorded on shipboard they are passed on. If there is any discrepancy or any dubiousness of manner, the suspect is pounced upon by waiting officials," *Harper's* explained, "questioned closely, and either sent upon his way, or pushed into the cage to await final investigation by the established board below," detained in the "cage of the rejected." The magazine emphasized the obliviousness of the new arrivals whose fate depended on the quick decision of a single harried inspector.

While the 1891 and 1893 laws established inspection protocols that remained in place for decades, less is known about how agents initially translated gatekeeping laws into the durable policy directives that had a profound effect on the migration of working-class peoples to the United States.[4] Over time, the "qualitative" restriction of specific racial, social, and economic conditions transitioned to a period of "quantitative" or enumerated exclusion by the 1920s.[5] The U.S. government had to establish a structure to evaluate immigrants before the rationale and the apparatus for numerical exclusion could be erected, but this early era of qualitative gatekeeping is less understood. Italian encounters with federal agents at Ellis Island show how the 1891 and 1893 laws empowered the administrative state to carry out the work of exclusion shadowed by the banality of bureaucratic decision-making.

Historians working at the intersection of labor history and immigration policy have clearly defined the distinctiveness of U.S. immigration law, in the broad administrative power that statute and case law created for agents to carry out increasingly strict gatekeeping of working-class migrants.[6] Congress initially issued a series of restrictive laws beginning in 1882 that facilitated exclusion at the border. The Chinese Exclusion Act of 1882 prohibited the admission of a "lunatic, idiot, or any person unable to take care of himself or herself without becoming a public charge." In 1891 Congress revised the law to give immigration agents the right to exclude any person "likely to become a public charge," granting agents broad discretion to invoke what became known as the LPC clause. After renewing and tightening Chinese exclusion in 1892 by requiring all Chinese to register regardless of citizenship, the 1893 U.S. Immigration Act required immigration inspectors to solicit information about occupation, marital status, literacy, money on hand, and a doctor's examination of physical health to determine qualification for admission. The 1893 Immigration Act also created a Board of Special Inquiry to hear cases that could not be determined by a single inspector.

Key to the gatekeeping apparatus, the Board of Special Inquiry assumed an incredible amount of power over working-class immigrants' lives through the unique authority the statute and the courts afforded to gatekeepers. In a report to the Italian ambassador in November 1894, five months after he arrived at Ellis Island to serve as the first chief of the Office of Labor Information and Protection for Italians, Alessandro Oldrini called the Board of Special Inquiry "the referee of the fate of many emigrants and the cause of their ruin."[7] Data collected by the Office, located in the main processing building on Ellis Island, offers a rare snapshot of the gatekeeping process in its crucial early years.

The Board of Special Inquiry bore no resemblance to a court of law in composition or procedure; four inspectors heard cases while dressed in dark suits and caps bearing the bureau insignia rendered in silver.[8] The number of people excluded grew dramatically from 1892 (when federal management and record keeping began) to 1910, jumping from 22,515 people in the period 1892–1900, to 108,211 excluded between the years 1900 and 1910, approximately a fivefold increase.[9] A larger number of cases came before the board as a direct result.[10] LPC exclusion formed the largest type of case heard.[11] A finding against the immigrant brought about an order for immediate deportation. Excluded migrants passed their remaining time on U.S. soil in the detention pens of the inspection station, which *Harper's* had reported as "great cages" full of "the rejected."[12] The LPC clause gave inspectors and the board wide leverage to move against those immigrants deemed undesirable with the power of the "finality clause" in the 1891 act that unilaterally ruled immigration inspectors' decisions final.[13] Cavalier Egisto Rossi, the second-in-command and, after 1896, the chief agent of the Office of Labor Information and Protection for Italians, described as many as four hundred Italians detained in a single day and ordered to return to Italy under the LPC clause in 1895.[14]

Italians entered into a new regulatory world shaped by these legal precedents. What happened when migrants came face to face with the inspector? In the era before coordinated federal enforcement began in 1891, "state officials' discretion dictated who could enter and stay in the nation and who would be removed," establishing the procedural model for the new federal system.[15] Tasked with enforcing increasingly restrictive laws, the Immigration Bureau created a distinctive bureaucracy that "lobbied against the interests of legal immigrants," historian Roger Daniels argued, "especially those of color and those who seemed to them [the officers] un-American."[16] Herman Stump, the first superintendent of immigration, told Congress in 1892 that he viewed his new role "to secure more searching and scrutinizing inspections, made with a view to a more faithful and stricter enforcement of the laws."[17]

Immigration law has long occupied a special place within the administrative state. The Office of the Superintendent of Immigration, created by the 1891 Immigration Act and expanded by subsequent legislation, was allowed from the very beginning a special privilege: to exercise independent administrative discretion to deal with arriving immigrants and decide without significant legislative or judicial oversight who can and cannot enter the country.[18] As legal historians Lucy Salyer and Torrie Hester have argued, when Chinese migrants used writs of habeas corpus to challenge exclusion laws in federal courts, Congress steered immigration law onto a secondary track under the control of a new Bureau of Immigration that allowed its officers vast administrative discretion.[19] Isolating immigration law from judicial oversight greatly diminished the power of the courts to reverse decisions in exclusion and deportation cases, which blunted the Chinese strategy of attack on the growing gatekeeping apparatus and strengthened federal power.

Over a relatively short period, the legal basis for broad gatekeeping power would be firmly established. At the same time when the federal government assumed gatekeeping authority from the states, three Supreme Court cases articulated the legal principles that propelled the first superintendent of immigration as he sought "stricter enforcement of the laws": *Chae Chan Ping* in 1888, *Nishimura Ekiu* in 1892, and *Fong Yue Ting* in 1893.[20] While the first two cases set a "lasting precedent" that supported administrative authority without significant judicial oversight in immigration matters, the *Fong Yue Ting* decision established a far more powerful basis for unchecked gatekeeping at the nation's borders.[21] The 5–3 majority decision in the case ruled the powers to exclude and to deport "rest upon one foundation, are derived from one source, are supported by the same reasons, and are in truth but parts of one and the same power," and thus *Fong Yue Ting* affirmed the immigration agency's right to deport and Congress's right to create entry and exclusion policy.[22] By 1893 the legal basis for deportation rested firmly in national sovereignty, from which the power to deport still derives today.[23] Italians became the first group of non-Chinese to encounter en masse this new regulatory world defined by remarkably unchecked power to interpret and apply immigration law. Italians soon found themselves trapped in a legal cage defined by vague exclusionary provisions, where inspectors of the immigration service held the key.

For the United States, as for many other receiving countries at the time, immigration laws became a tool to shape U.S. society but also to establish its right to determine who could (or could not) enter the country and who could naturalize. Chinese were the first targets of immigration restrictions because many Americans saw them as the quintessential "other." Italians, called "the Chinese of Europe," became one of the primary targets of nativists' zeal for restriction.[24] By the beginning of the twentieth century, immigration laws measured and categorized aspiring immigrants by socioeconomic class, literacy, criminality, political beliefs, diplomatic standing, physical and mental health, and sexuality. Officially rejected because they could not guarantee they would be able to provide for themselves financially, the poor, and unmarried or unaccompanied women, became the primary target for expulsion, making the LPC clause about social control, and further expanding the right of the state to exclude.[25] In 1896 Ellis Island commissioner Joseph Senner turned to the pages of *North American Review* to affirm the effectiveness of the new gatekeeping policy enforced by his officers. "I do not share the apprehensions of the distinguished and learned Senator [Henry Cabot Lodge] from Massachusetts, who is at present Chairman of the Committee on Immigration and Naturalization, that 'a great, perilous change in the very fabric of our race' is impending from further immigration," Senner wrote. "I can safely say that since the enactment of the law of 1893 no substantial number of undesirable immigrants have been permitted to enter the United States."[26]

At the same time, the royal Italian government responded on the ground to Italians increasingly targeted for exclusion by American inspectors. Their primary tool was a network that operated through the Office for Labor Information and Protection for Italians located inside the Ellis Island station and placed under the close supervision of the ambassador. A second tool came in the overseas application of Italy's first attempt to enact anticipatory remote control through the emigration law initially passed in 1888 and significantly expanded in 1901.[27] The Office was the only outpost of a foreign government permitted to operate at the federal station in its first decade of existence. More commonly, immigrant aid groups provided assistance at the Castle Garden station before 1891, and after U.S. authorities forced the Office to close in 1899.[28] In the middle of the 1890s, as federal officials at Ellis Island turned law into a functioning system to administer immigration regulation, a handful of Italian bureaucrats worked in close proximity on-site at the station. The work of this largely forgotten staff of men directly influenced the work of immigration inspectors who carried out their duties otherwise unobserved and unchallenged.[29] For a few critical years, the Office worked to protect Italian migrants from rejection at the border. This close Italian-American relationship also placed a handful of government agents in the position to witness, and react to, the implementation of early U.S. immigration policy as it was being transformed from law into action.

Italian records tell the story of how inspectors applied their discretion to European immigrants in the earliest years of Ellis Island, filling in the history of East Coast enforcement contemporary to the most significant decisions in Chinese exclusion cases brought about on the West Coast. In the first five years of unified federal immigration policy, Italians, through their dominating presence at Ellis Island, negotiated and shaped that policy on behalf of their emigrants. A total of 61,631 migrants from Italy presented themselves at the border for inspection by the newly professionalized agents of the Immigration Bureau in 1892, the first year of operation at Ellis Island, making up 10 percent of the total number processed. Numbers continued to rise through the end of the century. By 1894, Italians accounted for 15 percent of all arrivals, and 25 percent in 1899.[30]

A binational perspective incorporating the Italian response to the practice of rejection at the border illuminates the early construction of a gatekeeping apparatus in the United States. The activity recorded by the Office of Labor Information and Protection for Italians reconstructs the foundations of U.S. gatekeeping as it expanded from Chinese exclusion to target far larger numbers of European migrants. An examination of Italian power to negotiate and shape immigration policy expands the history of working-class migration. The limits of American authority to enforce border controls become clearer. While the LPC clause created a cage in which tens of thousands of Italians were forced to sojourn at the gates to America, the ability of a small, focused group of officers of the diplomatic service to shepherd their migratory countrymen through the cage frustrated U.S. authorities. The transnational history of these sometimes-competing forces more clearly defines the scope and limitations of early gatekeeping. While *Fong Yue Ting* had affirmed that the power to regulate immigration rested solely in Congress's hands, the history of the Office of Labor Information and Protection for Italians raises an important question about the unchecked power of the administrative state.[31] Bureaucrats newly freed from judicial oversight and endowed with the power of exclusion by Congress had a check on their authority that, quite surprisingly, came from a single-room outpost of a foreign government calling itself the Office of Labor Information and Protection for Italians.

### The Office of Labor Information and Protection for Italians

Housed in a single room on the first floor of the immigration station, the Office of Labor Information and Protection for Italians became the base of Italian presence and power, the physical expression of Italian attempts to shape American immigration enforcement. In a report to his government titled "Relations of the Office for Italians with the American Immigration Authorities," the Office's first chief agent, Alessandro (Alex) Oldrini, described the comments of two key bureaucrats, the commissioner of Ellis Island and the commissioner of immigration (both of whom kept their offices on the island).[32] The Office represented to the American authorities "'a State in the State,' a government concession that has no precedents," Oldrini declared, and Ambassador Saverio Fava confirmed, in a report destined for the minister of foreign affairs in Rome.[33] Reflecting on the first year of the Office's operation, Oldrini observed the frequency with which American immigration officials invited him into meetings and conversations about the island's operations. No "argument then of greater tranquility" existed between the Americans and the

Italian Office, Oldrini opined, than the invitation to attend a meeting of Ellis Island commissioners convened by Superintendent of Immigration Herman Stump the day after Stump's return from a trip to Rome.[34] Stump had invited Oldrini to speak to the level of coordination between the two nations, how Oldrini had "prepared with effective tips the best way to achieve the purpose of coordination of Italian and American immigration laws according to the criteria of the American Government," which anticipated more explicit forms of "remote control" coordination. From 1894 until the U.S. government forced the closure of the Office in 1899, Italians established a clear presence on the ground at Ellis Island, which functioned at the intersection of American and Italian authority.[35]

The Italian government responded to the practice of exclusion at Ellis Island in the early years of the immigration station's operation at the same time as they sought to comprehend the rules of gatekeeping. As the primary site to determine entry for European immigrants from 1892 until it closed in 1954, Ellis Island received a lot of attention from the Italian government. A handful of men led the dialogue: officers of the Ministry of Foreign Affairs including the ambassador to the United States in Washington, the minister of foreign affairs and his undersecretary in Rome, and, at Ellis Island itself, Alex Oldrini and his successor, Egisto Rossi. The consul of New York and the U.S. secretary of state were notably absent, as the Italians dealt directly with the Immigration Bureau, located until 1903 in the Treasury Department. The presence at the Office of the Chief Agent (accompanied from time to time by an assistant) as employees of the Italian Foreign Service but outside of the diplomatic corps brought Italians into a unique position to observe the process of inspection and question cases of exclusion. While this oversight had a very mixed effect on the overall treatment of Italians in the system, the Office of Labor Information put pressure on the United States to better define its process.

The origin story of the Office of Labor Information and Protection for Italians reveals how Italian oversight challenged American authority and, at the same time, helped strengthen it. The Office began with a request Ambassador Fava sent to the U.S. secretary of state in April 1894 "to establish in the ports of arrival 'Bureaus of Labor' or other similar offices, duly authorized and recognized by the federal authorities," to encourage newly arrived Italians to settle away from crowded city centers.[36] Three days later, on April 22, Fava wrote an upbeat message to the minister of foreign affairs, Baron Blanc, confirming his decision to enter into "amicable agreement" between the two governments to create an office that would redirect Italian migrants to "agricultural centers" on landing at Ellis Island. Fava conveyed to Blanc verbal assurances from Commissioner Stump that Congress would favorably receive the proposal.[37] In June 1894 Ambassador Fava, through his personal relationship with New Hampshire senator William E. Chandler, chair of the Senate Committee on Immigration and one of the most prominent advocates of immigration restriction then in the Senate, negotiated a proposal from Treasury Secretary John G. Carlisle, who oversaw the Bureau of Immigration and served as the final arbiter for any exclusion law appeals.[38] Following the unanimous passage of SR 207 on June 11, Carlisle notified the ambassador he had directed Commissioner Stump to open what Carlisle described in straightforward terms as an information bureau. The space would be a "room on the first floor of the Immigration Station on Ellis Island . . . to be designated as a place for the display of such circulars, advertisements and printed matter, forwarded by State Boards of Immigration, transportation lines, corporations, and individuals, offering inducements to immigrants for settlement and employment, as may be approved by the Commissioner of Immigration at said port."[39]

What the secretary wrote next is more telling. Carlisle informed Fava, "In this room you can have stationed one or two persons who can interview and advise with Italian immigrants, who have been allowed to land, and give them such instructions as will promote their welfare."[40] Carlisle's inclusion of the phrase indicated his adherence to the 1891 and 1893 U.S. laws that defined inspectors' duty to admit only those "clearly and without a doubt entitled to admission."[41] The letter emphasized that American agents "will be directed to cause all Italians, destined for the port of New York, to pass through this room before they are permitted to hold communication with any person not connected with the Immigration Service."[42]

The Office was initially intended to allay concerns on the part of both governments about the susceptibility of Italian migrants to the padrone system. Three years after the Chinese Exclusion Act became law, Congress moved under pressure from organized labor to limit another group of migrant workers. Advocates for the 1885 Alien Contract Labor Law believed it would prevent the exploitation of ignorant workingmen by padrones, an Anglicization of the Italian word for "bosses." This important step in the creation of qualitative limits on immigration prohibited the entry of men who had contracted to work with a specific employer prior to their arrival in the country. The law shaped the public discourse that initially linked Italians in particular to the exploitative padrone system. Newspapers often led with shocking headlines that detailed the worst cases of abuse. In June 1895 Foreign Minister Blanc wrote to Fava about how upset it made him to read judgments against Italian padrones in the "New-Jork [sic] press."[43]

Growing anxiety in Rome regarding the American climate and gatekeeping enforcement over the summer of 1894–95 led the Office of Labor Information and Protection for Italians at Ellis Island to focus its efforts not on snuffing out the padrone system but on the application of U.S. gatekeeping law. More broadly, Fava's reply to Carlisle revealed a careful dance of power as he watched the progress of legislative changes to immigration policy. His letter used delicate language that did not directly challenge the American administrative authority to reject emigrants either in principle or in practice. "I am deeply grateful to you for this kind communication, and I shall have the pleasure in replying later to such portions of the same as relate to the opportunity afforded me by you one or two persons stationed in said room in order to promote the welfare of Italian immigrants," the ambassador wrote.[44] Fava's missive initially appeared to embrace the Treasury secretary's sovereign power at the top of the chain of bureaucratic authority over gatekeeping.

In June 1894 Congress debated how to attack the padrone system in between discussions focused on the need for additional restrictive legislation, with the Italian delegation following the overlap closely. On the same day Carlisle informed Fava of his special entitlement, he announced the Treasury Department had formed an "Immigration Investigating Committee" composed of Commissioner Stump, Commissioner of Immigration for New York Dr. Joseph Senner, and Ellis Island Assistant Superintendent Edward McSweeney to test the application of existing legislation. Fava knew this and thought Rome should as well, so he folded the notice published by the Government Printing Office into his report dated June 14.[45] At the same time, Fava was corresponding with the man he called "my dear Senator" Chandler about the progress of restrictionist legislation targeting padrone labor practices, widely believed to be both perpetrated by, and victimizing of, Italians.[46] Chandler issued a resolution asking for the Senate to issue a statement on the padrone system. The brief Senate discussion of Resolution No. 207 captured Senator Chandler, Republican from New Hampshire, praising his friend Fava as "the energetic and courteous Italian Ambassador," and highlighting "the recent 'deep interest' shown by the Italian government in uprooting the padrone system."[47] The discretionary powers of immigration inspectors grew, in part, through the work of senators like Chandler who introduced legislation to strengthen enforcement of the Alien Contract Labor Law to combat padrones.[48] In a personal letter to Fava, Chandler highlighted what he called the "creditable cooperative movement of the two governments" to this end.[49] Initially, neither Rome nor Washington anticipated how Italians might resist or challenge U.S. policy through what Fava called an "amicable" relationship.

Fava saw the Office as a sign of preference granted to Italians facing increased scrutiny under U.S. immigration law. In a long report marked "urgent" to his own government back in Rome the day after receiving Secretary Carlisle's letter, Fava noted how "these measures constitute a considerable concession made to us."[50] While Carlisle had added a clause in his original letter clarifying that only those Italians "who have been allowed to land" were eligible for the Office's services, and stipulated that all immigrants regardless of origin could use the services of this office, the right for Fava to designate two Italians to staff the room was a move that the ambassador interpreted as covert evidence of American favor.[51] Fava told the prime minister that the power of selection conferred on him was "intended to reject possible protests against the protection that actually, if not openly, our emigrants will receive from the federal authorities," indicating preferential treatment.[52] Two days later the *Washington Post* publicized his ideas when it ran the headline, "Baron Fava Cares for His Countrymen." Fava clipped the article and underlined one phrase: "at the request of Baron Fava, two or more Italians, *representing the Italian government*, will converse and give information to Italians."[53] Notably, the language of the *Post* reproduced almost verbatim his private, internal correspondence with the prime minister.[54] It is likely that Fava leaked his letter to the press.

The first chief agent of the Office, Alex Oldrini, was a man who had lived in New York for some time, who claimed a role in Giuseppe Garibaldi's failed revolution for Italian unification in the 1850s, and spent many decades engaged in philanthropy in the city. Often referred to as "Professor," in 1894 he authored a chapter on the Italian educational system for the U.S. commissioner of education where he listed as credentials his membership in the Geographical Society of Italy, among other honorifics.[55] Beyond these brief notes, however, biographical details remain elusive. His marked influence over the U.S.–Italian relationship and the power he managed to exercise out of a single room on Ellis Island is striking, all the more so given his almost total absence in the historiography on migration and gatekeeping.

An Italian presence at the largest port of entry to the United States established a new kind of relationship between sending and receiving states that Italians would exploit to monitor American immigration enforcement. Detained immigrants could request testimony from family members already in the country, or the assistance of representatives of immigrant aid societies that formed among the mushrooming population of foreign-born in New York City. Italians were the only group that had reliable assistance at the island in these matters in the 1890s. What began as a hope for preferential treatment by immigration authorities quickly gave way to practical efforts by the Italian government to help migrants navigate the inspection process and avoid exclusion by the LPC clause. In June 1894 the ambassador was worried by the newspaper headline "Decline to Feed Immigrants. Steamship Companies Refuse to Pay for Their Meals in the Detention Pen"; it described an increase in detentions even though overall immigration was down from the previous year.[56] When Italians later filled the "detention pen" Oldrini and Rossi were quick to point out in reports to Rome that the "patronage" of the Office hurried the release of most of the migrants.[57] While the officers might have been inclined to praise their own work, their assessments of its positive impact are borne out in the documentary record. Being on the ground at Ellis Island allowed Oldrini and Rossi to cultivate a relationship with U.S. authorities that gave Italians insight into a confusing system of immigration enforcement.

While the U.S. government had taken care not to publicly acknowledge special treatment for Italians, the agents of the Office saw clear benefits. A series of letters and newspaper clippings sent between December 1894 and May 1895 between New York, Washington, and Rome focused on the relationship between the Office and the men the Italians called the "American Authorities" at Ellis Island. Oldrini, citing a report from Foreign Minister Baron Blanc, emphasized the ability of the Office to encourage more harmonious relations with a weak Italian state that needed the United States to accept its migrants.[58] An editorial from an unnamed Italian American newspaper found in the ambassador's archives called the Office "a victory for us, because only Italy has a control on immigration to the ship, and so the emigrant is not only guided at boarding at home but also at the landing abroad."[59] The same newspaper concluded with effusive praise of the royal government's prudent actions. "The Federal Government has admitted a check to the office of 'Immigration' at Ellis Island for Italian immigration. This control is exercised scrupulously and courteously at the same time by Prof. Oldrini," the author assured readers, "and his work and that of Ambassador Fava in Washington and the Italian Government should be praised very much."[60] While the article lauded Oldrini (which is probably why he kept it), more importantly it acknowledged "a check" on an American gatekeeping authority otherwise free from outside challenge. Oldrini's true value was more accurately described by an American editorial that emphasized his long tenure of residence in the United States, command of the English language, and thorough "understand[ing of] the immigration laws and the bureau's rules."[61] Most significantly, the Office's first chief agent identified the practice of exclusion—the rejection of emigrants at the border—as the point where U.S. and Italian law overlapped and where "remote control" began. "[It is] in the most delicate question of exclusions," Oldrini reported to Rome a few months after opening the Office, "over which more than other points, bring into contact the legal criteria of Italy and the United States."[62]

**TABLE 2.1. Italian Exclusions by Type and Year**

**THESE FIGURES** capture trends in U.S. immigration policy enforcement against Italians in the early years of federal control. Showing the haphazard and messy application of gatekeeping law, these statistics examine the reasons for rejection and the rate of exclusion as a percentage of all Italians who presented for inspection over five fiscal years. Both tables derive from data published by the Ellis Island commissioner in this period, J. H. Senner, and unpublished data collected in annual reports of the chief officer of the Office of Labor Information and Protection for Italians at Ellis Island over the years the Office operated.

| Fiscal year | Group | Number excluded | Reason for exclusion | Percentage of total excluded | Total number of emigrants arriving | Percentage of total arrivals that are excluded |
|---|---|---|---|---|---|---|
| 1891–1892 | Italian | | | | 61,631 | |
| 1892–1893 | Italian | | | | 69,437 | |
| 1893–1894 | Italian | | | | 42,074 | |
| 1894–1895 | Italian | 731 | not given | 100.00 | 33,902 | 2.16 |
| 1895–1896 | Italian | 977 | LPC Clause | 77.72 | 66,425 | 1.47 |
| | | 280 | Alien Contract Labor Law violation | 22.28 | 66,425 | 0.42 |
| | | 1257 | total number excluded | 100.00 | 66,425 | 1.89 |
| 1898–1899 | Italian | 1,024 | LPC Clause | 71.01 | 76,489 | 1.34 |
| | Italian | 330 | Alien Contract Labor Law violation | 22.88 | 76,489 | 0.43 |
| | Italian | 88 | Contagious Disease | 6.10 | 76,489 | 0.12 |
| | Italian | 1,445 | total number excluded | 100.00 | 76,489 | 1.89 |

SOURCES: Alessandro Oldrini, Primo Rapporto Statistico Annuale dell'Ufficio di Ellis Island (1 August 1895), box 111, folder 2198; Adolfo Rossi, 2.o Rapporto Annuale, dal 30 giugno 1895 al 30 giugno 1896 (10 September 1896), box 111, both in Archivio storico diplomatico dell'Ministero degli Affari Esteri, Rome. For total immigrants arriving: J. H. Senner, "Immigration from Italy," *North American Review*, June 1896; Rossi Annual Reports.

## TABLE 2.2. Immigrants Admitted and Excluded, 1890–1900

THESE FIGURES compare Italian emigration to the overall movement of migrants to the United States in the decade 1890–1900, combining different data sources to capture the scope of enforcement. The number of Italians landed and subsequent percentage excluded are compared to the number and percentage of Chinese migrants landed and excluded in each year.

| Year | Total immigration | From Italy | Percent Italian of total number immigrants | Total LPC excluded | Number Italian excluded | Percentage Italian excluded | From China (see note below) | Percent Chinese out of total number of immigrants | Total Chinese admitted | Percentage of total Chinese arrivals excluded | Total number excluded |
|---|---|---|---|---|---|---|---|---|---|---|---|
| 1890 | 455,302 | 52,003 | 11.42 | n/a | | | | | | | |
| 1891 | 560,319 | 76,055 | 13.57 | n/a | | | | | | | |
| 1892 | 579,663 | 61,631 | 10.63 | 637§ | | | | | | | |
| 1893 | 439,730 | 72,145 | 16.41 | 577§ | | | | | | | |
| 1894 | 285,631 | 42,977 | 15.05 | 417§ | 731‡ | 1.70 | 6,840 | 2.39 | 5,559 | 18 | |
| 1895 | 258,536 | 35,427 | 13.70 | 177§ | 977‡ | 2.75 | 2,732 | 1.06 | 2,075 | 24 | |
| 1896 | 343,267 | 68,060 | 19.83 | 977 | 1257‡ | 1.84 | 3,925 | 1.14 | 3,510 | 11 | |
| 1897 | 230,832 | 59,431 | 25.75 | | | | 5,880 | 2.55 | 5,478 | 7 | |
| 1898 | 229,299 | 58,613 | 25.56 | | | | 5,553 | 2.42 | 5,273 | 5 | |
| 1899 | 311,715 | 77,419 | 24.84 | 1024** | 1445** | 1.86 | 4,875 | 1.56 | 3,925 | 19.50 | |
| 1900 | 448,572† | 87,714* | 19.55 | 977 | | | 4,867 | 1.08 | 3,802 | 22 | |
| 1892–1900 | | | | | | | | | | | 25642† |
| 1901–1910 | | 2,329,451* | | | | | | | | | 119,769 |

NOTE: Definition of total immigrants is unclear and may be aliens landed. Ngai discusses this in table A1 note

SOURCES:

* Figure from Betty Boyd Caroli, *Italian Repatriation from the United States, 1900–1914* (Ann Arbor: University of Michigan Center for Migration Studies, 1973), 33 and 38, tables X, XII, and XIII.

† Mae Ngai, *Impossible Subjects: Illegal Aliens and the Making of Modern America* (Princeton, N.J.: Princeton University Press, 2004), table A1–2, 273–74. Ngai defines the figure as a measurement of "aliens expelled," which included deportations, exclusions, and removals.

‡ Data from Egisto Rossi, "2.o Rapporto Annuale, dal 30 giugno 1895 al 30 giugno 1896 [2nd Annual Report from the Office of Labor Information and Protection, from 30 June 1895 to 30 June 1896]," 10 September 1896, box 111, pp. 3–4, Archivio storico diplomatico dell'Ministero degli Affari Esteri, Rome (ASDMAE). Data is for fiscal years 1894–95 and 1895–96 at Ellis Island arrivals only.

§ From J. H. Senner, "Immigration from Italy," *North American Review*, 1896, 655. He says "Number returned within one year." Chinese migrant figures taken from Lucy Salyer, table 1: Chinese Admitted to the United States, 1894–1901, in *Laws Harsh as Tigers: Chinese Immigrants and the Shaping of Modern Immigration Law* (Chapel Hill: University of North Carolina Press, 1995), 67. Salyer reports figures unavailable for 1891–93.

** Data on Italian exclusions was tabulated for fiscal years 1895–96 and 1898–99 by Egisto Rossi in his annual reports, ASDMAE.

## "Those Days of Exceptional Invasion"

Egisto Rossi, second chief agent of the Office, focused on "the two principal services of the Office; that is, the information branch and the patronage." His language, in the style of high Italian common to diplomatic exchange at the time, diminished the outsize role that he and the Office played in shaping application of American gatekeeping law. Over the following lines of text Rossi described how he facilitated the entry of Italian migrants through Ellis Island: 25,865 persons processed in the busiest months of 1896 alone.[63] The Italian government's close work seems to have reduced the number of detainees ultimately rejected. They believed their work prevented more stringent application of exclusionary law, and the records the Office kept show this may have been the case.[64]

For the first eighteen years of operation, LPC or "likely to become a public charge" was the most common reason for exclusion at Ellis Island.[65] As Congress never defined the amount of money a person had to carry, Immigration Bureau inspectors were free to use the LPC clause at their own discretion to reject migrants. As little as $10 or as much as $40 in cash might be demanded as proof of self-sufficiency.[66] Gatekeepers' focus on keeping out the poor has a longer history, tracing back to the abject poverty of Irish migrants arriving in the mid-nineteenth century, which spurred states (in charge of immigration policy until 1891) to focus their mechanisms of exclusion on economic condition.[67] By the late nineteenth century, Italians had begun to replace Irish migrants for legislators seeking to keep out the most destitute. The Italian government tried to warn emigrants of the function of the LPC clause, issuing circulars intended for distribution at ports of departure by agents of the government and shipping lines.[68] When in December 1894 Oldrini reported about the circulation by the Ellis Island commissioner, J. H. Senner, of "secret instructions" to his inspectors, Oldrini recommended that his government focus on what he called the problem of "Public Charge . . . particularly where is the question of the money that every adult immigrant should have on arrival."[69] While he doubted the ability of Senner's guidance to "in and of itself have a special influence on the said officers," he acknowledged that this moment, with Congress at a standstill arguing over the passage of "additional restrictive legislation . . . it is useful here to point out that the special circulars and regulations of the immigration department have the effect of law."[70] Repeatedly over the next several years, the Office stepped in to educate emigrants so that they would be better able to navigate the entry process at the gates to the United States. Seeing the effect of these actions, after 1901 the government in Rome, acting through its Ministry of Foreign Affairs, would take over this role.

Italians made up the majority of the detained at Ellis Island for several of the station's early years as inspectors adjusted to the protocol outlined under the 1891 and 1893 statute. While specific details of individual cases have not survived, an overall assessment of the focus of U.S. inspectors can be surmised from the Italians' commentary. Fava took note in Oldrini's December 1894 report of the impact that exclusion had on Italian migrants. By the next year, Egisto Rossi, second chief officer at the Office of Italian Information and Protection, chose the months of April and May 1896 to highlight trends in the Office's second annual report. These months noted a new record in traffic from Italy to the United States. Rossi emphasized the role the Office played in supporting Italian migrants put in front of the Board of Special Inquiry when inspectors questioned their admissibility based on the LPC or Alien Contract Labor Law.[71] The statistics seem to indicate that Oldrini and Rossi used their intimate knowledge of the staff and procedures at Ellis Island to effectively coach migrants through the board's interviews. "How effective this sort of patronage for our emigration was during the year now closed," Rossi concluded to the MAE, "can be seen from the statistics" that formed the bulk of his comprehensive report.[72]

While a significant percentage of arriving Italians were initially detained for further questioning, the majority of these people ultimately gained entrance to the United States. Office reports paint a clear picture of conditions at the island and the functioning of the gatekeeping apparatus, showing how American inspectors struggled to process arrivals during temporary spikes. One newspaper corroborated Rossi's claims, reporting in the spring of 1896 how the detainee situation had reached a point of crisis so great it necessitated the creation of a "temporary detention pen."[73] In three short months, Rossi observed, Italians numbering "far beyond the emigration totals of the other main European nations in the aforementioned quarter" poured into the station.[74] U.S. officials responded to "such an extraordinary confluence in a relatively short time" by detaining more people.[75] The spike in Italian arrivals "was the cause of serious concerns on the part of the Immigration Commissioners and of greater rigors in the examinations of our emigrants. Hence the extraordinary number of those detained [in March, April, and May 1896 . . . who] arrived in contravention with the American laws, and therefore obliged to undergo further examinations."[76] Despite the heavy-handedness of inspectors who initially detained 33 percent of arriving Italian migrants, slightly fewer than 7 percent of the detained were ultimately rejected, meaning that inspectors refused only 2.24 percent of all passengers in the busiest months of the second-busiest year for Italian migration then on record.[77] This figure, however, was double that of the general rate of European exclusions, which was 1 percent.[78]

The Italian experience shows how widely, but not stringently, inspectors applied the LPC tool in the first few years of enforcement at Ellis Island. While only 6.7 percent of the detained were indeed rejected, of those sent back 77 percent were excluded under the LPC clause.[79] "Suffice it to say that in some days this number ascended to more than 400, of which no small part were sentenced to return to Italy under the accusation of pauperism, i.e. 'public charge,'" Rossi reported. While for these migrants "the patronage of the Italian Office was of invaluable help," the effectiveness of the interventions seemed only to strengthen the gatekeeping apparatus. In Rossi's words, "the more effective [the Italian Office] became, the more rigorous these Authorities were in granting admission to our emigrants during those days of exceptional invasion, for which the Federal Commissaries had to provide new premises and new dormitories, and increase the number of service personnel at Ellis Island" in direct response to growing numbers of Italian migrants. Rossi concluded his account with a note of cautious praise for his government's efforts. "On that occasion [Ellis] would have been called a more Italian than American island, where, despite such a great agglomeration, cause of so many exaggerated fears in the American and Italian press, there were no regrets of any sort."[80] In undertaking its work of "welcoming, advising, and directing emigrants upon their arrival," the Office had to take care not to be too successful, which they feared would encourage additional inadmissible migrants to undertake the journey. Reflecting the larger debate over how to regulate emigration then unfolding in Italy, leaders struggled to affect the flow of emigration without altering its "spontaneity . . . [and] becoming an instrument of propaganda" that would encourage even more migration from the kingdom that could further stoke restrictionism in the United States and overwhelm Ellis Island officers, forcing even more stringent application of the law.[81]

Officers of the Italian government working in the busy halls of Ellis Island queried the Americans constantly as they sought to understand the frequently changing character of U.S. immigration policy. While an internal report produced by the Immigration Restriction League actually confirmed Italians' concerns of more stringent gatekeeping, noting a doubling in the overall rate of rejection from 0.5 percent of arrivals between 1892 and 1893 to 1 percent between 1894 and 1895, it appeared that Italians were measured against an even higher bar.[82] Italian officials took particular notice of the shifting application of the LPC clause. Italian statistician Luigi Bodio (who went on to become the first commissioner of emigration in 1901) pointed out the difference in enforcement of the LPC clause he observed between 1894 and 1895. Writing to an American audience in a version of an article he published in Italy in *Nuova Antologia* the year previous, Bodio sketched out the shifting picture of enforcement, highlighting a trend that Oldrini had warned the ambassador about back in December 1894.[83] "In 1895 our 33,902 emigrants disembarking at Ellis Island had with them $362,000, that is, a little more than $10 apiece, including those who were rejected as 'paupers' and 'undesirable immigrants.' In the year preceding, the average to each individual was practically the same," yet the number rejected was lower.[84] Senner, the Ellis Island commissioner, reported in the pages of the *North American Review* in June 1896, "Solely [due] to the strict enforcement of the latest law (of March 3, 1893) . . . Italians . . . form the largest percentage of the detained." Like Bodio, Senner also used the pages of a widely circulated magazine to make his case to the public. He argued that his agents' enforcement efforts were working when he cited "the number of persons returned within one year after landing as public charges decreased from 637, in the fiscal year 1892, to 577, in 1893, 417 in 1894, and 177 in 1895. This is self-evident proof of the increasing efficiency of the immigration service in preventing from year to year undesirable immigrants from landing."[85] By late spring of 1895 the frequency of rejection led the leaders of the MAE to adopt a new term—*emigrazione clandestina* or illegal emigration—in reports that tried to identify migrants who skirted the rules set for exit and were thus more likely to be rejected by U.S. inspectors. Fava and his government remained focused on preventing exclusion at the border.[86]

At the same time that Italian officials recorded a surge in arrivals, and the ensuing struggle of the immigration service to contain them, four Italian detainees attempted a daring escape that highlighted both the conditions of detention and the influence of Oldrini and the Office. The episode in May 1895 roiled the remaining hundred men, women, and children held in a temporary "detention pen." The American press covering the escape story offered a sympathetic view of the Office even in the midst of a largely unflattering portrayal of Italian migrants. Nothing short of an address delivered by the chief agent of the Office of Labor Information and Protection calmed the "uproar."

> Over 100 Italians made a determined effort yesterday to break out of the detention pen at Ellis Island. They rushed against the gates in a body, yelling and waving their arms to scare the guards. The place was in an uproar in a moment, the scared women and children huddling into corners, and the attendants running about for extra guards. Finally, the Italian representative at Ellis Island, Prof. Aldrini [*sic*], mounted a desk and spoke to his angry countrymen. This had a quieting effect, and in half an hour there was quiet again in the pen. Four men had escaped over the railing earlier in the day, and made their way to the New-Jersey shore.[87]

This episode reveals how the Italian presence at the Office mediated gatekeeping as it oversaw the sometimes chaotic execution of U.S. policy, and the results of that work. The next year, Rossi described how the Office "watched with the utmost diligence" to protect those rejected at the border. His annual report highlighted how the Office navigated migrants through the sometimes literal "cage of the rejected." If their detention or exclusion appeared to be "without legitimate reasons," or ordered without a hearing before the Board of Special Inquiry, the Office intervened. "Our Office is obliged to bring [these cases] to the attention of the authorities, and to promote their cause in the best ways."[88] The only legitimate reason for exclusion, in Rossi's eyes, was "due exclusively to finding [oneself] in evident contravention" of American law. By the winter of 1896, two years after opening the Office, Rossi did not question the underlying principles of gatekeeping and focused instead on fair application of the law.

Oldrini and Rossi tried to make the Americans adhere to the letter of their own law, denying inspectors the discretion they sought to wield. The actions of Senner's agents became the subject of attention on June 1, 1895, when Oldrini typed onto his letterhead a copy of the Code of Conduct distributed "to all Officers Privelege [sic] Holders and Employees U.S. Immigration Station Ellis Island N.Y." and included it in his report no. 59. Oldrini highlighted point "1. The most humane and considerate treatment must be accorded in all cases to immigrants. They must not be justled [sic] or pushed and women and children especially shall be most patiently and kindly treated."[89] Senner's directions compelled Ellis Island officers to report any "improper act" and emphasized his expectations for their behavior. The culture of the inspection service at Ellis Island, while not rife with corruption in this period, was tilted in that direction, with certain habits surviving the transition from state to federal control.[90] As the leadership on the island struggled to maintain order and discipline within the ranks of inspectors, the records of exclusion provided by the Italian Office show how LPC was widely but not stringently applied in the 1890s, and how Italians worked with U.S. gatekeeping.

One case of LPC exclusion, the story of "penniless immigrant" Giuseppe Mintello ordered by the Board of Special Inquiry to be deported back to Italy, grabbed the attention of the American press in March 1897. Here, as in other cases, the Italian Office played a decisive role in securing the migrant's freedom. Despite earning the "sympathy of members of the board . . . he could give no satisfactory assurance that he would not become a public charge," and he was summarily refused entry.[91] But "the immigrant did not despair. Before he was taken from Ellis Island he wrote a long letter to Commissioner Senner, in which he recited a story of misfortune that touched the commission. Dr. Senner referred it to Dr. Rossi of the Italian Bureau on the island. Dr. Rossi recommended that Giuseppe be allowed to remain in this country." Rossi was so trusted by the Ellis Island Commissioner that Senner agreed to release the man at the last minute. Mintello was already aboard a steamship that "was to sail in six minutes" when a call patched through from the Anchor Line's dock across the water in Brooklyn. "The gangway had been drawn in, but the message of good cheer reached the ears of the Captain and of Giuseppe at the same time. A rope ladder was flung over the side, and Giuseppe scrambled down with his scant baggage and hurried away, happy in the privilege of seeking his fortune in the New World." Here the article ends.

Another piece published a week later in Texas gave a similar story but included the tale of an Austrian subject excluded under the Alien Contract Labor Law, a man named Andras Kadalcheck whose brother committed suicide the night before he was set to testify in front of the Board of Special Inquiry.[92] Both men were able to persuade Senner to intervene and reverse their standing deportation order using his administrative power.[93] In Mintello's case Senner "was moved to rescind his decision," while the commissioner "took pity on [Kadalcheck], and, cutting short the rehearing, allowed the man to land." Both of these stories testify to the arbitrary nature of gatekeeping in these early years.

Taken together with the records of the work of the Office of Labor Information and Protection for Italians at Ellis Island, Giuseppe Mintello's happy ending to a tragic tale, and the press's interest in cases like his, show how transnational forces mediated the inspection process and thus the application of gatekeeping law. Trapped in a cage of legal enforcement of the LPC clause, Italians used informal diplomatic relationships to force the United States to better define the rules of exclusion in an era where officers applied guidelines in unpredictable ways. Meetings, letters, and reports generated by the two-room Office of Labor Information and Protection requested clarification on the admissibility of specific categories of people under the law, a part of the larger Italian strategy that sought to understand American policy as it was being enacted. While historians such as Jane Hong and Julian Lim have begun to demonstrate in forthcoming work how transnational actors influenced U.S. immigration policies of Asian exclusion, the sheer number of Italians dwarfed Asian migration at the turn of the century.[94] The physical presence of "a State in a State" on Ellis Island mediated American gatekeeping as the system exercised its bureaucratic muscle.[95]

Informed by the work going on at Ellis Island, Luigi Bodio published an impassioned article first in Italy in December 1895, later translated into English in April 1896, which laid out a strong case for his government to protect immigrants. Bodio's view reflected a significant strain within the Italian government more broadly.[96] "If our peasants and workmen have greater difficulty in finding work in foreign lands, this state of things obliges us to be more careful in protecting our emigrants and removing the obstacles they encounter," Bodio argued. He set out a clear and direct agenda for consuls to carry out on behalf of the Italian nation. "In short, far from discouraging emigration, we should aid it in every way, improving its quality and making it an aid beyond the sea to the influence of the mother country. It is a safety valve for class hatreds and social unrest, an efficacious instrument of human equality," he wrote. "For us Italians, coming late in our development, it is also a school. The higher classes should see to it that it is kept healthy and is not left without protection."[97]

On June 15, 1897, a massive fire ripped through Ellis Island. Since the flames destroyed almost all of the station's buildings including the main arrivals hall, the Office opened a temporary immigration processing station at the Barge Office on Battery Park, at the old Castle Garden located at the base of the island of Manhattan. The fire fundamentally disrupted the work of the Office of Labor Information and Protection for Italians. Luigi Bodio lamented the loss of the Office's carefully prepared records that he would no longer be able to use to analyze the immigration stream.[98] At the temporary Barge Office quarters Rossi struggled to carry on, even after Rome sent him funds to replace his typewriter that had burned.[99] He found the new location compromised by many of the same issues that drove the U.S. government to relocate to Ellis Island in the first place in 1892 (namely, inability to keep at bay predatory employers who gathered right outside the building and enjoyed easy access to new arrivals).[100] Rossi complained that all emigrants should be required to meet with agents of his office first.[101] Yet this was unenforceable without the cooperation of the American authorities who suffered a disruption in order themselves.[102] A year after the fire, the immigration authorities had come to see the Office not as an aid but as an interference. Mixed messages between New York, Washington, and Rome in April and June 1898 first augured the Office's closing, then reversed course when Fava reassured his government that it would remain open.[103] Fava, temporarily back in Rome, sent his chargé d'affaires to the secretary of state to argue against Treasury Secretary Gage's decision, which he planned to issue April 15, 1898, to revoke the Office's authorization.[104] Newly confirmed commissioner of immigration Terence Powderly was partially responsible for forcing his hand. Powderly and the Knights of Labor, the union he had led that had fought to reduce the volume of labor migration to the United States as a way to protect workers' wages, had not looked kindly on the Office. Gage blamed what MAE historian Laura Pilotti called "the misunderstandings that arose between the agents of the office and the federal authorities of the port of New York on the interpretation to be given to

American immigration laws."[105] These crosswinds could not be contained as the Immigration Bureau did not want to yield its discretionary power under pressure from a foreign government. Finally, effective January 1, 1900, the U.S. government formally shut the Office down citing jealousy of other nations.[106] While diplomatic wrangling managed to delay the closure for a year and a half, functions had effectively ceased in the winter of 1898–99.[107] While American newspapers blamed the Office's inability to rout the padrone system, the Immigration Bureau did not want other countries to request the same privileges of oversight and proximity to the gatekeeping system that Italians had come to enjoy.[108]

## Conclusion

As Alessandro Oldrini looked out at the lines of people Superintendent of Immigration Herman Stump called the "worst classes" awaiting inspection on August 28, 1894, he picked up his pen and wrote to the embassy in Washington. He did not try to hide his mocking of Stump when he broke into colorful euphemisms punctuated by the liberal use of exclamation marks. Seeing Stump's fears of immigrant invasion as frankly ridiculous, Oldrini told the ambassador, "We know that Stump would make suggestions to the Italian government, regarding its emigration, on the best way to diminish the flow of migrants because Congress reported the superintendent 'feels very ugly about it.' Good lord, what jackasses!" he exclaimed in frustration. Oldrini struggled to understand why a country with territory as vast as the United States would ever need to restrict the flow of immigration—even that deemed undesirable. "With 3/5 of the country a desert between two oceans!!" he shouted from the page.[109] This letter was quite a contrast with the formal correspondence the two men frequently exchanged. As *Harper's* depiction of the "pathos . . . in the cage of the rejected" had emphasized, immigration inspectors held the power to permit or deny the entry of thousands of arriving immigrants each day. Reports peppered with frustration at the action of these inspectors filled the pages of confidential messages exchanged between the ambassador in Washington and the foreign minister in Rome, uncovering the transnational and sometimes competing forces of immigration restriction.[110]

A binational perspective on the regulation of immigration illuminates previously shadowed corners of this early era in federal immigration policy. Julie Greene has argued that "mobility became a key terrain of struggle" for workers on the move in the Gilded Age; at the same time, U.S. policy makers were constructing a gatekeeping regime under the close supervision of officers of the Italian government who were in constant communication with Rome.[111] Italians' concerns on the ground at Ellis translated into the language of their correspondence as they negotiated an asymmetric partnership between the two nations connected by migration.[112] Beginning in 1901, Italian law mandated government agents in the newly created emigration commissariat apply the same criteria to inspect departing migrants as inspectors would at Ellis Island to prevent embarrassing and costly rejections at the border.[113] From the very beginning, the Italian presence shaped the development of key gatekeeping practices: inspection, detention, and deportation. A handful of men in the Italian diplomatic service interacted daily with both the architects of gatekeeping and the foot soldiers tasked with interpreting the law at Ellis Island. Their closeness yielded an incredible record of documents and reports on a period little understood yet crucial to the development of a robust gatekeeping regime at the U.S. border as the laws and practices of Asian exclusion expanded to target Europeans.

The relationship between a tight circle of influential bureaucrats—Stump, Fava, Oldrini, the secretary and undersecretary of the MAE, and the undersecretary of the Ministry of the Interior—shaped Italian migrants' interactions with American authorities. In late August 1894 the chief agent of the Office of Labor Information and Protection for Italians jotted off a quick telegram to the ambassador in Washington seeking guidance. "A visit to the [ship] *Victoria* this morning asked me to advise what to do regarding Italians. Restrict number coming I hear Congress says, that direction received in force at Ellis [Island] today; after lunch I will leave tomorrow I will follow in its entirety your advice [signed] Alex Oldrini."[114] This cable, in its brevity and its casualness, shows how intensively Italian officers of the foreign service worked to manage the growing tide of migration and mitigate the threat of exclusion. Back in Rome, Giuseppe Solimbergo told his fellow members of Parliament assembled in December 1894 that the Office "represents a true diplomatic success of our government."[115] In the first two years of the Office's operation, Ambassador Fava exchanged not a single letter with the U.S. secretary of state regarding immigration. Indeed, the ambassador often went directly to Stump, sometimes with letters he labeled "personal," bypassing the expected channel for diplomatic communication.[116] Signs of their friendly relationship appear in letters that praise each other's work, and Fava and his underlings weighed in constantly on American activity. The secretary of the Treasury (who oversaw immigration at the time) wrote to Fava on April 12, 1895, "to express my satisfaction at the harmonious relations existing between the Immigration officials of our respective Governments, and the mutual benefits already resulting therefrom."[117]

In a typical letter to Stump, Fava outlined his plans for cooperation with American authorities, and when one reads between the lines, his words highlight a striking degree of direct coordination between Oldrini's Office and U.S. leadership. "I am glad to hear that Dr. Senner has been instructed by you to have Prof. Oldrini interview all Italians going to the State of New York," he began. "This I am sure, will prove very useful for the suppression of the padrone's system: all this," Fava emphasized, "to have Dr. Senner well satisfied, as I know you are, that the government of the U.S. can implicitly rely on the sure and active cooperation of the Italian Bureau of Ellis Island, which is placed under my own direct supervision, for the purpose of suppressing the evil which it is the intention of both our governments should disappear."[118]

Careful not to claim too much power, before sending off his letter the ambassador edited two crucial clauses in the final version, replacing direct statements of action with passive voice phrases that distanced his government from direct intervention. Where he initially wrote "the government of the U.S. will always find the sure and active cooperation of the Italian Bureau," Fava replaced "will always find" with "can implicitly rely on." Where he first used the phrase "have decided to destroy" in reference to the binational goal of ending the padrone system, the final letter read in the third person, "it should disappear." This exchange captures the overall state of relations between the two nations. The friendly, even conciliatory, tone of official correspondence with American leaders failed to translate into markedly favorable treatment at the hands of U.S. immigration inspectors. Yet the presence of the Office blunted the power of LPC as a tool of gatekeeping, leaving the door ajar to what *Harper's* called the "cage of the rejected."

The relationship between Italy and the United States in the 1890s reveals the limits of both Italian and American authority to control migration, the boundaries of American gatekeeping in its early years anticipating the rise of "remote control," and the limitations of Italy's efforts to bypass the immigration authorities. As a result of direct observation of the practice of gatekeeping at Ellis Island between 1894 and 1896 by the officers of the Office of Labor Information and Protection, the Italian government would soon shift into a more interventionist strategy to prevent exclusion of its migrants. In 1896 Egisto Rossi celebrated the success of his efforts to force the United States to apply clear and consistent reasons for exclusion. It was not until the establishment of the Office of Labor Information at Ellis Island that the royal government was able to offer, in the words of its second chief agent, "invaluable help" on the "days of exceptional invasion" that made the island "more Italian than American."[119]

The disastrous fire at Ellis Island in June 1897 has sharply limited scholars' studies of the mechanics of enforcement in its earliest years. For this reason most historians rely on European exclusion cases heard after 1900.[120] While the outcome of cases decided by the Board of Special Inquiry before 1897 cannot be studied systematically, the daily interactions with the American bureaucracy captured by men like Oldrini and Rossi shine a light onto the otherwise darkened history of early gatekeeping. The federal government has long created a "cage of the rejected," enlisting foreign powers to carry out the work of border control.[121] In the summer of 2019, the United States began exercising its administrative power to create a policy requiring some migrants with asylum claims to stay in Mexico. Who is allowed to enter (where they are held in horrendous detention facilities) still seems arbitrary and capricious in the twenty-first century, much as it did in the early years of Ellis Island. Journalists have struggled to bring details about the "Remain in Mexico" policy to light. The specifics have come from the handful of lawyers granted access to detained migrants: only ten to fifteen cases out of more than seven thousand migrants sent to wait in Ciudad Juárez, just across the border from El Paso, had met with counsel by early July 2019.[122] The Biden administration has struggled to end the policy. As contemporary crises at the southern border tragically demonstrate, the cage is not just a metaphor. While early immigration law enforcement in the United States fell under administrative oversight, the practice of gatekeeping has never been a domestically isolated phenomenon. The Italian record shows that this process has long been affected by transnational forces, as the pressures of Italian officers shaped the application of exclusion law.

# CHAPTER 3

# From Ellis Island to
# Sunnyside Plantation, Arkansas

As gatekeepers expanded their targets from Chinese to Italian migrants in the 1890s, the architects of anticipatory remote control tried out two new strategies to resist formal exclusion at Ellis Island. The Italian ambassador began to suggest diverting Italian migrants to agricultural colonies organized for their benefit in the American South as a way to bypass the increasingly punitive inspection regime at Ellis Island.[1] Moreover, Italian officials in Rome and Washington, D.C., working with the colony's founders, attempted to navigate around the prohibitions of the Alien Contract Labor Law of 1885. Precisely how and why the attention of Italian and U.S. government officials, and the destination of migrants themselves, shifted from Ellis Island to Sunnyside Plantation in Chicot County, Arkansas, speaks to fundamental questions in the history of immigration policy: Who do we keep out? Who do we invite in? How does "desirability" determine policy?

Significantly expanding the scope of previous scholarship on Sunnyside Plantation that examined aspects of its history in isolation, this chapter will connect the reasons why Italians came to the South to the impact of their presence in national immigration politics.[2] The history of Italian colonization in the American South connects to the larger history of federal immigration policy. Sunnyside Plantation offers a significant case study of the role that "undesirable" immigrants and their government played in constructing a gatekeeping nation.

At the same time, the Italian government's attempts to enforce one section, Article 17, of its 1888 emigration law demonstrate the limits of international cooperation to manage migration. The twelve-thousand-acre cotton plantation called Sunnyside was but one arm of the Italian government's response to gatekeeping enforcement measures that targeted working-class migrants. Through its support of Sunnyside Plantation, its work through the Office at Ellis Island, and a renewed focus on enforcement of a section of the first national emigration law of December 30, 1888, the Italian government responded to the decisions to admit or exclude made by U.S. Immigration Bureau agents and their Board of Special Inquiry. Article 17 gave emigrants who were refused entry at the U.S. border legal standing in Italian courts to recoup their costs as well as additional damages for the failed journey.[3] The law allowed prefects to force emigration agents to return fees to emigrants rejected at the U.S. border. Agents who sold tickets to passengers they knew could not pass inspection risked prosecution in Italian courts. The 1888 law also required emigration agents and subagents to secure a government license to operate as the Italian state tried to get a handle on increasing migratory traffic. While it was not yet a "remote control" law in structure, it was applied to try to address problems arising from American border control measures. In this way the efforts to use an older law in a new way in the summer of 1895 were an important step in anticipatory remote control, as they show how the Italian government adapted their own laws and procedures to respond to American policy.

As the largest migrant group to arrive in the United States at the turn of the twentieth century, Italians traveled a great distance, both physically and metaphorically. The relationship between Rome and Washington, and Ellis Island and Sunnyside Plantation in Chicot County, Arkansas—a physical distance of over twelve hundred miles—in the mid-1890s shows that while early immigration law enforcement in the United States fell under administrative oversight, the practice of gatekeeping was never a domestically isolated phenomenon. The revived interest in Article 17 was part of a period of intense strategizing by the Italian government in response to American policy making.

At the turn of the twentieth century, as native-born Americans moved to restrict the free entry of Italians and other "races unsuited to our civilization," the South actually began to recruit immigrants whose presence, proponents believed, would provide the kind of labor they desired and solve the "Negro problem" by rebalancing the region's racial composition. At the same time, influential leaders in Italy promoted colonization in the U.S. South as a solution to the most pressing social problems caused by mass migration—overcrowding, poverty, disease, and exploitation. Men at the highest level of the royal Italian government, ambassador to the U.S. Baron Saverio Fava and Minister of Foreign Affairs Baron Blanc, directed their officers to "protect" Italian migrants with *tutela* as their stated policy goal. Priest Vincenzo Grossi called out from the pages of the influential Italian magazine of politics and culture, *Nuova Antologia*, for the protection of the migrant laborers by sending them to the land. Grossi argued that the southern U.S. states had "the climate and economic conditions best adapted to the temperament and moral and intellectual training of Italian immigrants, and of the Mezzogiorno types in particular."[4] Leaders' goals in Italy and the southern United States coalesced in the program for rural colonization that became a form of distribution policy. Throughout this chapter I use the term "colonization" to align with the language used by its proponents, and to remain consistent with the ways in which its organizers discussed it both publicly and privately at the time.

Between 1895 and 1898, representatives of the Italian government arranged for the recruitment of several thousand Italians from lands around Rome for Sunnyside Plantation. To do this they had to navigate around gatekeeping law—particularly the Alien Contract Labor Law of 1885—as these policies directly shaped the development of the cotton plantation colony. The relationship between the Office of Labor Information and Protection for Italians and its most visible project outside of New York City, Sunnyside Plantation, challenges the perception of the unchecked power of the administrative state while broadening the geographic focus of early gatekeeping to include the rural South.

Colonization recast Italian immigrants—who the *Washington Post* in 1891 had claimed on authority were "eight times more murderous than other Europeans"—into valuable new settlers for the American South.[5] A journalist from the *New York Herald* contrasted Italian migrants with Black labor. The newspaper clarified that while "honest and respectable negro tenants" existed in the Arkansas delta, "as a class, however, negro labor is unsatisfactory." The Sunnyside Plantation colony was carefully designed and promoted to prove that imported Italian families approached cotton farming as a landowner would, taking care in their cultivation because they had a personal stake invested in their crop. Their desirability depended on their ability to permanently resettle: "On the other hand, the Italians that [Sunnyside owner] Mr. Corbin brought over have become purchasers of land on the installment plan, and for that reason, if for no other, must become better producers," the *New York Herald* reported in June 1896.[6] If the experiment could turn seasonal laborers into farmers, it could also prove that bird-of-passage Italians could assimilate and should be admitted into the United States. This belief contributed to making otherwise undesirable immigrants attractive and sustained the effort to divert Italians to Arkansas.

Colonizing migrant Italian families in Arkansas posed a direct challenge to racial and labor norms, but in unpredictable ways that reveal more about the construction of restrictive immigration policy. From the Italian diplomatic archive a detailed history of the plantation experiment and the parallel effort to apply Italian emigration law to address exclusion at the U.S. border emerges that is missing in English language sources. During a time of unprecedented European labor mobility, the colonization project and Article 17 enforcement tried to prevent and fix the problems migrants encountered as they entered the United States. But when scholars, pundits, and the public view the legal and bureaucratic-administrative structures of gatekeeping as a domestic phenomenon, crucial policy actors outside of the state's borders are overlooked.[7] Foreign actors have long been active in shaping immigration policy. Italy acted as a mediator during the construction of a gatekeeping regime in the United States, testing out novel solutions to the challenges presented by increasingly strict border controls that were influenced by ideas about desirability.

## Connecting Ellis Island to Sunnyside Plantation

The same Italian diplomats engaged in the larger effort to resist U.S. moves toward immigration restriction detailed in chapters 1 and 2 helped organize Sunnyside Plantation. This work developed out of the asymmetric partnership between Italy and the United States in the 1890s.[8] In June 1894 Ambassador Saverio Fava discussed rewarding migrants who chose to go to agricultural colonies, offering the first endorsement of an idea that would become Sunnyside in the same report where he outlined plans for the soon-to-open Office of Labor Information and Protection for Italians at Ellis Island. His long missive to the foreign minister in Rome indicated how much hope Fava and his government had for the new Office to ameliorate pressure to restrict Italian migration.[9] He encouraged Foreign Minister Baron Blanc to act quickly to staff the Office as the Immigration Bureau had already leaked to the American press news of their support for the endeavor. It would be best to staff the Office with agents who knew U.S. law and social customs well, Fava reasoned, deferring to Blanc to send two people from Rome but also offering to recommend men in New York Fava already knew to be qualified. He also proposed a head tax that would fund an account to help migrants navigate a number of challenges and support colonization efforts. Among the benefits the ambassador named for this fund, "a special case would be set up to assist the emigrants to their landing, to facilitate them in their attempts at colonization, to reward those settlers who would make themselves worthy [to earn it]; to provide for hospital and repatriation expenses, to help the workers in cases of accidents and industrial and agricultural sites." This tax would be similar to a levy authorized by an 1882 Italian statute that had expired in 1894, just ahead of the Office's opening. Fava calculated that such a tax could easily raise 75,000 lire a year from the profits of "the companies in the south that derive such fat gains from the transport of emigrants," he reasoned, "[so they] can pay it without serious damage."[10] Yet Fava was still looking for a location for his colonization project. Soon enough, an offer to create just the sort of "worthy" colony Fava wanted to support would emerge.

In October 1885 Austin Corbin, millionaire developer of the Long Island Railroad, assumed full ownership of a massive twelve-thousand-acre parcel of prime cotton land in the Arkansas delta when the owners defaulted on $133,305 in bonds underwritten by the Corbin Banking Company.[11] This foreclosure began for him a long relationship with the Arkansas plantation located more than a thousand miles away from Corbin's ornate eight-story bank headquarters in New York.[12] The tract was surrounded on three sides by the oxbow-shaped Lake Chicot that had formed when the Mississippi River changed its course in the far distant past. Cotton grew very well in the rich, dark alluvial soil that still nurtures the roots and bolls of the valuable plants today.[13] By October 1886 Corbin had founded the Sunnyside Company to begin to harness a profit from his new land. As a neophyte planter himself, Corbin assumed the conventions practiced previously on the plantation and in the surrounding area, and he hired local African Americans to serve as day laborers, sharecroppers, and tenants.[14] Almost immediately he ran into problems, likely because of the tenants' view of the company as "foreign" and their resistance to working under overseers controlled by a faraway landowner.[15] When the plantation failed to turn a profit, Corbin leased convicts from the state of Arkansas for one year only, in 1894.[16] Corbin, a man whom one biographer described as having "unusual vision and initiative," would soon shift his focus to a new source of labor.[17] Perhaps the railroad magnate and New York City financier was attracted by the challenge of running a cotton plantation, as Sunnyside was a unique property in Corbin's burgeoning portfolio of real estate investments, so he began to look beyond the region's racialized pools of tractable workers.

Around 1894 Corbin befriended a Roman nobleman and politician named Don Emanuele Ruspoli.[18] Corbin likely met the Italian noble through New York high society circles frequented by Ruspoli's American-born wife.[19] Ruspoli often traveled with her back and forth between New York and Rome where he held the ceremonial title of prince of the city. At some point Ruspoli introduced Corbin to Alessandro Oldrini, the royal Italian government's agent at Ellis Island. According to the report of an Italian language newspaper tucked away by the ambassador in his files, "It then became that, following the argument of Prince Ruspoli, he suggested to [Corbin] to import the labor of Italian families and divide the tract of land into small plots equal in size."[20] With the support of his friend Ruspoli, Sunnyside's owner appealed to the Ministry of Foreign Affairs with a plan to import to Arkansas around seven hundred settlers chosen directly from Ruspoli's own vast landholdings in the Lazio region around Rome in central Italy.

When the owner of this large plantation on the Mississippi River approached the Italian embassy with a plan to organize an agricultural colony on his land, the ambassador and his officers happily cooperated. Here was a millionaire, the owner of the Long Island Railroad and his own eponymous banking house, who could provide land, houses, tools, and general furnishings for as many as a thousand people. Praised by Alessandro Oldrini as "a man of great means," Corbin was also willing and able to arrange for the direct transfer of families from their native villages in Lazio to his land at Sunnyside, bypassing the confusion and possible threat of rejection under the "likely to become a public charge" clause or the Alien Contract Labor Law at Ellis Island.[21] Corbin's proposal dovetailed nicely with the emigration initiatives of the Crispi government. Southern agricultural colonization had the potential to provide for the physical, psychological, and economic well-being of the Italian peasant and his family. Beginning in 1887, in his first of two terms as prime minister, Francesco Crispi adopted a new approach to governing designed to combat Italy's pervasive rural poverty. Crispi looked beyond Italy's borders as he, according to historian Mark Choate, "promoted an aggressive foreign policy as a way to solve Italy's internal problems, especially its unimproved agriculture, endemic unemployment, and backward social structures in the South." Furthermore, the offer to divide Corbin's large twelve-thousand-acre tract into approximately twelve-acre plots per family directly addressed the problems these people struggled with as poor farmers in Italy. Crispi "hoped the creation of overseas settlements would liberate Italians from the archaic great estates and tiny, scattered landholdings that polarized rural society and strangled economic development."[22] By promoting colonization abroad, Crispi and his government tried to alleviate the pressure of their growing population on government services and improve their country's economy.[23]

Through much of 1894, as Corbin, Fava, and Oldrini worked together to establish an Italian colony in Arkansas, the Italians made the case to their colleagues in the MAE. Oldrini summarized the details of a meeting in February 1894 that demonstrated how much Corbin wanted to try a different kind of labor if he could get Italians—whom the men called "real colonists"—to the plantation. "Corbin provided me with figures that the part [of Sunnyside] now cultivated with *convict labor* renders 6 percent per year." Oldrini speculated about the possibilities. "The contract ends in February. He does not see doing this with 'convicts' and wants real colonists, if he could make the sacrifices to have it . . . I believe . . . that not only could he pay their transport from New York to the South but little by little also from Italy."[24] This kind of facilitated migration clearly violated the Alien Contract Labor Law, but it could be carried out with the support of the ambassador, the men hoped. The same day that he received Oldrini's report of the meeting, Fava sat down to draft a memo announcing the Corbin plan to the entire MAE. The ambassador emphasized how Corbin's plan could enact an informal redistribution policy he believed clearly aligned with Crispi's reform agenda: "At the very least it is not up to him to indicate how much the Italian government wants to see our emigration arrive in the agricultural centers of this continent." Fava encouraged his consular agents stationed throughout the United States to "use every tool available to us immediately and give maximum publicity to the serious proposal of Mr. Corbin" to promote the opportunity.[25] By September, in a confidential report to Rome, Oldrini emphasized the overwhelming impact he believed agricultural colonization would have on Italian migrants in the United States: "It is this movement that could serve as an 'object lesson' to all of our migratory population," he began, "at this point, clearly documented, irrefutable, of the benefits that could be derived from agriculture in the United States," especially for the struggling worker whose employment "at this point is too intermittent to permit the emigrant to assure their family a modest security."[26]

Oldrini worked closely with Corbin and his plantation manager, George Watkins, to lay out the specific terms of the Sunnyside labor contract at a meeting in November 1894. Each family would pay 6 percent interest on a mortgage underwritten by the landowner's banking house. Corbin estimated each family would pay $150 annually, and at a 6 percent interest rate tenants could expect to become the owner of a twelve-and-a-half acre plot in twenty-two years. The proposal proved appealing when less than two months later, on January 11, 1895, the New York Times reported 575 families "engaged to occupy" Sunnyside plots. The actual number was 150 families (totaling 562 individuals) who had signed the contract and left their village together, bound for Sunnyside, in December 1895.[27] Later that month the families landed at Lake Chicot, on the western bank of the Mississippi River just north of the town of Greenville. With winter setting in around them, the emigrants went about making more comfortable the simply furnished two- and four-room cabins that had been issued to each family by the Corbin Company. Inside a wood frame dwelling, Domenico Pirandolfo, his wife, and their four children stocked their kitchen shelves with coffee, flour, salt, and sugar purchased from the plantation's commissary and waited for the planting season to begin. The men who had brought Pirandolfo, his family, and their neighbors to Arkansas had big hopes for these migrants.

Alessandro Oldrini personally escorted the first group of settlers to their new homes, connecting the royal Italian government to the physical process of migration and acting as a shepherd through the gauntlet of gatekeepers who could exclude the contract holders under the provisions of the Alien Contract Labor Law of 1885.[28] This important piece of legislation prohibited the importation of immigrants who had contracted to work with a specific employer prior to their arrival in the country. While the mortgage provision made their contracts quite appealing, it also pushed signees into a category of migrant specifically prohibited under the law.

The potential to earn sizable profits from a successful cotton harvest from its seemingly limitless supply of fertile soil drew myriad speculators to the Yazoo-Mississippi delta throughout the nineteenth century. Yet the territory was isolated and subject to unpredictable floods, and the region north of Natchez offered few of the trappings of conventional Anglo society.[29] An early Sunnyside settler told an oral history interviewer that the sound of the frogs on the plantation at night scared her husband's uncle so badly, he boarded a train and never returned.[30] Those who risked farming there made and lost huge fortunes; volatility was the one constant. Italians could only increase the monetary value of planters' land by cultivating more of it, and because these immigrants came under the promise of becoming landowners of their own small plots, employing them under such a contract meant that the planter would expose himself to less risk each year. He had a guaranteed annual income living in each of his tenant cabins.[31] The presence of this mortgage provision became crucial to the contentedness of the Italian tenants and to their government's claims that the terms of colonization made them exempt from exclusion under the Alien Contract Labor Law.

Sunnyside's original vision complemented the immigrants' own hopes, dreams, and expectations, and Ministry officials repeatedly agreed that the path to ownership was the essential clause in every contract made with an Italian. In an internal report to the ambassador in 1894, Alessandro Oldrini, head of the Office of Labor Information and Protection for Italians at Ellis Island, emphasized how the Sunnyside experiment's "purchase plan . . . will also ensure the advantages of ownership to the emigrant and because [of it] the families that will come do not have to fall under the Contract Labor Law."[32] The Alien Contract Labor Law and the prohibition of persons "likely to become a public charge" were the two most often invoked statutes to enforce Italian exclusion. Italian officers and their American counterparts sought, through careful wording, to assure that the families intended for Sunnyside would be classified as "Land Owners" and not manual laborers by the U.S. commissioner of immigration.[33] Association with sharecropping carried extremely negative connotations for one's racial and economic status in the South, and therefore it was not surprising that the Italians tried to avoid any and all association with that title in order to set themselves apart from this category of Delta labor. But more specifically, the motivation came from the explicit need to sidestep the 1885 Alien Contract Labor Law. If the U.S. immigration agents meeting their ship classified the families intended for Sunnyside as manual laborers, they would be denied entry into the country and sent back. If, however, Fava and Corbin could make the case that the families were farmers and therefore not workers in the sense of the law, their safe passage would be guaranteed.

The "Land Owner" designation was purposefully defined through the stipulation in the contract that a percentage of the year's rent would be put toward a twenty-one-year mortgage underwritten by the Sunnyside Company on each farm and paid on 6 percent interest annually per twelve-acre plot.[34] This language was crucial: the Sunnyside Italians were supposed to be small-time proprietors, not inadmissible contract laborers. More than just a short-term alternative to native black labor, the Italian worker was to be a permanent solution to the region's post-emancipation "labor problem."

For the next few years Fava continued to pour his energy into the Arkansas plantation experiment. Father Pietro Bandini, sent by Rome to minister to the Sunnyside colonists, reported excellent conditions in April 1896.[35] On April 17 Bandini informed Ambassador Fava: "I visited with all of the individuals of the colony and they seemed to me all satisfied and content."[36] Summarizing Bandini's findings for his superiors in Rome, Fava wrote:

> The impartial indications coming [out of Sunnyside] reassure us of the good organization of this, our first agricultural colony in the United States, and of the useful providence of the [Sunnyside] Company for the well-being of our colonists without regard to cost[.] This is indicative of the sort of favored and optimal conditions of the families of this colony and also indicates the probability of good things to come from the enterprise that colonizers Corbin and Ruspoli offers.[37]

Such positive reports led the Italian government to support the Sunnyside Company's request for seventy-two additional families to arrive in the winter of 1896.[38]

From far-flung places observers encouraged the Sunnyside plantation experiment. Italian-language newspapers in Texas and New York reported on the colony as the ticket to material success in America. *Il Corriere Italiano* announced news of "The Italian Colony in Arkansas" one month after Sunnyside received its second infusion of settlers in January 1897, adding seventy-two families to the 150 already present for a total population of 232 thirteen months after its founding. According to *Il Corriere Italiano*, Prince Ruspoli had given the Sunnyside migrants his personal guarantee that they would be able to acquire their plots if they followed the mortgage payment plan established by their contracts.[39] Using similar language to Sunnyside's boosters in the Italian government, the Texas newspaper emphasized, "If more and more co-nationalist peasants now at this hour are experiencing a life of hardship in the home country or in America, they can find an honest income and good profits to come with the cultivation of the soil." In April 1896 Ambassador Fava had praised the plantation experiment in a report that emphasized the role that cotton farming in the South could play in improving peasants' lives.

"See the goodwill that comes from rendering them less uncomfortable in the new residence[;] it proves, beyond a shadow of a doubt that . . . they can find notable profits to come" at Sunnyside.[40]

But things were not as they seemed. Like much of the land lining the river, Sunnyside had benefited from the Delta's renowned topsoil, which thousands of years of uncontrolled annual flooding had built to a depth of several feet. With water surrounding the area on three sides, rich alluvial floods were almost guaranteed, but this natural fertility came at a price to anyone attempting to actually live there.[41] Sunnyside's location greatly impacted the health of the settlers. Diseases like malaria and other fevers flourished easily in the semi-swampland of the Plantation. The Italian families had come from the *meriodionale*, an area with a cooler and drier climate in comparison to the Arkansas delta, and they lacked natural immunity to lowland maladies. River water, while plentiful, was not a reliable nor particularly healthy source of drinking water, and the lack of potable water at Sunnyside proved over time to be an intractable problem. Corbin suggested a rainwater barrel system that was attempted in the early years of the colony.[42] Management tried several methods without success to obtain a reliable supply of fresh water while Fava and Oldrini, encouraged by Father Bandini's lobbying, pushed for the installation of artesian wells. The management promised it would dig wells, but this expensive work was continually postponed as the plantation struggled to turn a profit. This unresolved health issue eventually created palpable friction between Sunnyside's owners and managers, the consulate, and the tenants.

In his April 1896 report Bandini had detailed Corbin's efforts to install pumps to bring drinking water to each settler's cabin from the Mississippi River. "The engineer assured me," Bandini told Fava, that "in a few days [drinkable water] will be distributed to every single house."[43] On July 15, almost a month after Corbin's sudden death in a carriage accident, his son-in-law George Edgell forwarded to the ambassador his own hopeful assessment of the state of the water supply. He even addressed the plan to negotiate for a new influx of Italian settlers that he had been discussing with the ambassador.[44] The company had another hundred settlers they wanted to bring to Arkansas and had informed the Ministry of this plan; Fava recommended Corbin wait until the water situation was resolved.[45] In a sudden turn away from the easy cooperation that had marked the first year and a half, the Sunnyside Company now needed to reassure current settlers and the Ministry before they could grow the colony any further.

Some macroeconomic factors also influenced the course of the farm labor experiment. Despite initial hopes for plantation profits, the two seasons from 1896 to 1898 were bad years for cotton in the entire region. A worldwide cotton price depression dragged down values for the whole of the 1890s. [46] Even the officers at the MAE recognized that some of the struggles at Sunnyside were due to factors out of their control. "This summer is exceptionally dry and windy, not only in Arkansas, but in New York and in general in the whole United States," Oldrini lamented to Fava in August 1896.[47]

The success of the experiment also depended in no small part on the treatment Italians received from southern landowners, and the gap between promise and reality soon stretched into a chasm. With only one narrow land bridge connecting Sunnyside to the rest of Chicot County, the Sunnyside settlers had enormous difficulty leaving the plantation.[48] The company had constructed a river landing at this single access point, and riverboat travel, the quickest and most reliable method of transportation to and from the plantation at the time, still took two hours to reach the nearest city of Greenville, Mississippi.[49] Corbin, who had made his fortune developing the Long Island Railroad, promised to connect up the plantation's short track with outside lines. But two years after the first settlers had arrived, the railroad still only ran from one end of the plantation to the other and thus remained a three-mile-long road to nowhere.[50] Over time, the very qualities that made Sunnyside ideal for cotton culture also left the plantation isolated and its inhabitants easily controlled. Sunnyside would not be the perfect solution to the problems of emigration that Fava had hoped for. As the colony struggled the government in Rome was trying a different strategy back in New York Harbor.

### Article 17

Simultaneous to the efforts to successfully establish Sunnyside, a new strategy emerged that tried to avert exclusion at Ellis Island using a then seven-year-old Italian law. Despite being on the books since 1888, the provisions of Article 17 had been only loosely enforced before 1895 in response to the growing problem of exclusion at Ellis Island. The 1888 law targeted agents who encouraged inadmissible migrants to depart for the United States. Prefects, local government officials, charged emigration agents operating within their territory for an offense on another nation's territory, confirmed by an agent of the U.S. immigration service. Each case required the Ministry of the Interior to cooperate with the ambassador and the Office at Ellis Island; the larger goal was to stop the emigration of any person who could not gain entry to the United States under the American statute. Even though the offense led to exclusion at the U.S. border, Article 17 defined the crime as one committed on Italian soil before the migrant departed. While the law gave the Ministry of the Interior control over prosecution of these cases, how specifically to carry out Article 17 was still an open question.

Article 17 focused on points of contact before departure and stayed within the clear jurisdiction of Italian courts, but prosecution of its cases required transnational cooperation. For the law to have an impact migrants needed to know about the law's protections and agree to report emigration agents. Officials in the Interior Ministry had to gather evidence from abroad. The undersecretary of state in Rome, G. Adamoli, attempted to put this process into motion. In April 1895 Adamoli told Fava to instruct his consul in New York to collect complaints for prosecution under the 1888 law, and for Oldrini to inform immigrants when landing of the law's protections.[51] A general report authored by the undersecretary noted a discrepancy between the press's coverage, like the story of a group of migrants who reportedly retaliated against U.S. immigration officers by beating them with heavy bags of macaroni in May 1894 to avenge the deportation of their friends.[52] Yet there had been no attempt to bring forth a case under Article 17 by the rejected men against the ticket agent who sold them their passage. Adamoli reasoned that the comparatively small number of cases reported to consular agents resulted from migrants' lack of knowledge about the law's protections.[53] The Italian government wanted to make it easier for emigrants to report violations to consular agents to increase the effectiveness of the law.

The government's efforts seemed to pay off as the messages from Rome stimulated a robust response in New York. In the late spring of 1895, a little over a year after the macaroni incident and at the same time that Fava and Oldrini threw their support behind the Sunnyside colony, Oldrini began invoking Article 17 to respond to the exclusion of emigrants by U.S. agents at Ellis Island. The Office of Labor Information and Protection immediately became the clearinghouse for Article 17 cases. Oldrini prepared a document with instructions to distribute to rejected emigrants, which he shared with Fava on June 1. "I have the honor of submitting to you three printed copies of the instructions given to rejected emigrants with the data from the Board of Special Inquiry as you requested, your excellency," he wrote with more than a hint of pride. The law offered free legal assistance to emigrants to pursue their cases for damages, and Oldrini felt his Office was particularly critical to the effort to inform excluded migrants of their rights. He capped off his report with a note that highlighted his specific efforts to support Article 17 cases: "Beginning this month each emigrant is supplied by me with notes which they will need on their return" to pursue their claims in court.[54]

Oldrini approached the two most influential agents of American gatekeeping at Ellis Island, the station commissioner, Joseph Senner, and the chair of the Board of Special Inquiry, Joseph McSweeney, with news of the Italian government's plan to begin enhanced enforcement of Article 17. Oldrini discussed the law with these key officials on the island, and his report to Ambassador Fava spoke to his hope for the law's potential. Oldrini reported that both McSweeney and Senner were pleasantly surprised to hear about the application of the Italian law. Senner had expressed his satisfaction with its provisions.[55] McSweeney asked about the timeliness of the action, pointing to the long-standing complaints migrants had against transatlantic shipping lines. Even though the 1888 law targeted emigration agents who worked for the shipping lines rather than the companies directly, McSweeney seemed hopeful that the Italian government would lend support to these claims.

For more than seven months Oldrini had been pushing the power of Article 17 to mediate U.S. gatekeeping policy. He summarized his view in a report to Ambassador Fava in November 1894: "So I believed that by accentuating the consequences of the *exclusions* of Italian emigrants from the United States," he concluded of his conversations with American officials, "I could get the Officers of the Special Board of Inquiry and other inspectors, as well as the commissioner himself, to be more cautious in their final decisions."[56] Furthermore, Oldrini wanted to expand the scope of the 1888 law to hold his own government more responsible for regulating the traffic, "observing that the legal responsibility should fall not only on the emigration agents, if there were inducements to emigrate, but more on the navigation commissioners who know better than the first the immigration laws of the United States, and therefore should not accept with their eyes closed the emigrants sent to them by the agents." Fava hoped this attempt to impose financial consequences to exclusion on the shipping companies would be followed by further action in Parliament to "discipline the emigration question."[57] Oldrini wrote in report no. 79 of efforts to write a new law, "a more general one to prevent emigration agents or maritime companies or others from profiting off of the movement of 'undesirable elements,'" using the English phrase he had seen repeated so frequently in the American debate over immigration. He summarized the legislative debate in Rome as it engaged with questions of punishment and compliance: "Adding that the new immigration law to be presented to the Italian Parliament will be even more severe in this regard, the provisions concerning damages . . . will be strictly applied in all cases where the complainant will prove or the arbitration commission will judge that there was an incentive given to emigrate [by the agent or company]." The asymmetric partnership took shape in these internal discussions, revealing a distinctly transnational influence shaping migration control through anticipatory remote control measures like in the changing application of the 1888 law and the consideration of new legislation designed to address Italy's "emigration question." As American officials tightened their control of the borders, Italian leaders, spurred in part by the experiences of migrants with the U.S. system, debated changes to emigration law.

The new focus on Article 17 enforcement emerged from the increased scrutiny of U.S. and Italian law by the MAE. Throughout the spring of 1895 the MAE circulated internal reports that tracked proposed amendments to U.S. law while Ministry publications circulated notices meant to accurately guide migrants through the gauntlet of American inspections.[58] The ambassador sought specific information from the immigration commissioner on the reasons his officers excluded migrants. He focused on the decisions of the Board of Special Inquiry, where unclear cases ended up. A few edits in Fava's handwriting scrawled on a dictated letter to Commissioner Stump highlight how Italians attempted to understand American enforcement as Italians became targets for detention and exclusion. A translator in the ambassador's office wrote the following in English:

> In order that the Arbitral Commission of Emigration, existing in Italy [to enforce Article 17], should be well acquainted with the reasons for which the Italian emigrants, arriving in the U.S. in contravention with the American laws, are sent back ["refused" was the original word] by the Special Board of Inquiry, I would be most obliged to you if you would, if there is no objection [original phrase: "there being nothing to prevent it"], forward to Prof. Oldrini a *typewritten* copy of the decisions taken by the Board of Inquiry on this matter.[59]

At this point the letter switches back to Italian. Where the translator wrote "non è sufficiente," Fava edited the line to read "è insufficiente," which changed the meaning from "is not sufficient" to "is inadequate." The sentence in the final letter read in English: "Until now the Commissioner of Immigration of the Harbour of New York kindly gave to Prof. Oldrini only notice of the said decisions; but this system is inadequate to enable him to send an exact report to the Arbitral Commissioner about the reasons of the repulse of the emigrants." The record shows the crucial role of Italian authorities at Ellis Island in the discovery and prosecution of Article 17 cases. Fava wanted to collect data the Italian government could use to enforce Article 17 but that could also illustrate, as never before possible, the specific rationale U.S. immigration agents used to reject Italians at Ellis Island.

The first major case presented itself in the late spring of 1895. A complaint against emigration subagents and business partners Antonio De Martini and B. Bertini from Chiavari, a small coastal town in the province of Genoa, caught Foreign Minister Blanc's attention. Accused of selling transatlantic tickets to eighteen migrants in no shape to pass inspection on the American authorities, Blanc contacted Fava who in turn brought Oldrini into the case after the excluded men incurred additional debts during their brief detention in New York. Blanc suspected a significant degree of underreporting of Article 17 violations, and this case looked like it could spur more effective enforcement. Baron Blanc initially led the recommendation for prosecution from Rome after reading, in his eyes, far too many press reports of migrant abuse that went unpunished. Blanc was a very high-level official to be involved in this case—it must have been important to him to enforce Article 17. (He otherwise does not appear much in the diplomatic correspondence dealing with day-to-day issues.)

While the 1888 law has received some attention from Italian scholars writing about migration, it deserves a closer look. Scholars writing in English tend to ignore or dismiss the law. One article described the legislation as "inadequate and incomplete."[60] Maddalena Marinari described the pre-1901 MAE as taking few protective actions on behalf of migrants abroad.[61] Yet the 1888 statute set the precedent of preemptive reaction to U.S. policy, which would be the foundation for "remote control" of U.S. borders from outside the nation.

Article 17 offers another way of looking at gatekeeping enforcement through the De Martini and Bertini case. Blanc reached out to Fava and Oldrini to determine the extent of the agents' malfeasance, shut down their activities in Italy through the local prefecture, and find their victims and allow them to collect damages. Blanc characterized De Martini's actions as unlawful but ultimately done without malice. He described how De Martini acted "with negligence, but in good faith" in selling steamship tickets to eighteen people who were denied legal entry into the United States.[62] This episode shows how, despite the efforts to disseminate accurate information about American policy, it was hard to predict the reaction of U.S. immigration authorities at the border. In an effort to avoid punishment, De Martini and Bertini may have tampered with the witnesses; each victim swore to a statement declaring the two men had sufficiently addressed the emigrants' material needs. The statement avoided a direct answer to the charge of selling tickets to men and women who could not pass inspection. It read, "We certify that from Mr. B. Bertini we found what we needed, both in maintenance and in assistance, for which we declare to have nothing to report, neither against him, nor against other people, including Mr. Antonio De Martini." The undersecretary of state noted this statement was "strange" and likely coerced.[63]

The muddled facts of the case and the need for cooperation with Ellis Island officials made prosecution of De Martini and Bertini harder. "This Ministry will wait for Your Excellency [Ambassador Fava] to make the truth of the facts clear," Blanc wrote, "with the means that it will consider most appropriate, so that the Authorities of the Kingdom will know exactly if any repayment is due from De Martini to the above-named emigrants, and in what amount. I would add that the aforementioned subagent was formally warned" to stop sending migrants who could not lawfully enter the United States. Within a month of the first notice, on June 1, Fava ordered the Office to block the operation of these agents. Undersecretary Adamoli demanded the ambassador immediately inform the MAE of any judgments by the Arbitration Commission against an emigration agent working in Italy. With his frustration palpable, he admonished Fava to send all news of judgments immediately and simultaneously to Rome and to U.S. officials at the Bureau of Immigration. Having read first in New York newspapers about judgments made in Italy against Italian emigration agents seemed an embarrassment.[64] Duly warned, Fava crafted his reply to Oldrini the same day he received the correspondence.

Two months after his first notice, the ambassador wrote Stump to request clarification of the exact reasons for rejection at the border. In his handwriting the letter reads, "When the said Commission will be perfectly acquainted with these reasons they will be better able to punish, according to the Italian Law, those agents who are the cause of the illegal departure of the emigrant from his country."[65] Over time, the gatekeeping strategy known as "remote control" would coalesce around these small attempts to enforce Italian emigration law, facilitated by the Office at Ellis Island at the intersection of Italian and U.S. law, what Oldrini had called "a State within a State."[66]

The application of Article 17 was one part of a larger effort by the Italian government to use the Office of Labor Information and Protection to correct problems migrants experienced at the border resulting from "ignorance" of American laws and to facilitate distribution beyond New York. A bulletin published by the MAE in April 1895 and intended for consuls in the United States offered a series of practical advice and informed the consuls about changes taking place within the Italian bureaucracy to better address conditions in the United States. The bulletin gave directions for consuls to advise migrants on how to purchase railroad tickets for destinations beyond New York City.[67] The island location of the immigration station had led to unforeseen problems, like if a passenger bought in Italy a ticket for domestic train travel in the United States. These tickets were often fraudulent, resulting in delays and added costs. The bulletin called such problems "troubles of a particular kind that bear damages on the emigrant, sometimes heavily."

The Italian government was also amending its procedures to facilitate migrants' entry into the United States. Moving forward, the Ministry of the Interior announced it would send official notice to all prefects, responsible for issuing passports and determining that a person was eligible to emigrate and had fulfilled his military service requirement, asking them to convey to emigrants that they should avoid purchasing train tickets before departing. It told passengers what to look for when buying a ticket for Ellis Island so they did not add unnecessary time and expense to their journey. Oldrini translated the bulletin and sent it to Commissioner Stump to inform him of the Italian government's directives for protecting immigrants.[68] Sharing this information helped Oldrini build a special rapport with officials at Ellis Island. The record of Article 17 enforcement can be read as evidence of Rome's evolving views on emigration regulation and the pressure the United States put on Italy to reconsider its policies.

Oldrini began to develop a single sheet that would condense the Ministry bulletin and guide emigrants through their landing on American soil.[69] His focus on practical advice reflects the frustration of Italian authorities at how unpredictably Americans enforced exclusion law. The information made several specific recommendations designed to address, or ideally to prevent, exclusion decisions. The Office would receive orders for railroad tickets paid for and ordered before departure. Oldrini warned, "Do not wait until the emigrant has arrived at Ellis Island and is already excluded due to lack of means or train tickets."[70] In a June 1895 report written while pursuing the De Martini and Bertini case, Oldrini identified some strategies to prevent unscrupulous agents from adding extra charges.[71] This would preserve their limited funds to aid in the inspection process and prevent unnecessary delays (and associated costs for lodging, food, and travel) after landing. Oldrini advised migrants to send any funds they wanted to carry into the United States to Western Union's Ellis Island office. This strategy, designed to avoid LPC exclusion, allowed migrants to show inspectors a receipt to collect their currency on the island as proof of support. If a migrant was detained for further questioning, Oldrini encouraged family members already in the United States to appear in person where they could give testimony before the Board of Special Inquiry if called to do so. Oldrini reminded aid agencies that emigrants could request a second or even a third examination to reassess a decision for exclusion. If these appeals failed to secure admission, the migrant could direct his or her case to the federal commissioner at Ellis Island.

Within a week's time Oldrini adapted his bulletin into a standardized form the Office could distribute to immigrants excluded from entry. He happily shared the news of his work with the ambassador, tucking the notice into one of his regular reports. Oldrini's *avviso* or "advisory" letter informed the emigrant of his right to claim a refund of cost and agent fees paid for his or her

*Ufficio di Informazione e Protezione per l'Emigrazione Italiana*

Autorizzato dal Governo Italiano e dal Dipartimento d'Immigrazione degli Stati Uniti.

ELLIS ISLAND, NEW YORK, STATI UNITI D'AMERICA.

New York, _____ 1895.

**EMIGRANTE RESPINTO.**

NOME ...............

GIUNTO COL VAPORE ......................... DAL PORTO DI ................. IL .................

RESPINTO   "   "   ..................   "   "   " NEW YORK ...................

CAUSA ......

.........

## A V V I S O.

A termini dell'Art. 17 della Legge Italiana d'Emigrazione (30 Dicembre 1888. No. 5866-Serie 3a) gli emigranti Italiani che verranno respinti in patria da Ellis Island, per decisione delle autorità Federali Americane di Immigrazione *potranno intentare un'azione in rifusione di danni e spese contro l'Agente di Emigrazione che vendette loro il Biglietto d'Imbarco per gli Stati Uniti.*

Il reclamo, su carta semplice, senza bollo, è esente da ogni tassa e dovrá essere presentato al *Prefetto della Provincia dove l'Emigrante stipulò il Contratto con l'Agente o Sub-Agente; non più tardi di un mese dall'arrivo al porto di destinazione.*

I danni sono riconosciuti e liquidati da una COMMISSIONE ARBITRALE di cui fanno parte:—*Il Prefetto,—Il Presidente del Tribunale,*

*Il Procuratore del Re presso il Tribunale,—Due Consiglieri Provinciali.*

La sentenza sará definitiva; nè contro di essa sará ammesso Appello o ricorso per Cassazione.

N. B.—In tesi generale, il Ricorso avrá effetto favorevole all'emigrante ogni qualvolta questi potrá provare di essere stato respinto da Ellis Island, New York, senza sua colpa o perché mal informato dall'Agente o Sub-Agente, quindi giudicato come appartenente ad una delle categorie escluse dalle leggi d'Immigrazione degli Stati Uniti.

IL CAPO AGENTE

*Chief Agent.*

FIGURE 3.1. Chief Agent Alessandro Oldrini, *Avviso: Emigrante Respinto*, 1895. Migrants rejected at Ellis Island by U.S. immigration officials and denied entry into the country could use this form to claim refund of their fare from emigration agents on their return to Italy, a protection offered by the Italian 1888 emigration law. The form contained instructions and collected information necessary to process a claim under Article 17 of the law. Legazione Sarda e delle rappresentanze diplomatiche Italiane negli U.S.A. (1848–1901), box 111, fasc. 2195, Archivio storico diplomatico dell'Ministero degli Affari Esteri, Rome, reprinted with permission.

attempted trip, and also served as material support to a claim the emigrant could pursue on return in front of an arbitration board in his prefecture.[72] "Damages are recognized and paid by an ARBITRATION COMMISSION," the letter advised, "whenever he can prove to have been rejected by Ellis Island, New York, without his fault or because he was misinformed by the agent or sub-agent, then judged as belonging to a set of categories excluded from United States immigration laws." Oldrini designed the *avviso* with blank spaces to fill in for each case. At the bottom of the form letter he included preprinted guidance that defined the Office's role. A section labeled "Advice for Immigrants" listed four priorities for the Office: helping immigrants with "1. Letters, train tickets and funds, 2. Remittances, 3. Admission to Ellis Island, 4. Exclusions and Appeals," highlighting the Office's mission to check U.S. exclusion law, which in 1895 included enforcing Article 17.[73]

The ambassador wanted to get more specific and actionable information to use to decipher the rules of American gatekeeping. Yet the answers never came: the transcripts of exclusion cases heard by the Board of Special Inquiry never made their way to Fava's desk in Washington, and the inspectors' rationales remained mysterious. Despite its potential, the period focused on Article 17 enforcement was intense but short lived. Sending information specific enough for legal proceedings across the ocean and from one department (Foreign Affairs) to another (Interior) where cases were prosecuted proved too difficult.

In a telegram to Fava, Oldrini acknowledged that the only way to truly know the details of a decision would be to request the specifics of the proceedings of the Board of Special Inquiry for each case where an Italian was rejected and repatriated.[74] Fava followed up with a letter to Stump on June 18, 1895, requesting the records. Fava sought, for Oldrini, "an exact report . . . about the reasons for the repulse of the emigrants" that the enforcement commission of the Interior Ministry could use to "punish, according to the Italian law, those agents who are the cause of the illegal departure of the emigrant from his country."[75] Oldrini was to provide the data from American border officials that would shape the exercise of Italian emigration law. Two days later, Superintendent McSweeney replied to Fava's request and said they could not send the files but Oldrini was welcome to make copies from the transcriptions located at the island.[76] As partners in gatekeeping the Italians had to follow the Americans' rules.

Unfortunately, records attesting to the U.S. government's response to Article 17 are scant. By 1910 the Dillingham Commission's investigation into European sending countries resulted in a brief but fascinating sentence embedded in the fourth volume of the forty-one-volume report. "It is well known that the Italian Government not only seeks to regulate emigration in the interest of the emigrant before embarkation and during the voyage at sea, but also that it undertakes to prevent Italians from going to countries or sections of countries where it is believed they will not prosper or receive adequate protection."[77] This is the only mention of Article 17 in the whole report, and it emphasizes the changes implemented in the 1901 emigration law that significantly expanded the scope of Italian oversight of emigration. The Dillingham Commission report indicates that U.S. officials later saw the Italian law as a potential aid to their gatekeeping efforts—as long as Italian authorities continued to cooperate with American desires.

The next major Article 17 case came more than a year later, but this time the prosecution was carried out with much less urgency. From Rome the Ministry of the Interior accused Connecticut banker Gennaro Agnone of violating Article 17 when he sent a letter to Italian bankers in the United States "in order to encourage illegal emigration from the Kingdom." Two months passed before the Interior contacted Fava about the case. While the letter carried the same urgent tone as the correspondence around the De Martini and Bertini case, the delay and scant supporting material in the archive indicate the difficulty of prosecution, likely because of the coordination required between the Interior and Foreign Ministries. Unlike the De Martini and Bertini case, where Italian officers directly observed the exclusion of eighteen people at Ellis Island, here was a more vague case where the government lacked the names of any of the purported victims. "As soon as the R.[oyal] Government can know the name of these [Agnone's] correspondents, it will not fail to take, in their regard, all the measures that the homeland laws allow," the undersecretary of the interior told Fava. The ambassador was encouraged to provide a copy of Agnone's circular to American authorities so that Agnone's "correspondents" could be identified and prosecuted under an unspecified U.S. statute described in the letter only as "acts to prevent speculation equally harmful to Italy and the United States." "I look forward to being, in due course, informed of the measures taken toward Agnone," the letter concluded.[78] There was no follow-up.

The lack of prosecutions in the De Martini/Bertini and Agnone cases can be explained by the social ties that bound migrants and ticket agents as neighbors in the same village. "The connection between the peasants and the subagents of the villages was so distinctive, however, that very few appeals were presented despite frequent and open violations of the law," historian Grazia Dore has explained.[79] She concluded the law had no real punitive effect. Enforcement depended on two unpredictable factors: the willingness of emigrants to bring their claims against their neighbors forward to prefects in the same village they had just tried unsuccessfully to leave, and the arrival of corroborating evidence from New York. Legal historian Dolores Freda has examined court records that show how few Article 17 cases were successful. Not many people appealed their exclusion once back in Italy under the 1888 law, and a handful of decisions actually went against the migrants, which must have discouraged more prosecutions.[80] Even though it focused on preventing the departure of emigrants, the 1888 emigration law gave the state a weak mechanism to rein in exploitative immigrant agents and labor recruiters, and by the 1890s this structural limitation was apparent.[81] With the inadequacy of the 1888 law now clear—its protective measures required extensive international cooperation—Rome would use this experience to craft a second, much more wide-ranging law in 1901 as some observers had long recommended. Italians' experiences with U.S. border controls would precipitate a larger reenvisioning of the system that governed emigration from the country.

## Conclusion

Despite their creative efforts to navigate restrictive immigration policy, Italians still struggled against a shifting and evolving gatekeeping machine.[82] By the end of the 1890s, reports emerged from the Office of Labor Information that inspectors were rejecting Italian migrants on the grounds that their promised work violated the Alien Contract Labor Law of 1885. In the early part of the decade an immigrant landing without enough money to pass inspection could provide evidence of an arrangement or solid promise of work, typically through family members or friends. This promise had usually been enough to gain entry. The structure of the Sunnyside contract meant that incoming colonists bypassed Ellis inspections and these kinds of legal challenges. The immigrant would instead be taken directly to the plantation with the approval of both governments. Rossi emphasized that Italians required "protection most especially of the rights of our emigrants during the various procedures and formalities they must undergo as soon as they disembark on Ellis Island in order to gain their admission to the territory."[83] No one with a destination of Sunnyside would have to navigate the entry process on his or her own.

The "protection" that Rossi and his government sought extended well beyond the port of entry. Sunnyside Plantation was intended to serve as a model colony, and moving Italians to the South required extensive cooperation between governmental and private interests in a sort of anticipatory remote control. In the pages of the southern business weekly *Manufacturer's Record*, influential landowner Charles Scott of Mississippi used language that echoed the attitude of the Italian government. He advised "the success of the experiment depends primarily, in my opinion, on the sort of treatment received by the

Italians at the hands of the Southern planter."[84] Another frequent contributor to *Manufacturer's Record*, Lee J. Langley, wrote, "If the impression goes out that the Italians are not fully protected and fairly treated in Mississippi, Louisiana and other Southern states, the tide of immigration will be turned away from our shores."[85]

Anticipatory remote control was taking shape by the late 1890s. The history of Sunnyside's Italian colony is intertwined with the history of the Office of Labor Information and Protection for Italians and the attempts to enforce Article 17 of the 1888 Italian Emigration Law. A direct connection between Ellis Island and Arkansas emerged out of strategic responses to the growing system of qualitative immigration restriction. Before the U.S. gatekeeping strategy shifted from "qualitative" to "quantitative" restriction, the arrival of Italian families to the Arkansas delta was driven by the goal of the Italian government, particularly its U.S. diplomatic mission, to understand the shape of American gatekeeping policy in the late nineteenth century. By 1899 the Italian government expressed a "desire to cooperate most heartily in preventing the departure for the United States of all persons inimical to its interests."[86]

# CHAPTER 4

# Colonization, the Literacy Test, and the Evolution of Gatekeeping

Beginning in the spring of 1895, Egisto Rossi, the second chief agent of the Office of Labor Information and Protection for Italians, noticed a problem. Over that spring and into the summer, as ships regularly departed Naples for New York with "thousands of emigrants of the lowest species" aboard, U.S. immigration authorities had increased their capacity for screening and detention in response to these new, unwanted arrivals.[1] As many as 50 percent of the passengers aboard the ships, which were commonly called "tramp steamers," Rossi noted, had been denied entry by officers at Ellis Island over these months. For more than a year the American and Italian American press had predicted trouble to come at the station when the volume of migrants increased the following spring and summer.[2] But, as Rossi reported to his government, the Office had prevented major unrest on the island through its relationship with bureau officials.

Looking back over the year in his comprehensive annual report of the Office for the Ministry of Foreign Affairs, Rossi described how "in those days of exceptional invasion" Americans scrambled to increase both the capacity at Ellis Island for more screening and the space to detain those who did not pass. Over three months in the spring of 1896 Rossi saw "an extraordinary influx in a short time," which was a "cause of intense concern" to the immigration commissioners.[3] American agents immediately applied a "more rigorous tests of our emigrants" designed to exclude more people at the gates under the "likely to become a public charge" or LPC clause. The cheap cost of a one-way ticket, he explained, encouraged migrants to depart on a whim, arriving with little but the proverbial clothes on their backs. Rossi lamented how these passengers lacked a clear plan or destination. They invoked the suspicion of immigration inspectors as these passengers who landed with only "a few rags to cover themselves" could not provide friends' or relatives' addresses to vouch for their plans for settlement and work in the United States.[4]

Italians in the mid-1890s encountered the expansion of early immigration enforcement against the poorest migrants. At the same time, Italian migrants became the object of intense scrutiny by the Immigration Restriction League as evidence of the need for a more restrictive policy approach to gatekeeping. Meanwhile, the government in Rome continued a long and difficult debate over how to respond to rejections at the border by American authorities.[5] The project to settle Italian migrants on southern lands presented a solution to problems like the kind Rossi observed at Ellis Island. Yet the kinds of migrants that southerners desired were certainly not the passengers of the so-called tramp steamers.[6]

Evolving federal immigration policy influenced how recruited "colonies" of Italian migrants fulfilled regional labor needs in the American South parallel to the evolution of gatekeeping law. Italian reactions to practices at the border shaped the MAE's support for the redistribution of migrants onto southern land in a program that supporters called colonization. The project of southern colonization had its origins in the post–Civil War period, but the brief period from the winter of 1896 through the fall of 1897 provides a clear view of the dynamics that counterposed the program's possibilities against its limitations. Because colonization required the cooperation of U.S. and Italian authorities, it would also influence the practice of border controls in both nations over time and continue to refine the asymmetric partnership.

In his report following an October 1896 special mission to Rome at the invitation of the "friendly government" of Prime Minister Marquis di Rudinì, the commissioner-general of immigration, Herman Stump, described how di Rudinì sought the Americans' advice on "the proper interpretation of certain provisions of our immigration laws." Stump made the rounds among the highest officers in the Italian government during his week in the capital. On a late October afternoon he met with the minister of foreign affairs and then with di Rudinì three hours later. "After a conference with these gentlemen, in which the immigration laws of our country were fully discussed, and the reasons given for the deportation of Italians, the ministry expressed its earnest desire that persons who would not be permitted to land in the United States should be restrained from embarkation," Stump reported, "and that such regulations as the ministry had the authority to enforce should at once be promulgated, with a view to preventing further undesirable immigration, and at the same time save the persons who intend to migrate a fruitless voyage."[7] Following on several months of internal governmental correspondence emphasizing the need for more guidance from the Americans, immediately following Stump's trip, the prime minister issued a proclamation, dated November 8, 1896, clarifying the conditions under which prefects should issue the *certificato penale* document required by U.S. agents as proof that a migrant was not in violation of the conditions outlawed in the 1885, 1891, and 1893 statute—in other words, that they were not a contract laborer or too sick, too poor, too criminal, or, by the late 1890s, too illiterate to pass inspection at the border.[8]

Colonization in the American South links back to the early history of gatekeeping through the literacy test, introduced in Congress in 1897 and championed by the country's first restrictionist lobby, the Immigration Restriction League (or IRL), founded in Boston in 1894.[9] The national campaign for a literacy test organized by the IRL complicated the Italian government's efforts to facilitate unrestricted migration as the Office for Labor Information and Protection struggled to maintain its privileged status within the Americans' expanding immigration control regime. Italian officials saw their support for colonization as a strategic step, in the words of vice-consul at New York Gustavo Tosti, "to transform our immigrants into . . . farmers and small landowners," not "farm workers."[10]

This chapter continues the history of Sunnyside Plantation by placing it in the larger context of regional efforts to recruit foreign labor after the Civil War. It moves from Italians' hopes for the plantation, the subject of the previous chapter, to an examination of white southerners' desires for an imported labor force. At regional meetings in the 1880s and 1890s, white landowners described their resistance to working with free Black workers after emancipation, defined their "labor problem," and explained why Italian labor was superior. Regional interest in colonization spurred the formation of public and private organizations dedicated to recruiting foreign labor directly from Italy. The permanency of colonization sets it apart from other temporary labor recruitment programs in the Americas that exploited migrants' in-between legal status and differed from Brazil, a major point of comparison, where state-sponsored recruiters, subsidies, and infrastructure brought Italian families to farm coffee in the same period.[11]

This chapter offers the first comprehensive examination of Italian colonization in the American South, a region critical to Italian–U.S. relations at the turn of the twentieth century. It organizes the scattershot history of European immigrant colonization in the region beginning in 1865, before returning to Sunnyside Plantation, Arkansas, in 1896 when the second wave of four hundred recruited colonists arrived and Italian diplomats responded to ongoing problems between migrant farmers and plantation management.[12]

This chapter expands our understanding of Gilded Age exploitation of migrant workers who lacked legal status by exploring the effort to settle Italian families permanently on cotton land in the Arkansas delta as a lesser-known "circuit" that allowed Italians to traverse gatekeeping law.[13] Supporters of Italian colonization in the United States promoted it as a solution to the South's "labor problem" and described it in language intended to avert legal restrictions then in place, primarily the Alien Contract Labor Law, at the same time as the law's gatekeeping efficacy was being challenged.[14] The intersections of state power revealed in the history of colonization show how federal immigration policy was still very much in flux in the mid-1890s and why the South matters in the history of national policy.

Going back in time to examine a longer history of colonization places Sunnyside in its larger context. Beginning in the winter of 1895, thirty years after southerners issued the first solicitations for foreign settlers, officers of the royal Italian government had cooperated with a group of landowners to transplant villagers from central Italy to Chicot County, Arkansas. This endeavor sought to replace the traditional farm labor pool—that is, landless Blacks and whites—with a stable and still tractable labor force. The reformers who implemented the plan offered a labor contract that persuaded whole families to migrate from Italy together and settle permanently on a piece of land transferable to them through a twenty-one-year mortgage. The employment contract established the characteristics of a distinctive approach to land and labor management in the South, and it was essential to the kind of facilitated entry that Egisto Rossi attempted to use in order to manage migration into Ellis Island.[15]

The Alien Contract Labor Law was the gauntlet through which any Sunnyside Plantation–bound Italian had to pass. As the original and the largest settlement, Sunnyside received a lot of attention from the MAE and in the press. Recruiters believed the contract terms allowed migrants to claim exemption to the Alien Contract Labor Law, a belief that boosters emphasized to the press as a reason that imported Italian families were superior to native-born labor. But the U.S. government questioned this interpretation. In late November 1895 Alessandro Oldrini had traveled from Ellis Island to Louisiana to await the second major wave of settlers set to arrive on a special journey of the *Chateau Yquem*, an Anchor Line steamer that crossed several times a year between Italy and New York but had made a special detour to carry the Sunnyside-bound families directly to New Orleans. "When asked if he thought there was any possibility of trouble regarding the landing of the immigrants," the *World* newspaper reported, "the professor said: 'I do not anticipate the slightest trouble in landing them. Every member of the party paid his or her own fare, and each family has a contract with the Sunnyside Company for twelve and a half acres of land.'"[16] Oldrini resisted the reporter's assumption that it was strange for the ship to bring its 562 passengers to New Orleans. He told the New York–based *World* newspaper "that it was not strange at all" and cited the cheaper cost to deliver the families by steamboat than cross-country rail. Oldrini had taken the railroad down from New York to smooth the border inspection in front of a suspicious Bureau of Immigration. "A special agent is here from Washington to examine the immigrants on their arrival," reported the *World*, "for it is the opinion that the Contract-Labor law has been violated." Likely due to Oldrini's intervention, the *Chateau Yquem* passengers overcame the suspicion of illegality and were ultimately permitted to land.[17]

As the contract necessitated the coordination of Italian and U.S. officials at the border, Oldrini felt confident that his work to smooth the admissions process at Ellis Island would help him do the same at New Orleans, and that the contract would demonstrate without a doubt that each family had sufficient means to enter the country. Over the 1890s New Orleans developed a reputation as an easier point of entry for Italians, where inspectors applied restrictive laws less stringently. By the first decade of the twentieth century, some steamship companies plying the route between the two countries had developed a regular schedule to and from Louisiana.[18] Consummately, the increasing focus on New Orleans, Louisiana, and Arkansas as a site for Italian settlement showed how the asymmetric partnership between the nations continued to focus on the South.

## The History of Italian Colonization in the American South

The project that would eventually bring more than five thousand Italians to the U.S. South by 1920 began as a campaign to recruit European immigrants immediately after the Confederate Army surrendered at Appomattox in 1865.[19] At a time when wage-paying jobs in the country's rapidly growing industries lured millions of immigrants to the United States, early attempts after the Civil War to entice peasant farmers to the South resulted in few successes. By the late 1860s the region's largely agricultural economy settled into a system that apportioned workers along race and class lines carried over from the antebellum period. Formerly enslaved Black men and women formed a vast underclass that worked the land alongside landless poor whites who also toiled as tenants and sharecroppers. Ownership of the most valuable land remained in the hands of a white elite.[20] Over time, however, this postwar system of nominally free labor exhibited major flaws. Landowners became frustrated that they could no longer control their mostly Black labor force as the dominant crop—cotton—lost value on the world market.[21]

The English and Scandinavian migrants that white southerners initially desired never came in large numbers, and by the turn of the century, Italians seemed willing to work in ways that these landowners preferred. "They are capable of improvement in many ways, which is not the case with the negro," Georgia planter Lee Langley emphasized in the pages of the *Manufacturers' Record*, a Baltimore-based weekly business magazine with enterprising subscribers across the South. "They are not hard to teach, as a rule. They want to make money, which is their sole object, and they try to follow instructions, and it is inevitable that if they make any, the landlord will, too," observed Langley in 1904.[22]

White southerners organized themselves into associations to recruit new sources of labor from outside the region. Large regional organizations made up of private citizens propelled public discussion of colonization in the 1880s and early 1890s. Groups organized for public benefit while others worked on behalf of private investors. State boards of immigration worked to promote their respective jurisdictions. Southern railroads recruited Italians to buy the land along their roads. (Railroads calculated a future profit from settlers' farms, figuring these families would use their line to transport goods to market and grow paying traffic.) Some industries, sugar and turpentine in particular, sought single male foreign workers from Eastern Europe, Central America, and the Caribbean whose status made them particularly ripe for exploitation.[23] But because of the large role the diplomatic service played, individual landowners connected to Ambassador Fava or Alessandro Oldrini at the Office accomplished much more than the regional meetings whose activities the diplomatic service tracked. The records that tell the story of Italian colonization are overwhelmingly the product of fastidious officials employed by Italy's diplomatic corps who kept close watch on developments in the region. The shift in focus to Italians as a desirable permanent labor force for farming would complicate the growing push for immigration restriction in the United States.

In the decades following the demise of slavery, state governments and loosely organized groups of landowners initially turned to European immigrants then flooding U.S. shores in their search for an alternative to an African American labor force. European labor recruitment took many forms. In 1865 a venture calling itself the Southern Land, Emigration and Product Company of New York published a catalog, the first example of the South being marketed directly to immigrants as a desirable destination for settlement. Newspapers began to use their editorials and advertising space to promote companies like the Southern Land Company.[24]

While public calls for cultivators for idle lands appeared in the *New Orleans Times-Democrat* as early as 1865, requests for settlers put forth in the late 1860s and 1870s met with ambivalence within the South.[25] Soon a narrative emerged that the region was hostile to foreigners. Historian and key architect of the Lost Cause, Walter Lynwood Fleming, explained why in *Political Science Quarterly* in 1905. "Southern people desired no immigration either from the North or from foreign countries" due to their "general dislike of outsiders" and the "bitter feelings" remaining from the Civil War.[26] By the early twentieth century his analysis helped advance the view that the region was hostile to immigrant labor despite several decades of focused efforts to recruit foreign workers.[27]

The history of colonization challenges the narrative of immigration restriction and desirability. From the 1860s through the mid-1920s, a small but vocal group of men proclaimed the benefits of resettling European immigrant families to whomever would listen.[28] The colonization movement positioned itself apart from employers who preferred single men and in doing so won the support of immigration restrictionists, including the cofounder of the Immigration Restriction League, Robert DeCourcy Ward.[29] Ward managed the contradiction between his views and his group's calls for immigration restriction by describing recruited migrants as productive new settlers distinctive from the masses of abject poor arriving on the "tramp steamers."[30] He declared in the *Atlantic Monthly* in 1905, "What the South most wants to-day is not the newly arrived, ignorant, and penniless alien, but the settler with means of purchase." Ward described the caliber of immigrant welcomed in the South: "the immigrant with money, coming from Northern Europe, skilled in intensive and diversified farming," he emphasized, "and who can depend on his own exertions, manage his own business, market his own products, and save money."[31]

The work of Boston's Immigration Restriction League largely reinforced the ugliest stereotypes of Italians in an era when "criminality and violence were the supposed dysfunctional traits of Italian immigrants."[32] The IRL cultivated a reputation steeped in New England's academic culture that it used to its advantage as it campaigned for a literacy test to restrict undesirable European immigrants. Yet the IRL differentiated between generalized immigration and what one supporter of colonization had called "good settlers of the right stock" in 1883.[33] Ward's description of a process for land redistribution conveyed his vision: "As the large plantations are cut up into small farms, thrifty tenants, not ignorant and pauper laborers, are needed." Ward echoed and amplified views Ambassador Fava had also expressed since forming the Office of Labor Information and Protection in 1894. These two men saw colonization in similar ways. According to Ward, "the Italian seems to be well fitted to do much of the work which needs doing in the South, and in many parts of the southern country where Italians have settled they are praised as industrious, thrifty, frugal, good citizens, and as having increased land values."[34]

Proponents of colonization framed Italians differently from other groups in language that elevated Italians in contrast to Black workers. Langley's 1904 *Manufacturer's Record* article described working with Italian tenants. Langley emphasized, "Thus far I have found them good neighbors and good tenants. They are frugal and industrious, and when working as tenants they are always willing to do their part. I find it a great improvement and cheaper than the negro labor of today that wants a dollar per day for a half-dollar's work."[35] The solution to what Mississippi planter Charles Scott called the "scarcity and inefficiency of negro labor," he argued, lay in plans to increase the quality of available white labor with Italians.[36] Langley argued in the pages of the *Manufacturer's Record*, "The majority of farmers have done away with negro labor. Why?" Langley asked. "Because they are a shiftless, worthless sort, whereas the Italian laborer is a success. His sole object is to make money, and he knows it must come out of the ground: therefore he is always at work when his work is needed."[37] Robert DeCourcy Ward accepted Italians as thrifty colonists for the South even if he and the IRL rejected those who arrived at Ellis Island as illiterate paupers. Ten years before he published his article in *Atlantic Monthly*, Ward made Italians the subject of the IRL's first major study of inspection procedures at the island, which provided, in their pamphlets, direct evidence of the need for a literacy test.[38]

The Italian government recognized that colonization could tell a better story about Italian migrants in the United States. From the initial opening of the Office of Labor Information and Protection in the spring of 1894 through 1896, its key function was to serve as a clearinghouse for what Fava described as any viable plan.[39] One of Oldrini's first official duties was to send a formal letter informing "Governors and Mayors, State Boards of Immigration, Agricolture [*sic*] and Trade: Transportation Lines; Corporations and Individuals throughout the Union" that his Office was equipped to handle any offers of "inducements . . . with preference to Western and Southern states, the climate of which is temperate, and where immigration is more wanted."[40] Oldrini told all interested persons and organizations to "directly communicate with this Bureau, furnishing at their earliest convenience" detailed information for any proposed settlement. Oldrini signaled his government's willingness to help put Italians onto farms. He specified that those interested in "lead[ing] willing Italian immigrants to enter into reliable and durable agreements" should provide comprehensive information to his Office.[41] In an 1897 interview with the *Atlanta Constitution* he listed the desirable characteristics Italians had as small farmers: "Let it be permitted at this stage to state a well known fact, viz: that Italy furnishes a contingent of emigrants about 90% of whom are good land tillers and laborers. Also that, as a rule, they always prove to be a sober, orderly and a thrifty working class of men."[42]

In the late nineteenth century a small number of state boards worked to actively facilitate new colonies. The state boards offer another view of the mechanisms of immigration control during the transition from state to federal management of U.S. borders. An examination of their function and the challenges they faced illustrates that transition. In Virginia and South Carolina publicly funded boards of immigration initially operated in the United States and Europe as clearinghouses for the kind of information Oldrini later requested, mainly notices of available lands. Virginia was the first state to officially promote colonization within its borders by passing legislative support for private organizations in 1866.[43] State funds went toward a State Bureau of Immigration; however, funding for this organization depended over the next few decades on the shifting interests of the legislature. Virginia established a pattern of using recruiters later adopted by South Carolina. A *New York Times* article from August 15, 1867, "Immigration to Virginia—Agents to Visit Europe," reported that the organization, anticipating an unreliable stream of state funds, expected to raise its operating budget of $10,000 through private subscriptions.

The state of South Carolina followed a similar pattern. In 1867 the Commission of Immigration operated with public funding.[44] By 1878 this office had disappeared, replaced by the legislature with a charter to the South Carolina Immigration Association. In the early 1880s this organization was subsumed by the Bureau of Immigration, when it became part of the Department of Agriculture. The joint Department of Agriculture and Board of Immigration issued monthly reports for the years 1882–86, sometime after which it dropped "board of immigration" from its title. A similar bureaucratic arm, the S.C. Department of Agriculture, Commerce and Immigration, reemerged around 1904. It actively sought settlers with annual *Yearbook* publications, sent at least one person on a recruiting trip to Europe in 1904, and may have stationed an agent in London.[45] From 1905 until 1907 an industrious man named E. J. Watson led this organization, and it appeared to dissolve temporarily after he left the helm. By 1909 the state legislature restructured the department, this time dropping the "immigration" title in favor of "Agriculture, Commerce and Industries." That department functioned until the early 1920s.[46] State legislatures changed the funding for these boards and altered their duties every few years, limiting their impact.

Private organizations also tried to recruit migrants. The James River Valley Immigration Society of Virginia (JRVIS) illustrates how such privately funded recruitment functioned. Like the state boards, private organizations saw their task as the explicit promotion of available lands and opportunity in a defined territory.[47] The members of JRVIS raised money through the sale of stock, which they then used to advertise land available for purchase to immigrants.[48] The organization would act as a land broker, arranging sales between private owners and immigrants seeking to farm in central and southeastern Virginia. JRVIS, incorporated on August 8, 1888, and operating for two years, divided its territory into twenty separate districts. The organization tried to secure lands to offer for sale through a complex structure of local agents. But less than a year after drafting their charter, JRVIS officers became concerned about the future of the organization given "the difficulties now surrounding us."[49] A few days earlier, in February 1889, seventh vice president (out of eight) Alex Bondurant had written to Henrico County officer W. E. Grant (one of four). Bondurant wrote, "The great trouble I encounter with our land owners is, they fear sales will not be made—and for that many seem unwilling to make the experiment of placing their lands in the hands of any land company." Bondurant recommended that JRVIS convince hesitant landowners by settling a handful of immigrant families in the area who could create a model settlement. "If I can get the society to send some bona-fide purchasers and can make a few sales, I feel sure our landowners will then have full confidence in the enterprise."[50]

While JRVIS faltered in southeastern Virginia, facilitated migration to Brazil in the same period, from the 1870s to the turn of the twentieth century, provides a useful model for comparison. State cooperation was always an essential part of São Paulo's immigrant recruitment strategy for coffee plantations during the transition to free labor. In the decade before emancipation the regional legislature in São Paulo passed laws in 1871 and 1872 that offered money "to aid planters who might wish to obtain immigrant workers."[51] Unlike in the United States, the provincial government played a major role from working cooperatively with private landowners to building infrastructure like landing stations to facilitate the arrival of these workers. Indeed, the coffee growers believed their government had a duty to spend public money to secure a new labor force during the transition from slavery, and that is exactly what happened.[52]

Beginning in the 1870s two brothers and large coffee planters, Antonio and Martinho Prado Jr., assumed leadership in the effort to bring European workers directly to the São Paulo region. Martinho Prado took on the role of president of a new society established in July 1886, the Sociedade Promotora da Imigração. As in the Delta, the leaders came from prominent landowning families, but in São Paulo the society cooperated with a government immigration office to create a quasi-governmental agency. The society created promotional materials in Portuguese, German, and Italian that offered significant incentives for families to migrate to farm. These incentives included free room and board for as many as eight days, transportation to the rural districts where plantations were located, and free medical care, all paid for with public funds. With a recruitment office in Genoa, a system to process and pay for travel subsidies, and pamphlets calling for families to farm, this highly coordinated effort successfully recruited 124,000 Italians in 1887 and 1888, the latter being the year of emancipation.

After 1891, following the adoption of a new Brazilian constitution, the provincial government in São Paulo fully assumed the role of immigration promotion and recruitment. State subsidies continued to be a critical factor shaping family migration, making affordable or even free the cost of an entire family's passage to the São Paulo province over the next ten years.[53] Italy was the most common sending country to São Paulo before 1900, supplying 73 percent of all migrants to the region. But this predominance faded after 1903, in part due to changes in Italian migration policy that limited migrants' access to free or reduced passage.

The history of recruited migration in the São Paulo coffee industry emphasizes the importance of the travel subsidy to Italian family migrations in the late nineteenth century, and to the ability of the Italian government to directly shape emigration flows to Brazil. The volume of migration showed great sensitivity to two separate measures enacted by the Italian government. The first, a ban on Sociedade Promotora–sponsored labor recruiting and offers of free passage instituted by the first Crispi administration in response to consular reports of poor conditions at landing stations, was in place from March 1889 to July 1891; the second, the "Prinetti decree," adopted in 1903 and named for the minister of foreign affairs, banned offers of travel subsidies but allowed migrants to travel who could pay their own passage. The Prinetti decree effectively ended the era of family migration by cutting off access to Brazilian subsidies that Italian families clearly needed.[54]

In contrast to Brazil's state-sponsored recruitment program, the work of private citizens who organized immigration associations in the U.S. South in the mid-1880s had far less authority and limited access to public funds, and it never offered to pay an immigrant's passage. Instead of facilitating people on the move, these regional U.S. organizations tried to influence the discourse around immigrant desirability. They have never been viewed in this way or even taken very seriously by historians. While their work is largely forgotten today, the strategies they used provide insight into later efforts to control who could enter the country and where they settled. The Southern Immigration Association and the Southern Interstate Immigration Bureau organized independent conventions in Nashville in 1884 and Montgomery in 1888 to discuss plans to colonize Europeans on southern soil. Over the course of the next several years, three other meetings took place, in Augusta, Georgia; Asheville, North Carolina; and Baltimore, Maryland. The delegates who met at Nashville and Montgomery left behind a detailed record of their conversations, debates, and resolutions. The *Proceedings of the Southern Immigration Association* and the *Proceedings of the Southern Interstate Immigration Convention* provide an understanding of this phase of the movement in the South.[55]

At both conventions delegates directly tied regional improvement to immigrant recruitment, a goal reflected in the organizations' names. President of the Southern Interstate Immigration Bureau, F. B. Chilton, described the larger impact immigrants would have in the region. Chilton wrote in an open letter to southern newspapers, "This is no local movement but one . . . through which the resources of the South will be heralded to the world, and its influence felt throughout civilization."[56] Andrew Jackson McWhirter, president of the Southern Immigration Association, described in grandiose terms how immigration would "be the great revolutionary power in the political economy of the South." A colleague from Little Rock foretold of a time when "the resources of our dear Southland" would be harnessed "by the bringing in of capital, muscle, and intelligent, enlightened, skilled labor" and transformed into "sources of light, and strength, and power, and wealth."[57] The southern immigration conventions described migrants whose labor in the region would "make her waste places blossom as a rose."[58] These predictions, largely unrealized, show how eagerly some white southern men looked outside of the region after the Civil War to rebuild the economy, showing greater interest in imported labor than investing in emancipated Black workers.

For almost three decades southerners interested in agricultural colonization promoted an appealing picture of immigrant Italian labor for the region. In December 1888 the men gathered in Montgomery opened their meeting with a resolution calling for small, immigrant-owned farms that could "add to the intrinsic value of [southern] lands and other property by cultivating and improving them."[59] By the early twentieth century Mississippians Leroy Percy and Charles Scott deftly used the media to downplay Italians' cultural and religious differences from the native-born population. Characteristics such as the migrants' Catholicism, language, and culture could be easily overlooked in favor of their strong work ethic, large families, commitment to their work, and use of family labor. The *Manufacturer's Record* ran a number of stories that encouraged such thinking. Georgia planter Lee Langley offered a positive comparison of national stereotypes. "The German is steady and frugal, the Frenchman impulsive and active, the Irishman everything that goes to human credit, the Scotchman stocky and solid, yet honest and conservative." Langley then turned to the subject of the Italian: "But from a land-tilling standpoint, from the point of desire of the love of a home and a willingness to make it by the sweat of the brow, I can see no reason why the Italian now in the South does not compare favorably with any one of them," he concluded.[60]

Langley and others painted Italians as industrious and motivated to contrast with the "shiftless" Black worker. As South Carolina's commissioner of immigration, E. B. Watson, wrote in the industry journal *Railway World* in

1904, "In the launching of this all-important movement, we are not laboring to drive out the negro, but are trying by the introduction of foreign people, who will become good citizens, to build up our waste places and benefit the common country."[61] The Southern Land Advertising Agency and Real Estate Exchange, based in Batesburg, South Carolina, distributed informational pamphlets to landowners interested in engaging with "the Great Immigration Movement, [which] Is looking to the development of the South: inducing immigration hither . . . [for] *an addition of the best people* to our white population."[62] Advocates for immigrant colonization offered a positive role for Italian migrants in the region as racist attitudes toward Blacks made them want Italians instead.

These effusively stated desires did little to affect the flow of migration that continued to move around the country according to established networks. The men who promoted the sale of lands in the South to industrious European immigrants could not understand why foreigners would reject the South to settle in the Western states. Some delegates blamed poor advertising and commonly held stereotypes about the region. McWhirter decried railroad agents' attempts to line their and their companies' pockets at the expense of the southern states. He described exaggerated promotional maps designed to trick migrants into thinking the Dakotas were akin to "Eden and Eldorado." McWhirter complained that on these maps "the cold and ice-bound regions of the Northwest, Dakota for example . . . is portrayed in roseate hues," confusing land seekers "with deeper red lines of the ethereal railways they represent, permeating their Eden and Eldorado."[63] In 1884 Charles Hooker, who represented Mississippi at both the Montgomery and Nashville meetings, pushed the Nashville convention to address critical concerns about publicity and public opinion head on when he declared, "We have two problems—how to utilize and make valuable the broad acres we have, and how we shall increase the population and increase the resources of agriculture, to make cheap and accessible the lands of the country?"[64]

The conventions criticized the success of railroad-sponsored bureaus, which were much more successful at selling farmland to immigrants, accusing their labor agents of using unscrupulous recruitment practices. Both the Southern Immigration Association and the Southern Interstate Immigration Bureau expressed disgust for the methods of the railroad companies, who actively discouraged immigrants from going to the South. As McWhirter complained in his opening address at his association's first meeting: "Immigrants are imposed upon by corrupt agents representing the railway and other real estate corporations of the great and unfathomable Northwest. . . . These agents often display maps of the United States, with the entire list of Southern States marked in Ethiopian darkness, with here and there a skull and cross-bones labeled *Yellow Fever District—Famine and Pestilence*."[65] Supporters of immigrant colonization in the South competed against other regions in a losing battle to recruit whom they saw as the right kind of immigrant.

In the absence of a competent state power to recruit and distribute immigrants, the expanding railroads stepped in.[66] Despite the distaste the southern immigration conventions had for their practices, in the late 1880s and early 1890s railroads were the only organizations with economic resources and administrative reach to recruit effectively, and their actions influenced the developing gatekeeping regime. Railroad companies published advertisements domestically and abroad and sent labor agents to Europe to recruit immigrant families. This laid the groundwork for shipping companies to facilitate the transatlantic movement of people. By the 1910s steamship companies became preferred by the U.S. government as highly effective enforcers that "made private [shipping] companies partners in the execution of U.S. immigration policies in the early 20th century." This system began with U.S. health service inspectors (who applied their own racist ideas of bodies and healthfulness to their work) and consular officers who were unpredictable in their application of exclusionary law.[67] Tracing back several decades through the efforts of the southern immigration societies shows how corporations and private citizens wanted to act as gatekeepers through their recruitment efforts. But they lacked an apparatus powerful enough to enact their vision for who they wanted to immigrate. While the nascent immigration bureaucracy translated congressional statute and federal case law into practice, independent, corporate, and state-level actors continued to engage in the work of gatekeeping by trying to shape the discourse around Italians and their desirability as migrants to the United States.

### The Asymmetric Partnership at Sunnyside Plantation

By engaging in arguments about the desirability of specific immigrant groups, colonization's supporters tried to influence migration patterns to advance distinctly regional goals. At the same time, while the leaders of the Italian delegation in Washington and at Ellis Island continued to emphasize the potential of Sunnyside, the asymmetric partnership shaped the trajectory of Sunnyside Plantation. Hopeful but hesitant to agree to send more settlers, over several months in the spring of 1896 officers of the MAE addressed complaints about contaminated drinking water. Then founder Austin Corbin died suddenly in a carriage accident in June 1896, throwing the plantation into a management crisis. Corbin's death became a moment to reaffirm the goals of the entire colonization experiment and its connection to the Office of Labor Information and Protection at Ellis Island. Securing land for citizen-colonists remained the central focus with a proposal by Prince Ruspoli in June 1896 to bring a hundred more families to Sunnyside. Ambassador Fava later wrote a report about Ruspoli's plan that drew a straight line through gatekeeping law to the plantation's purpose and future success. "As to the proposal by Ruspoli," Fava reminded the minister of foreign affairs, "the point of view shared by Our Excellency is of seeing to above all that it will not only be accepted permanently but that they will have obtained for them the necessary declaration from the Department of the Treasury that the new families will be admitted all equally as 'Land Owners,' if the Corbin heirs intend to translate into serious action and with honesty the vast plans of the late Mr. Corbin around the ultimate development that he had set himself to do to this agricultural colony."[68]

On June 12, 1896, the Ministry's undersecretary of state reminded Fava that the colony's success depended on securing a satisfactory source of drinking water.[69] Fava followed up with a personal meeting with Sunnyside Company president George Edgell, Corbin's son-in-law and heir apparent. His report established an important evidentiary trail the Ministry used to shape its relations with the company going forward. While the Ministry clearly expected that the colonists would receive the same or better treatment as they had under Corbin himself, and that the company would provide access to clean drinking water on the plantation, Fava waited for the results of a second visit by Ruspoli to Sunnyside to approve the recruitment of additional families later that winter.[70] From his post at Ellis Island, Oldrini wrote to Fava reaffirming his vision for colonization as a transformative force: "I believe firmly that we have in hand the method to open splendidly the countryside to the emigration of the Italian farming population for whom we have been working so hard," he wrote in August 1896. "[This] plan and what it will bring practically, [is] absolutely the best outcome to the emigrants."[71] In a decision that pointed to the growing disconnect between the vision for Sunnyside and the reality on the ground, that fall Fava approved the recruitment of seventy-two more families who arrived from Genoa on January 5, 1897, but only after Ruspoli visited the plantation and offered his approval.

The "circuits" that brought Italian migrants to Arkansas also gave them a voice to amplify their complaints and try to negotiate with the Corbin Company.[72] What had initially manifested as complaints over access to clean drinking water in the summer of 1896 expanded into broader complaints about treatment workers received at the hands of plantation management. Some of the newest arrivals to Sunnyside had quickly become disillusioned with the conditions they found there, and by the end of the year a few organized committees had sent letters to Fava in Washington and to the consul at New Orleans. Giovanni Delpidio wrote on behalf of a group of families who offered specific examples of how conditions on the plantation failed to live up to what they had been promised. The charges for passage to Arkansas and for housing, farm equipment, and furnishings far exceeded what the families believed they could earn. The Corbin Company had promised side work paid in cash wages, which had not materialized. Egisto Polmonari, along with fellow resident Giovanni Vivarelli, sent an itemized list of problems to the consul at New Orleans, G. M. Magenta, on November 22, 1897. "We put our trust in the highest goodness of you, our honored representative, because we want you to intercede and obtain for us from the Sunnyside company the repayment of damages, we will not say morally, but for physical torment we suffered, and for the unjust way in which we have been treated in this land. The damages our families have suffered in one year of production have deepened our debt unjustly, without any fault of our own," Polmonari's letter emphasized.[73] He claimed that families like his were living "in a miserable poverty." Company policies that undervalued cotton and overcharged for mediocre farmland had resulted in a situation where "we have been reduced to living like slaves," a phrase that specifically invoked the ultimate state of labor's oppression (and one that was very familiar to the Delta).[74] Polmonari and his committee focused on many of the same issues as Delpidio's group, and in February and March 1898, first Luigi Bruni and then Alfonso Mazocchi added their voices to the growing chorus.[75] Taken together, the complaints called attention to the disconnect between the promises of colonization and the reality of work growing cotton in rural eastern Arkansas.

The journey the letters and telegrams took from the plantation to Washington and to Rome also illustrate the tensions inherent in the larger asymmetric partnership between Italy and the United States in the 1890s. "I received your first complaint and your declarations made me incensed!" the ambassador wrote emphatically in a letter drafted the day Egisto Polmonari's complaint arrived in Washington. "I will take action to obtain more exact information about the true state of things at Sunnyside and about the causes of your complaints."[76] Perhaps looking to avoid a direct conflict over affairs in the South, with the disastrous 1891 lynching negotiations not far off in his memory, Fava left his post in Washington and delegated the problem for a time to his chargé d'affaires to untangle.[77] Three days later Fava sent as his representative Consul Baron C. F. Romano to meet with Sunnyside's management at their headquarters in New York City. On December 31, 1897, Romano reported to Fava's second-in-command on the session.[78] George Edgell, now the most powerful man at the company, had reassured Romano that "it was his strongest desire that the Society would flower" and that he knew "that is an impossible thing if these [terrible] conditions were true." Edgell promised that immediately following the 1898 cotton harvest—which was then more than nine months away—the company would undertake a careful study of conditions on the plantation. He concluded the meeting by reassuring the consul that Sunnyside management would do everything in its power to improve sanitary conditions, but he did not address Polmonari's complaints about debt.[79] While the Sunnyside Company had a prevailing interest in keeping these settlers in whom they had invested so much time and money content on the plantation, this was clearly a binational partnership, and Fava had information that was not positive. On January 2, 1898, Fava, now back in Washington, warned Edgell of the "complaints and reports which daily reach me from the Sunny Side Colony." While Romano was convinced that Edgell had done all he could and "any more than this he wouldn't believe can be done or said" for Sunnyside, the company's promises were weak and based only on the ability of the management team in New York to effect change on the ground in Arkansas. Fava would not allow the company to ignore the complaints: "These reports, if correct, seem to me should be thoroughly examined by the [Sunnyside] Company." Fava seemed to lament this delicate situation where the larger goals of the Italian government to resettle migrants were so dependent on the cooperation of a handful of people in Arkansas. "The welfare of these Italians," the ambassador concluded, "is an object of solicitude to the Embassy, it is also one of great interest to the Company, for on their welfare depends the success of the enterprise."[80]

The remarkable level of coordination between Ministry officers and the Sunnyside Company is revealed by what happened next. Before the promised study could take place, on March 24, 1898, Edgell did an about-face and authorized his officers to liquidate all outstanding accounts on the plantation.[81] The Sunnyside Company offered colonists two options. They could leave, and forfeit any mortgage payments but be released from their contracts, or families could stay, and re-sign for next season and carry over their debts. If some colonists still remained unsatisfied, Edgell promised that his company would "make provisions to repatriate [those] that cannot make it, who are most upset." Only 38 of the original 174 families now remained, the rest having left on their own between January and March in a single exodus led by Father Pietro Bandini to a new settlement in the Ozarks he named Tontitown. Edgell indicated that this decision to subsidize the repatriation of some remaining families had been based on Romano's recommendation: "This, I think, is strictly in accordance with our conversation when you were here, that we felt disposed to do all that we could to assist those to return to their native home who desired to do so."[82] Edgell reported that his company spent almost $750 to provide for safe passage of nineteen people to Genoa in April 1898.[83] From New Orleans, Consul Magenta facilitated the repatriation journey for fourteen of the nineteen who abandoned Sunnyside to return to Italy.[84]

Magenta's account of this episode makes fun of the frustrated peasants who, he said with more than a tinge of annoyance, disrupted his otherwise quiet morning.[85] He reported that a loud mob had arrived to his office in the Garden District after traveling together down the river from Greenville. That day Magenta had also received a package of cash from the Sunnyside Company to purchase steamer tickets and cover related expenses. The ship departed for Italy less than forty-eight hours later with the families who had abandoned the plantation aboard. While the company had released these settlers from their contractual responsibilities, the families did not leave happily. Even Edgell agreed that these people had a reason to feel they had been cheated out of a great opportunity.[86]

Fava lamented how the land's problems ran too deep to fix despite management's "good intentions." Just three months earlier he had reported his suspicions in a letter to Rome. "My personal impression is that the company has not been able to make better the hygiene of the place and can't make large concessions for it. And not for lack of good intentions, but because of the current financial situation being as it is, and the death of founder A. Corbin."[87] He alluded to a new effort to reestablish the plantation with "the proper resources." He found it hard to separate the plantation's reality from its promise.

While the experiment fell far short of its lofty goals, the idea of rural resettlement schemes as a way to resist changes to U.S. immigration law continued to percolate in the minds of a small group of Italian leaders. MAE officers had emphasized that the path to ownership was the essential clause in every contract made with an Italian. In the early stages of the experiment Oldrini had written to Fava: "You suggest to me the same 'purchase' plan will also assure the advantages of ownership to the emigrant and because [of it] the families that will come do not have to fall under the Contract Labor Law. [T]his plan is the personal work of Mr. Corbin himself. . . . He intends great things for his colonists in 15 or 20 years."[88] Ten years later, in 1905, Egisto Rossi, now the new head of an emigration council that oversaw all aspects of migration out of Italy, returned to the idea of colonization in the official organ of the council published by the MAE, the *Bollettino dell'emigrazione*. "One of our biggest problems now, an urgent problem, is that of achieving a better distribution of Italians in the interior parts of the United States. Only in this way can we both ward off new threats of restrictive legislation and also assure a better situation for our emigrants in the United States."[89] While Rossi and others were trying to encourage agricultural colonies to resist immigration restriction, the push to institute tougher gatekeeping measures grew more powerful. Italians were now facing new challenges in their efforts to navigate the U.S. immigration system that extended far beyond the swampy lands of Lake Chicot, Arkansas.

## The Literacy Test

Most importantly for the supporters of colonization in the U.S. South, the Immigration Restriction League generated a seemingly unstoppable force in public and legislative circles that swept the arguments for Italian farm colonies away in the push toward restrictionist policy, strategically closed off paths for Italian migrants, and ended the kind of close cooperation with U.S. officials that the Italian government had enjoyed. Formed in 1894 in Boston as the nation's first "anti-immigrant think tank and lobbying firm," the IRL proved exceptionally influential in limiting Italian migration to the United States through its campaign for a test to exclude "all persons between 14 and 60 years of age who cannot both read and write in the English language or some other language."[90] The IRL "weaponized statistics" in their campaign to prove that indigent immigrants, especially Italians and Jews, were dangerous; the organization's membership, drawn from the New England upper crust and the nation's most prestigious universities, used their renown and institutional status to carry out research to spread their message of restriction and fear.[91] The IRL carried out their work with the close cooperation of Ellis Island officials and powerful members of the U.S. government, like Senator Henry Cabot Lodge, an ally in the fight to pass a literacy test. After 1896 this test would become the cornerstone of the IRL's policy prescription for restriction. The Immigration Restriction League began its campaign for a literacy test with careful studies of Italians arriving to Ellis Island, and used its findings as proof of the need for a stricter law. The organization bent statistics to their view in their many publications and speeches to stimulate fear that too many dangerous immigrants were slipping through the cracks of a flawed inspection system.

The U.S. immigration service had given the IRL unfettered access to the Ellis Island station where they were free to closely observe agents at work, a privilege only previously granted, in part, to the Italian Office. Members of the IRL also used their access to Ellis Island to challenge enforcement practices then in use at the station. In April 1896, in the midst of what Rossi had called the "days of exceptional invasion," the IRL conducted an investigation of procedures at Ellis Island that focused exclusively on Italian arrivals.[92] Both the IRL and the Italian government worried about the effects of haphazard inspection procedures and sought to observe firsthand what was happening during the busiest months at the station. Commissioner Senner and Assistant Commissioner McSweeney allowed Prescott Hall, Robert DeCourcy Ward, and George Loring Briggs to observe inspection procedures, review official data, and interview migrants directly over three days of investigation.[93] The men observed that inspectors excluded only 197 out of 3,174 Italians who arrived at the island aboard four ships, a number they concluded was artificially low.[94] From their interviews the IRL investigators determined an illiteracy rate of 68 percent among these 3,174 persons even though the rate of exclusion was only 6 percent for this sample. To compare, the 1900 census estimated illiteracy among native-born whites at 4.6 percent and foreign-born persons at 12.9 percent. African Americans and other races, what the census referred to as "Negro and other," had an illiteracy rate of 44.5 percent.[95] The statistics were clear: Italian migrants were far less likely to know how to read in their native language than even African Americans and Native Americans, who had been systematically denied access to education by the state for most of the nineteenth century. What the IRL saw at Ellis Island led them to conclude that the existing law was "radically defective" in filtering out illiterate immigrants. However, the methods they used to determine this were less than scientific and would rightly be criticized as junk science today.

As gatekeeping moved from a regional issue focused on Chinese exclusion to a national policy that targeted migratory labor more broadly, Italians became the public face of the growing restrictionist movement. While enforcement action for the Chinese Exclusion Act was seen as a "regional concern" that lacked support in the interior states, contract labor was a different story.[96] The question of effectiveness challenged early immigration enforcement, and the resulting laws reflected these concerns.[97] Hidetaka Hirota argues that the enforcement limitations of the Alien Contract Labor Law played a large role in the nationalization of immigration control. The 1885 law was an insufficient barrier in part because it focused on tracking down laborers, an arduous task for inspectors, who also complained immigrants had been "carefully coached" to resist detection.[98] IRL reports highlighted the flaws and limitations of such an inspection-based system that screened immigrants at the point of arrival and depended on the decisions of individual officers.

The IRL proposed the literacy test as the only fiscally prudent, "uniform" system.[99] The IRL's work among Italians at Ellis Island had convinced the group that immigration inspectors needed stricter standards to do their work more effectively. Italians became the case study the IRL used to prove to Congress and the public that the gatekeeping system was flawed. By lobbying for what they believed was the more objective measure of a literacy test with the power to supersede inspectors' subjective admission decisions, the IRL pushed for a stricter national gatekeeping policy by presenting enforcement as a national, not regional, problem. In this way they cast the problems particular to Ellis Island as a national problem, which in the spring of 1896 as the IRL conducted its visits was the massive and sudden influx of Italian immigrants. The IRL's study of Italians arriving in New York became evidence of the need for a more restrictive federal policy, another key step in the transition from Chinese to European exclusion and with it the adoption of federal solutions to regional immigration problems.

Five years earlier a congressional investigation of inspection procedures at Ellis Island in March 1892 showed a haphazard and frequently shifting system. The so-called ten-dollar rule ascribed to Assistant Commissioner James O'Beirne is illustrative. O'Beirne, working as acting commissioner while Commissioner John Weber was away from the island, instituted a standard that required emigrants to have ten dollars in cash or be excluded under LPC. This in the short term led to the detention of three hundred people. But when Weber resumed his duties, he released all three hundred detainees. Presenting this episode as evidence, Senator William Chandler of New Hampshire, Fava's personal friend and the first chair of the Senate Immigration Committee, concluded in his first investigation of Ellis Island that exclusion "depends upon no statutory provisions, and is decided very much according to the personal feeling or judgement of the person who makes the decision."[100]

Four years later the IRL highlighted the arbitrary nature of enforcement in its arguments for the literacy test. Such a test, Prescott Hall argued in an IRL pamphlet published in 1896, would remedy the "unlimited and burdensome discretion" of federal immigration agents. Their report told a story in statistics of how current immigration policy remained "radically defective" at gatekeeping. Instead of murky policy open to inspector discretion, the IRL called for a more "uniform" test that would become a much more rigid barrier.[101] Government statistics revealed that only 0.5 percent of new arrivals were prevented from entering the country under the laws in place in 1892 and 1893. The addition of boards of special inquiry only had the effect of increasing that figure to 1 percent. "To rectify this situation," historian Vincent Cannato wrote, "the IRL continued to press for a literacy test."[102] Hall argued that the literacy test "is exact and definite in its operation; easily and simply applied." Somewhat like the arguments for disfranchisement then gaining steam in the American South that emphasized how removing Black voters from the rolls would clean up corruption, his pamphlet argued that the literacy test "diminishes the labor of the boards of special inquiry, and gives the immigration officials opportunity for a more thorough inspection." He also argued that the literacy test would alleviate the burden of immigrant separation at the border, because families will be able to know if members are eligible for entry before they leave. Both the IRL and the Italian government sought a clearer, more predictable system, but the results they hoped to achieve could not have been more opposed.

By the winter of 1896 the IRL began pressuring Congress to bring the literacy test bill to the floor for consideration, but it would be another year before a version of the literacy test came up for a vote. During this time Italians continued to be the primary example the IRL used to make the case for the new law. Over time the IRL would profoundly influence the structure of gatekeeping with its relentless focus on the tool of a literacy test, its use of statistics, and its technique of direct lobbying of Congress.[103]

Legislation introducing a literacy test requirement to enter the United States passed the House five times and the Senate four times between 1897 and 1917.[104] The debate over the initial attempt to pass a literacy test in February 1897 captured the climate around the early bill. R. B. Mahany of New York voiced the concerns of his fellow Republican lawmakers who saw the test as too blunt an instrument. "I stand here in protest against the passage of this legislation in its general scope. It is not just unjust to the immigrant but it is injurious to the people of the United States," he argued. Mahany, almost taking a page from Ambassador Fava, advocated for thoughtful "regulation" of immigration that would encourage redistribution "away from the crowded cities of the Union and place them where they can win prosperity for themselves and add to the glory and progress of the great Republic."[105] While his position had been informed by calls, in his own words, "for more immigration to fell the forests and plow the soil" of the Pacific Northwest, his testimony reflected the sentiment that a literacy test would restrict migrants entering at Ellis Island who were desired elsewhere in the United States. Concerns like these slowed the progress of the test. It would eventually take twenty-two years from first introduction to enactment. The House overrode a presidential veto two times, and two other times the override failed by fewer than seven votes. The Senate's sole successful override vote, in 1917, finally turned the bill into law. While economist Claudia Goldin has argued that the literacy test movement was the beginning of the quantitative push to limit European entry, examining gatekeeping from a broader definition shows how debates over early enforcement against Italians were reflected in the introduction of the literacy test. These connections point to the critical role Italians played in the rise of a gatekeeping nation.[106]

Through the literacy test campaign the Immigration Restriction League influenced gatekeeping for generations. The initial debate over the literacy test shows how border control transformed from a regional to a national concern best addressed through congressional legislation. At the same time, the IRL "invented a new way of spreading and legislating xenophobia," laying the foundation for a novel strategy as described by Erika Lee, the national public pressure campaign. The organization was fundamental in the history of American xenophobia for its impact and its style. The IRL employed direct lobbying of Congress to great effect and built a particularly strong relationship with Massachusetts senator Henry Cabot Lodge.[107] To the Italians the literacy test bill became known as the "Lodge immigration bill."[108] Lodge had spoken out following the 1891 New Orleans lynching to tie the massacre to lax immigration laws that allowed in too many criminals, and he later became a member of the Dillingham Commission formed to study the nation's immigrant population and recommend legislative action.[109] His views of gatekeeping and ties to the IRL had a durable impact that Fava noticed. Both the restrictionist IRL and the Italian government focused on the problems of uneven enforcement of gatekeeping law: the Italians, to try to better comprehend and enforce U.S. law; the IRL, to try to tighten the mechanisms that could keep migrants out.

The IRL's early campaign for a literacy test amplified criticism of the conduct of federal gatekeeping, where the focus remained on Italians arriving at Ellis Island. While the workers' newspaper *L'Araldo Italiano* reported in January 1897 that Dr. Senner had issued special instructions to his agents to detain and return anyone who "under a minimum pretext can be returned to their homeland under the current laws," the editorial, published under the headline "Ridiculous Zeal of the Ellis Island Authorities," also identified the Italian government as a key actor responding to increased detention at Ellis Island. The paper complained that in the temporary absence of the ambassador in Washington, Rossi and the Office were "limited in [their] defense of our co-nationals facing the preconceived ideas of the federal authorities," which were exacerbated by "this italophobia mania." Still, the editors of *L'Araldo Italiano* remained cautiously hopeful. Predicting a sharp increase in migration by spring, they concluded: "However, we hope that, if he can't improve this situation, Cavalier Rossi will be able to act to protect unjustly detained Italians, who certainly, given Senner's orders, will be coming in large numbers on the next arrivals of steamships from Italy."[110] The ambassador collected a flurry of Italo-American newspaper articles as Congress debated the literacy test in February 1897.[111] With a literacy test in place, the Office of Labor Information and officers of the Italian government would be severely restrained in their ability to intervene in exclusion cases, these newspapers argued. The literacy test electrified a new argument to tighten border controls and expand the tools of restriction even further, to concentrate the power to exclude in the hands of American officials and limit avenues to object to these decisions.

While the role the Office, and the Italian government more broadly, would play in managing migration across U.S. borders was still up for debate, attempting to counter anti-Italian restrictionism through a model Italian colony now seemed like a quaint solution to a burgeoning political movement to close the gates.

## Conclusion

Based in large part on the experiences of its migrants, the Italian government soon changed its approach to managing the exodus of its citizens. As the twentieth century dawned, the IRL's campaign to close what one contemporary American poet called the "unguarded gates" would also inject Rome into the work of gatekeeping in surprising ways.[112] Because it elevated the roles of consuls and labor agents, Sunnyside Plantation's recruitment and colonization scheme operated as an early system of "remote control" decades before the law codified consular roles in vetting emigrants.[113] The experiment at Sunnyside showed how the asymmetric partnership between the nations continued to influence, and be influenced by, events in the American South where diplomats paid a lot of attention. "Although the Italian government did not intervene frequently to protect the rights of immigrants," historian George Pozzetta has written, "authorities in Rome occasionally took active roles. Interestingly, those events that resulted in diplomatic exchanges often involved Italian immigrants who settled in the American South" in the 1890s.[114] The Sunnyside plantation drew Italian consuls and the ambassador into the action of "managing mobility," which in turn influenced the Italian view of U.S. immigration law.[115] In this way Italian colonization is an important preamble to "remote control" gatekeeping that would come to define the American system in the twentieth century.

The history of the movement to colonize Italians in the American South is a significant but little understood and largely ignored facet of the U.S.–Italian relationship at a time when Italy looked to the United States for models in foreign policy and economic development.[116] The history of Italian colonization also has important implications for labor history in the region. Outside of work on Latino migration in a labor history context, scholars have not given immigrant recruitment a recent treatment.[117] Only two books, both published in 1993, attempt to place Italian colonization in its full context but still miss crucial elements of the story.[118]

The history of colonization at this specific moment in the mid-1890s overlaps with the formation of the Immigration Restriction League and that group's targeted campaign to close the gates with a literacy test using Italians as an example for the need for more consistent restrictions. The IRL's campaign to bring more uniformity to immigration enforcement aligned with the Italian government's desire to better understand an arbitrary American system. Ultimately the experiences at Ellis Island and Sunnyside Plantation would push Italy to adopt new tactics to manage migration of its citizens to the United States as the partnership in gatekeeping between the nations continued to evolve.

# CHAPTER 5

## Partners in Gatekeeping

In May 1894 the *New York Times* reported an attack on immigration agents at Ellis Island. Identified by the bags of macaroni and beans they abandoned in their wake, this particular tale of retaliation highlighted some of the troubles with executing a policy of restriction. "Thomas Flynn, son of Alderman Flynn, had a narrow escape from being killed by revengeful Italians last night. He is a deportation officer at Ellis Island," the *Times* began.

> Recently a considerable number of Italians have been deported, and Assistant Immigration Commissioner McSweeney said yesterday that he had no doubt these assaults were committed by friends of the rejected immigrants. As a result, he is about to make application to have the deportation officers appointed Deputy United States Marshals, so that they may be in a position to carry arms and protect themselves in similar cases. Sometimes one or two of them have to take quite a squad of people back to the ship on which they came, and at present the only weapon they carry is a small cane.[1]

At the turn of the twentieth century Italians sometimes went to great lengths to resist the decisions of immigration inspectors.

The experiences of Italian migrants arriving in the United States in the 1890s transformed the kingdom's approach to managing migration, and by 1901 Italy had become a partner in gatekeeping. The Italian Parliament passed two emigration laws in 1888 and 1901 that significantly increased government oversight of people leaving the country. The political history of Italian migration law, and its connections to economic development in the country and abroad, sheds light on U.S. policy, helping expose the transnational origins of border controls. At the same time, domestic politics in Italy and the shift more broadly toward state management of migration there and in the United States influenced the foundations of key aspects of the international border control regime.

The origins of one of the most fundamental systems in a modern state—control over national borders—date to the turn of the twentieth century for both Italy and the United States. A focus on the relationship between Italy and the United States between 1891 and 1901 exposes the integrated development of systems that controlled the outflow and inflow of migrants, deepening and expanding our view of gatekeeping to include many kinds of border controls and counteracting what Zolberg called the "constraint [that] arises from the unidimensionality of the concept of restriction."[2] Examining the evolution of Italian law though the landmark acts of 1888 and 1901 shows how U.S. gatekeeping practice influenced the growth of emigration bureaucracy in a key sending state. Encounters with Italian migrants shaped emerging U.S. bureaucracy, sometimes reactively, in its first decade.

Working in response to Ambassador Fava's reports of migrants' struggles to avoid exclusion by federal immigration agents at Ellis Island, and encountering the limitations of its own emigration law, the Italian Parliament passed what scholars refer to as the "social law" in 1901. The Italian example is an opportunity to closely examine the interplay between U.S. immigration law and policy and a sending nation's emigration law. At the turn of the twentieth century, the growing interdependence of the United States and the world both extended and limited U.S. reach in matters of migration.[3] In Rome, debate that focused on not just how to manage migration but also why it should be managed animated several decades of policy making that was increasingly informed by experiences at U.S. borders.

Over time the feedback from the Office of Labor Information and Protection would encourage leaders in Rome to adopt a new legal strategy. The challenges of Article 17 enforcement and the limitations of the 1888 law demonstrated a need to move the management of emigration out of the Department of the Interior altogether and into the Ministry of Foreign Affairs. The emigration law of 1901 picked up where the 1888 law fell short. The 1901 law shifted the focus from emigration agents to the shipping lines, whose actions were easier to regulate and to prosecute if needed. It fundamentally changed the relationship of the Italian government to its citizens on the move. The opportunities, connections, and frustrations experienced by officials working in the 1890s are clearly visible in the 1901 law.

## Italian Emigration Policy from Unification to 1888

In late nineteenth-century Italy the "emigration question" occupied a permanent place in Italian politics. Prime ministers on the historical left and right first attempted to legislate solutions beginning in 1869, eight years after unification. At the close of the nineteenth century, political historians generally agree, the ideological differences between the parties were not significant, and the ministers of the Treasury and the Interior, as well as prominent members of Parliament and key Italian intellectuals, tried to engage in migration policy making. While some legislators emphasized the need to protect emigrants, they disagreed on the role the state should play in this effort and took a cautious approach that reflected the larger disagreements over whether and how to expand the power of the new national government. Interventions that regulated emigration were challenged as an unacceptable compression of the rights and individual freedom described as "the freedom to leave."[4] Emigration was free except for obligations imposed on citizens by the laws of the country, which traced directly back to 1857's royal passport decree and 1865's public safety regulations that gave the police the authority to oversee "public agencies" and was interpreted to include emigration matters as well.[5]

For the next three decades policy debates focused on the role of emigration agents and the language of protection, often adopting what legal historian Dolores Freda characterized as a limited "pro/con" point of view on emigration that sidestepped the role of the state in addressing the root causes of migration, notably, inadequate state services and limited economic opportunity.[6] The first major proposal to protect emigrants came from the minister of agriculture, Gaspare Finali, who pushed the state to denounce agents' exploitative actions. Finali's proposal would have increased state oversight in two key ways: it would have introduced a license good for two years that all agents had to obtain and required officials stationed in the main ports to check that agents followed the terms of the law and had committed no obvious fraudulent actions. Finali was the first to actively call attention to the emigration agents in this way, but the legislation failed to advance because the government fell soon after.[7]

The Finali proposal had an important effect on the debate that followed over how to regulate emigration. The two sides that would dominate the debate had formed. They were divided between, on one side, conservative and moderate leaders who thought the state needed to control migratory flows to preserve the domestic agricultural workforce and feared emigration was a menace to family and society, and in the opposite position, socialist and workers' organizations whose attention to the underlying causes behind Italian peasants' struggles led them to believe temporary migration was positive and a valuable benefit that helped undermine the power of the landed elites who controlled them. (Socialists and other radicals did not necessarily support permanent emigration, seeing it as a drain on the power of workers to wage class struggle in Italy.) These sharply opposing political views contributed to the hardening of the debate.

From this basis emerged the long-standing focus on regulating the activity of emigration agents. By focusing on agents, lawmakers reasoned, they could address the most visibly egregious problems.[8] Subsequent proposals in 1878 and 1879 regulated agents and licenses, and were combined into one single proposal in 1880 that distinguished between "spontaneous emigration" and "artificial or provoked emigration" that agents created by enticing people with overly optimistic promises of opportunities abroad.[9] Legislators fretted over the seemingly unsolvable problem of how to support emigrants without encouraging more emigration, and the Chamber of Deputies struggled to decide how to regulate the movement of people because it did not agree on the principle of regulation itself. As emigration increased in scale the government rehashed the debate but hesitated to make significant changes. For a time the emigration agent was Rome's scapegoat for everything that was wrong in the countryside that pushed Italians to leave. The question was how to protect emigrants from duplicitous and greedy agents whose "stormy marriage" with shipping companies packed ignorant people onto old, cramped ships, the kind Egisto Rossi of the Office of Labor Information and Protection called "tramp steamers," without encouraging even more emigration as a result of any new regulations.[10]

Outside of Parliament, officials in the Ministry of the Interior exercised their own power to regulate exit, which initially rested in the power to issue passports and enact laws of public safety, both in the Ministry's domain.[11] Very early in the history of a unified Italy, a circular issued by the Ministry of the Interior had allowed for prefects to refuse to issue a passport for travel to persons for whom there was "no justification that they had the means necessary to undertake the trip, or if there was any basis to suspect they would be returned from abroad for abandoning themselves to idleness, to mendacity or vagabondage."[12] (In this way the Ministry adopted the basic principles for exclusion that the U.S. Congress would also encode in the 1880s and 1890s.) In 1867 the Ministry added that prefects could act "to diminish . . . greatly the emigration of our nationals to America."[13] In 1868 the Ministry of the Interior acted again, this time asking mayors and other public safety agencies to "dissuade and if necessary to obstruct the emigration of Italians."[14] According to historian Corrado Bonifazi, "this is indicative of the diversity of views already present on the migration question" that had resulted just ten days earlier in the Menabrea Circular, issued by the prime minister, which was the first time since 1869 that Parliament had weighed in on the issue. Menabrea took the position that while the government at that time favored the freedom to emigrate, it was limited in its ability to act. Circulars, and not formal legislation, would be the primary method used to regulate emigration for the time being, an approach that Bonifazi pointed out is the same the Republic of Italy uses more than a century later to deal with the contemporary problem of immigration to the country.[15]

The debate over how to address the emigration problem took on a new form following the completion in 1871 of the very first census of Italians living abroad, conducted by consuls, which showed the scope of Italian emigration, estimated by the MAE at the time as between 432,000 and 478,000 persons in total.[16] By 1881 that number had grown to one million, and by 1891, to two million. The rapid rate of growth was clear to see, and previous efforts to regulate the flow through circulars could not stand up to the volume of migration. The time had come to pass a new law.

### The Freedom to Emigrate versus the Freedom to Let People Emigrate

The fundamental tension shaping Italian emigration law was the difference, as articulated in 1888 by Giovanni Battista Scalabrini (the influential founder of a Catholic order with the mission of ministering to migrants who also helped craft the first major revision to Italian emigration law in 1888), between "the freedom to emigrate versus the freedom to let people emigrate."[17] Throughout the late nineteenth century the government in Rome struggled with the question of how to permit emigration without encouraging it outwardly. Leaders in Parliament recognized that emigration in many ways aided the state, by connecting Italians seeking work with markets seeking workers whom the fledgling domestic economy could not accommodate. But the movement of people could not be entirely market driven as the government also fretted over growing complaints about exploitation, suffering, and petty swindles, and rejection by U.S. immigration agents at the border.

In 1888 Monsignor Scalabrini, then the bishop of Piacenza, wrote to his former classmate Paolo Carcano, the undersecretary of finance, about pending legislation to regulate emigration. Companies and their agents who encouraged migrants to leave were the problem, Scalabrini argued. Without a stricter law, the selfish business interests of the shipping companies that led them to operate crowded, substandard ships and reward agents who recruited more and more emigrants with false promises would continue to cause harm to many people. "A good law on emigration will be able to defend the emigrant from the frauds of the agents and, up to a certain point, make the exodus less bitter and less dangerous, which would already be a lot, but it is not all that is needed."[18] From Scalabrini's point of view Italy's leaders had to consider the emigrant over those who wished to exploit him.

The debate pitted landed elites who feared the loss of their labor force against the economic interests of the shipping companies, and reflected the major fault lines that had animated the emigration question over the previous two decades. The 1888 law, also called the Crispi Law after Prime Minister Francesco Crispi, faced criticism for its focus on agents. Francesco Saverio Nitti, a statistician who would remain an outspoken voice on issues of migration, called out the ways the law failed to address the real problems—poverty and lack of employment—that caused emigration in the first place. Future prime minister Sidney Sonnino exposed what he saw as the law's inherent contradictions. It failed to establish a special office for emigration, punished agents too severely, and was too restrictive, aspects that would, in his view, further encourage clandestine emigration that would operate completely outside of the realm of regulations. Agents were a necessary part of emigration, and while their powers deserved regulation, they should not be restrained too much, he believed. Changes instituted by the 1888 law required emigration agents to obtain a license granted by the Ministry of the Interior; subagents had to be clearly identified; no migrant could work in exchange for ship's passage; and sanctions could be applied in cases of exploitation.[19] Focusing on the "economic-political aspect and not the social one," the 1888 law left a gap that later reformers attempted to fill. Arriving at the 1888 law was itself a long and exhausting process for Parliament. Even though the law confirmed that "emigration is free, except for the obligations imposed on citizens by the laws of the country," and in spite of Scalabrini's exhortations, historian Daniele Fiorentino noted that "the protection of migrants remained at the margins of the new legislation."[20]

In the late nineteenth century passports were the most powerful tool the Italian government had to exercise control over migration, and the history of emigration law demonstrates how resistant leaders were to introduce stricter regulations. Only a handful of public safety laws and two circulars, the Menabrea Circular of 1868 and the Lanza Circular of 1873, addressed who could leave and how. Passports controlled citizens' legal exit, but changing their regulation was a slow process. The 1888 law stated that migrants could not be charged more than the published price for their passports, ending the practice of local officials adding fees.[21] Before 1901 a passport cost 2.40 lire for laborers, the equivalent of several days' wages. After 1901 the passport fee was eliminated, but passports were now legally required to emigrate. A person had to demonstrate their intent to emigrate by writing a letter or appearing in person in front of the mayor (*sindaco*) of his *commune*, who issued a *nulla osta*. This document to "indicate that there are no legal obstacles to the emigration of the applicant" was required for the prefect or subprefect in the applicant's province to deliver the passport. This new chain of command did nothing to interrupt the Ministry of the Interior's long-standing control over exit.[22] Changes to Italian passport law generated extensive debate in Parliament that kicked up tensions between liberal, authoritarian, and leftist attitudes toward the freedom of exit. Debate in 1900 and 1901 invoked fears of a return to overly restrictive controls on exit that "smacked of supposedly outmoded restraints on emigration typical of the pre-liberal period," associations the Zanardelli-Giolitti government strenuously sought to avoid.[23] The resulting passport law, which regulated passport controls for sixty-six years and passed alongside the new comprehensive emigration law on January 31, 1901, "appeared to be a departure from the widespread warm feelings toward the freedom of movement in Europe at that time."[24]

The new Italian laws were directly responding to the exclusion of Italian emigrants in ports in the Americas, especially the United States. Political scientist John Torpey drew a direct connection between Italy's legislative actions in 1901 and the impact of immigration exclusion practices in the United States. "Just as there were often 'external' determinants of emigrant health inspection, and indeed of citizenship laws that might be thought to be at the very heart of state sovereignty, passport requirements might be imposed in one state as a result of the restrictions laid down by another. Such was the case with the Italian passport law of 1901."[25] As the United States was instituting its own bureaucratic system to assess and enforce standards for entry, then Italy would endow agents of its own government with the power of "remote control." To this end, the 1901 passport law established that only police authorities at the port of embarkation could approve "a passport for emigration." The law instructed these authorities to limit the issuance of passports in accordance with the capacity of the transporting vessel and in agreement with the laws of the receiving countries. Agents were expressly prohibited from granting passports to persons who would not be allowed to enter the country to which they proposed to go if they did not meet that country's requirements for admission. Proponents of the law in Parliament like Eugenio Valli argued for its support using exclusion statistics gathered in the year previous from U.S. ports. According to Valli's testimony, U.S. inspectors refused twelve hundred Italians in the fiscal year just passed, 1899–1900. "In the United States, if they believe or suspect that there is a danger that the Italian emigrant . . . is likely to become a public charge, they will throw him out with the most remorseless brutality."[26] For Valli and other supporters of the new law, by issuing passports the Italian state would offer a "testament of the bearer's 'good conduct'" to facilitate their free emigration out of Italy to their destination.[27]

While health concerns also led to exclusion at the border, an aspect the 1901 law addressed with its extensive new bureaucracy to facilitate inspections at the port of departure and on board the ships to ameliorate the worst unsanitary conditions, the main thrust of the 1901 law was to encourage the unhindered migration of the laboring classes. As historian Aliza Wong pointed out, "in Italy the provinces that experienced the most emigration were not those that were the most heavily populated, but those that had been devastated by malaria, or those suffering from oppressive agricultural contracts."[28] At the turn of the century, migrants from cities chose to move within Europe following seasonal patterns while poor, rural dwellers left for destinations in the Americas and Australia.[29] Facilitating the free movement of working-class people was an act of self-preservation for the liberal government as the Socialist Party made inroads with national elections.[30] According to Torpey's analysis of the parliamentary debate surrounding the bill, the 1901 law "thus reflected not so much the reawakening of slumbering authoritarian habits as it did the ruling elite's acceptance of Italy's peripheral position in the Atlantic economy and its vulnerability to class-based movements of social protest."[31] The 1901 law failed to address the real problems behind the massive emigration of Italians: rural poverty and economic underdevelopment. Instead it tried to fix the problems of emigration itself as the underlying causes were just too complex for the government to tackle at that time.

Italy had a great need to facilitate migration to alleviate its internal and foreign crises. "Emigration," Wong's research has shown, "actually helped to improve the social and economic structures seen as problematic to the well-being of the new nation."[32] Foreign policy struggles buttressed domestic problems. Following the epic failure of the army to claim Abyssinia as a colonial territory in 1896, emigration also came to be seen as a way to build Italian influence abroad, what Torpey described in the period before the invasion of Tripoli in 1911 as "promoting an oddly imperialist sort of nation-building."[33] The 1901 law cemented the terms of the relationship between Italy and the United States, forging a new component of their asymmetric partnership. Rome looked to the United States, and its actions in Washington and on Ellis Island, as it actively shaped emigration policy. Historians have established how Italy saw the United States as a model for how a young country like itself could emerge as a world power and grow its economy.[34] This relationship was even broader as the terms of the asymmetric partnership are clearly reflected in 1901 emigration and passport legislation. The U.S. influence can be plainly seen in the provisions of the 1901 law. Beyond the models in foreign policy and economic development that the United States offered to Italy at the turn of the twentieth century, the government in Rome reluctantly embraced U.S. methods of migration control.

The 1901 law was far more expansive than its 1888 predecessor and put in place for the first time a formal state emigration bureaucracy in the Commissariat of Emigration housed within the MAE. The first leader, Luigi Bodio, had at the time of his appointment a four-decade-long career as a statistician who had published an irregular series of government reports on emigration beginning in the early 1880s.[35] While Bodio had long been respected within the government as "an active contributor to the scientific study" of emigration, he also struggled throughout the 1890s to secure the funding and appointments he desired to carry out his work. He faced personal attacks in Parliament for his leadership that by 1904 led to his resignation as commissioner-general.[36] The 1901 law, drafted by Bodio's longtime friends and collaborators Luigi Luzzatti and Fedele Lampertico, sought to secure the *tutela* or protection of emigrants, a long-standing goal of the Ministry of the Interior and now included in the portfolio of Foreign Affairs.[37] Bodio "made a fundamental contribution to formulating the first legislative provisions on the matter, promoting a policy aimed at," in Bodio's words, "leaving free flow to individual choices to emigrate, limiting the intervention of the State to the action of education, information and protection of migrants."[38] As an American supporter of Italian immigration noted at the time, "the design of this law was to remedy any defects noted in the operation of existing legislation, to institute the best feasible safeguards for the protection and guidance of emigrants, and especially to suppress any artificial promotion of emigration."[39] The 1901 law, like its predecessor, reiterated that Italy did not question the right of expatriation and emigration, but it introduced enough safeguards that its sponsors considered it a restrictive law to align with American gatekeeping policy.

With these new rules in place and the commissariat providing oversight, Italian migration to the United States continued to grow: three million Italians entered the United States between 1900 and 1915 alone. This arrangement allowed the government in Rome to exercise more power over the migration flow out of Italy, not to mention that it brought additional revenue the government could use to comply with other parts of U.S. immigration legislation. By 1901 the tension between what Scalabrini had described in 1888 as the "freedom to emigrate versus the freedom to let people emigrate" had led to a massive new government bureaucracy designed to protect, but not encourage, mass migration out of Italy. The structures created in 1901 would prove particularly durable and prescient in a world where the right to free movement across international borders would encounter new challenges and would soon come under much stricter scrutiny as receiving countries erected more and more barriers to entry.

## Growing the Migration Bureaucracy

After a long and difficult negotiation process the passage of the "social law" established long-standing legal and structural precedents for the management of emigration from Italy to countries around the world.[40] The 1901 law took into account the challenges of enforcing prior statute and strengthened the ability of the state to oversee migration. By 1901 the government was explicitly focused on protection (what it called *tutela*) of emigrants and set very specific requirements for transatlantic shipping firms to follow. It offered options to emigrants to hold the transport companies accountable for the cost, duration, and conditions of the voyage as well as whether they were ultimately accepted onto American soil. It formed a *commissariato dell'emigrazione* (or emigration commissariat) that issued annual licenses, set prices, investigated complaints, inspected facilities, and collected fees from shippers, which provided emergency monies for stranded or excluded migrants to access. Transatlantic shippers and their emigration agents took on more responsibilities for the protection of emigrants, which meant they now bore more financial and legal risk for their passengers who sought to cross national borders.

The components of the 1901 law demonstrate the influence of the experiences of migrants with the U.S. immigration service on the form and function of Italy's emerging emigration bureaucracy. The specific articles directly address what at the time were "the most frequent damages suffered by emigrants[, which] concerned rejection from the United States, loss of baggage and delays in boarding."[41] While the earlier law functioned on the principle that emigration was a function of trade, by 1901 that view had shifted, paralleling a similar transformation in the United States documented by historian Donna Gabaccia.[42] Prior to 1901 the Ministry of the Interior handled migration, but the 1901 law moved these duties to the MAE and expanded the scope of administrative power significantly. Previously limited bureaucratic activities grew larger and more complex as the 1901 law established structures and channels for oversight and enforcement. A close examination of what historian Mark Choate called "truly historic social legislation" points to the evolving partnership between the United States and Italy, and the dynamics of these two sending and receiving nations who acted as partners in gatekeeping.[43]

Over an eleven-year period from 1888 to 1901 Rome moved from carrying out very general oversight to enacting a complex emigration bureaucracy that largely paralleled similar developments in the United States. Most significantly, the 1901 law brought American requirements and standards to bear on the entire process of transatlantic migration from predeparture to arrival. The law formalized the paperwork issued at the village level; funneled departures to official ports; and required transatlantic shippers to sail with a medical inspector and a doctor (typically a surgeon in the royal navy). All of this was to ensure that no one departed who was inadmissible to the United States by reason of poverty or physical or mental disease, but if a passenger was refused, the law required shippers to return, refund, and compensate them for damages. The evolution of Italian emigration law demonstrated by the two landmark statutes of 1888 and 1901 reveals the extent to which Italy became a willing partner in U.S. gatekeeping in this critical decade. The articles of the 1901 law show a clear response to U.S. policy and to the threat of additional restriction. At the same time, the two landmark Italian laws reveal how this was a new aspect of relations between the United States and Italy at the turn of the twentieth century.

While the 1901 law built on the general structure of reporting and enforcement first established in 1888, it also took some new steps that reflect the influence of American gatekeeping practice. A reporting system was created in 1888 to gather information on the conditions, with an inspector from the Commission for the Protection of Migrants stationed at ports to hear complaints against emigration agents.[44] Agents of the commission issued passports and the *nulla osta* document required to depart the kingdom, an official declaration issued by the local *commune* testifying the applicant did not have a criminal record that would otherwise bar them from emigrating.[45] The 1901 law expanded this oversight dramatically and moved it out of Interior, where the 1888 law had placed the duties, and into the portfolio of the MAE. The law of 1901 regulated the exit of Italians by creating a new oversight council, the *consiglio dell'emigrazione* or emigration council, to oversee the emigration commissariat at the heart of this new structure, with its broad enforcement powers to improve the "safety, reliability, and decency of Italian emigration."[46]

The law established new bureaucratic structures that nested within each other and had discrete roles. The council had thirteen members representing relevant ministries within the Italian government (Foreign Affairs, Interior, Treasury, Marine, Public Instruction, Agriculture); three academics from the fields of economics, geography, and statistics who were appointed by the king; two members whose credentials were to be a resident of the city of Rome; and two members who represented the views of the "Italian Cooperative Societies and the first aid societies of the major seaport cities."[47] In August 1901 Luigi Bodio became director, a position he held for three years, although he struggled to carry out the mission to which he was appointed. [48] Long-running power struggles between the government and shipping companies surged again. "Soon the hostility of the powerful interests of shipowners and those who chartered vessels for the transport of emigrants emerged . . . made the action of the commissariat difficult," with his work further challenged by a lack of staffing.[49] The emigration council and MAE leaders recognized that the commissariat desperately needed more staff to carry out its work, but additional funding never came, since the MAE tied this budgetary request with other amendments to an emigration law that failed to pass in Parliament. Meanwhile, "Bodio's management of the commissariat was subject to heavy attacks in Parliament that included those of a personal nature."[50] These attacks led Bodio to step down from leadership and into the role of general member of the emigration council in June 1904. By 1905, Egisto Rossi, the former chief officer of the Office of Labor Information and Protection for Italian Emigrants at Ellis Island, assumed the role of head of the council.[51]

The relationship between the two governments had by the beginning of the twentieth century propelled the growth of dual bureaucracies to manage migration. In Italy the 1901 law went beyond any previous statute or decree to regulate the places from which and conditions by which Italian citizens could legally migrate on Atlantic crossings. A new element appeared in 1901: the law funneled traffic to three ports that government agents could more easily oversee and manage and outlawed departures from any other part or aboard an unlicensed ship. The law allowed transatlantic migrants at three official ports only: Genoa, Naples, or Palermo. Article 23 of the law forbade ships from taking passengers from any other ports without the explicit permission of the commissariat, which would establish that the request was "in the interest of the migrant" and not the financial interests of the shipping company. The system of official ports allowed the Italian government to monitor and build up its emigration infrastructure over the next twenty-six years.[52]

The 1901 law methodically and strategically addressed some of the most common problems faced by transatlantic migrants that had been reported by the Office of Labor Information and the ambassador's consular network. It is striking how closely aligned aspects of the 1901 law are with the reports generated by Fava and the agents stationed at the Office. Parliament acted on the reports that had been coming out of Ellis Island and Washington since 1894, which described the interactions with U.S. immigration agents as those agents worked to interpret and apply their own national law. Two American barriers played a significant role in the Italian legislation's construction of its own emigration controls. Articles 18 and 19, discussing contract laborers and passport controls, repeated that the clear responsibility for the immigrant refused admission fell on the emigration agents and their employers, the shipping companies. In this way American authorities extended the duty to police its borders, effecting anticipatory remote control. If immigration agents rejected a passenger and refused his or her entry into the United States, the shipping company had to pay for the return voyage. If an emigration agent sold a ticket to a migrant who the agent knew was not "clearly and without a doubt entitled to land," in the words of the American law of 1893, that agent could be held responsible for not just the cost of the wasted ticket but also for costs incurred during the trip such as extra nights of lodging. Migrants had to show a valid Italian passport to depart the kingdom, and Article 19 prohibited ticket agents from selling a ticket to a person not already in possession of a passport. The same law required the MAE to report to Parliament once a year who was leaving the country. This meant the Italian government would now track who was departing, and Parliament authorized a new Bureau of Statistics to study the migratory record. These new border controls yielded to American demands for official citizenship documents while also establishing their own system for managing and studying emigration.[53]

Article 19 illustrates how an unforeseen problem that arose at Ellis Island and was reported by the Office was later solved through Italian emigration law. The Office's first two annual reports described migrants who landed at the island holding what were essentially worthless vouchers. These slips identified a person, usually a hotelier on the Lower East Side, who would provide tickets for train travel when the bearer appeared in person at that establishment. Both Oldrini and Rossi recognized this made migrants an easy mark for a swindle: the hotelier could claim that the ticket holder had to stay over in their hotel before continuing their journey, or even refuse to honor the slips.[54] Rossi called this practice "a disgrace" in his 1896 annual report, where he described innkeepers and bankers who made migrants wait two or three days in the city for prepaid tickets valid for travel to be delivered.[55] The 1901 law decreed that emigrants have valid train tickets for the destination where they were arriving. No other agent or company besides the transatlantic carrier, referred to in the law as the *vettore*, or ship carrier, had legal permission to issue train tickets. Only the *vettore* could legally sell train tickets valid in the destination country, unless the tickets were free, and in that case they should be given to the passenger at the time and place of arrival. Making this law allowed the Italian government to solve problems migrants were experiencing. Migrants arrived at Ellis Island with what they believed were valid train tickets that did not cover the cost of transfer from the island station to the nearest train depot in New York or New Jersey where they could actually catch a train. Confusion about the location of Ellis Island—on an actual island—gave nefarious agents room to take advantage. Once those stationed at the Office of Labor Information and Protection for Italians became aware of it, they moved to curtail the practice. In 1899 Chief Agent Egisto Rossi wrote in his annual report that he was able to prevent this by requiring the hoteliers and bankers to send the money to the office or to come in person to deliver it to the voucher holder. Rossi went so far as to suggest the MAE set up an accredited "train department" on the island, but no one took up his idea.

The 1901 law addressed with specific penalties a whole series of problems that migrants to the United States frequently encountered. Beyond train vouchers the law established a series of specific conditions for ticket sales as the authors assumed transatlantic transit companies had the worst intentions and would try to swindle passengers at every opportunity. Article 20 listed a series of conditions: if a ticket was sold abroad from a *vettore* for an emigrant who needed to depart from the kingdom, the law stated the recipient should expect to depart on the first steamer that was going to the ticketed destination, even if something else was written on the ticket. Under Article 20 shippers had to honor passengers' stated destination. This provision addressed cases where people bought tickets for their relatives who were then allowed to be the first in line to depart. The Ministry's commissariat for emigration would set ticket prices, and Article 21 forbade shippers or their agents from demanding money from passengers beyond the officially printed cost. In case someone paid more, he could get back double what he paid plus compensation for damages. If a migrant could not travel because of illness in himself or his family, he could petition for his money back. If the train transporting him to the port of departure was delayed so much that he missed the boat, then he could also request a refund. In these ways the 1901 law responded to practical challenges under the philosophy of *tutela*; Bodio described the commissariat as having been "created for the protection of emigrants."[56]

The law's protections extended to the days before a scheduled trip. Railway lines were obliged to return a migrant to his or her original departure station along with luggage for no cost, and transatlantic carriers owed migrants the replacement cost for lost luggage. Even if a migrant decided not to depart on a prepaid ticket—for reasons other than illness or a delayed train—he or she had the right to claim half the cost of the ticket be returned, including half the cost of prepaid food. Navigation companies were also required to pay for food and accommodation at the harbor up to thirty-six hours before scheduled departure. (To the modern reader accustomed to twenty-first-century discount airline travel, these protections seem quite generous.) In the case of delays in departure, the shipping company remained responsible for passengers' extra costs for food and lodging. If a traveler had not left his house but had a ticket, he could receive an allowance of two lire per day if he reserved a full seat (passengers could reserve a full seat [*posto intero*], half of a seat, or a quarter of a seat).[57] If the boat's departure was delayed more than ten days, the ticket holder was eligible to receive a refund and ask for compensation for damages. In case the trip was amended for reasons outside of the migrant's control or for reasons of quarantine, such as if the boat stopped unexpectedly in a harbor on the way to the destination, expenses for food and accommodations had to be provided by the *vettore*, the shipping company. If the vessel shipwrecked the *vettore* was obliged to send another boat to carry migrants to their destination.

Article 14 of the 1901 law gave the MAE the job of approving the price of a ticket. Every four months the Ministry would issue a price based on information sent by the shipping companies on their fleet, the quality of transport, accommodations available by class, speed, and frequency of traffic. The law prohibited agents from charging more and required shippers to extend any discounts offered to all passengers on a particular voyage in Article 14. Article 14 required ticket prices to be published at least fifteen days before going into effect. To prevent price fixing among the shipping companies, the local committees established by the 1888 law could intervene to sell tickets for the published price. In this way, the commission took the place of the ships' representatives in an effort to prevent shippers from defrauding or tricking migrants. Unlike the 1888 law, the 1901 statute included a distinct enforcement mechanism: companies who did not abide by the government-established published prices would have their licenses to carry passengers revoked or given to their competition. Repeat offenders could be banned from obtaining a new license. A provision allowed the MAE to revoke shipping companies' licenses for violations, which inspired some of the hostility toward the agency charged with enforcement, Bodio's emigration commissariat.[58] Recognizing the pull to bend the law in the face of lucrative and growing transatlantic traffic, the authors gave the statute teeth. In most cases, it seemed, the emigrant was very much protected from the vagaries of the journey and conditions on board and were regularly inspected. As if to demonstrate its commitment to *tutela*, the law gave many tools to migrants to seek compensation. However, to take advantage of the law's protections, passengers had to take action because even if one of these protected conditions occurred, compensation did not come automatically.

The 1901 law stands out for its exacting specificity compared to its antecedents and its responsiveness to conditions reported by the Office of Labor Information. Shifting penalties to the shipping companies instead of the companies' emigration agents was a major change over the structure of the 1888 law. This change also eliminated the problem that had shown itself during the struggle to enforce Article 17 back in 1896: it removed the need for interministry coordination to prosecute cases of malfeasance and eliminated the pressure that migrants may have felt when called to testify against their own village neighbors who served as emigration agents for misleading them. Now, the commissariat oversaw enforcement directly through its network of officers stationed at the three designated ports. Moving the responsibility for observing American gatekeeping law from low-level emigration agents onto the firms who transported migrants had long-lasting effects. Italian policy established the precedent that by the 1910s outsourcing enforcement to shipping companies would be the primary strategy of American remote control when the U.S. government "made private [shipping] companies partners in the execution of U.S. immigration policies."[59]

## Navigating "the Uncertain and Vague Provisions of the American Law Concerning Immigration"

Four years before the passage of the 1901 law, U.S. and Italian officials arranged a special meeting in Rome to discuss U.S. immigration policy. That U.S. immigration commissioner Herman Stump boarded a boat in 1896 destined for the Italian capital illustrates the distinctly transnational development through the relationship between the two partners in gatekeeping of border control policy. The trip began with a request. That September Prime Minister Marquis di Rudinì wrote to Fava. "Owing to the uncertain and vague provisions of the American law concerning immigration," could the ambassador secure clarification from the Treasury Department so the Italian government could better understand the parameters of exclusion?[60] Specifically, the prime minister focused on decisions made by the Board of Special Inquiry at Ellis Island and inspectors' interpretation of the language in U.S. law. He asked how the board specifically applied the immigration acts of 1891 and 1893, particularly what constituted evidence of "moral turpitude" and infamous crimes. "Kindly send . . . a concise statement of the principles by which the Board of Inquiry is guided in determining whether the provisions of the law above mentioned are or are not applicable."[61] To answer his questions Fava requested that his friend, Commissioner of Immigration Herman Stump, conduct an official visit to Rome, where he would be asked to provide information so officers of the kingdom could give "precise and categorical instructions relative to the issuance of passports in strict conformity with the legislative provisions in question." The State Department and the Italian embassy arranged the trip. The secretary of the Treasury told Stump, "From the assurances contained in this letter I am satisfied that this friendly Government does not intend to permit its subjects to violate our laws, and desires at the same time, by the refusal of passports to such as are liable to be rejected and deported, to prevent them from embarking on a fruitless voyage." He then instructed Stump to travel to Italy for the proposed meeting.[62] By October, less than a month after Fava requested he visit, Stump would be on his way to Rome.

On November 2, 1896, the king arranged a special council meeting for the visiting American immigration chief. The invitees included di Rudinì; MAE secretary-general Commendatore Giacomo Malvano; Chevalier Alessio representing the Ministry of the Interior; director-general of the Italian Bureau of Statistics, Luigi Bodio; and the New York consul-general, Chevalier Giovanni Branchi. Describing Rome as a "friendly Government," the commissioner-general of immigration gladly sent Stump as his emissary. Di Rudinì's government had asked the Americans to explain "the proper interpretation of certain provisions of our [U.S.] immigration laws" to decrease the volume of deportations and prevent the clearly inadmissible from leaving Italy in the first place.[63] Stump was asked to explain the specific convictions that barred an immigrant from entry and how members of the Board of Special Inquiry determined LPC exclusion standards, so that the kingdom's Interior Ministry could communicate this information through its network of prefectures.[64] With this specific direction officials would know whether or not to issue a passport to a migrant intending to travel to the United States. As traffic increased between Italy and the United States, the U.S. government found that Italy would be a partner in gatekeeping.

The Italian–U.S. relationship in the 1890s shows how "remote control" emerged as a key component of early gatekeeping, rather than as a later addition to the management of migration to the United States.[65] The United States needed the cooperation of the sending state to enforce its own laws. By 1901 the Italian government codified the partnership with the passage of the new emigration law, which fundamentally reshaped how Rome managed migration to the United States. This landmark law incorporated the observations of the ambassador and the Office's personnel and responded to the challenges of enforcement the Interior Ministry had experienced. It decisively addressed the several-decades-long debate over what role the Italian state should play in managing emigration. In the late 1890s Italy moved to anticipate American immigration policy and laid a secure foundation for key provisions of the practice of "remote control." The story of Stump's trip is particularly illuminating. Stump felt reassured following his meeting that October with the prime minister that Italy would work to enforce American gatekeeping law on its own territory. He told Congress "the [Italian interior] ministry expressed its earnest desire that persons who would not be permitted to land in the United States should be restrained from embarkation."[66]

The transformation from a law to "police" emigration rooted in the power to regulate public safety to the "Social law" of 1901 reflected powerful changes in Italian politics as the government reexamined its legal relationship to emigration. In the 1890s the Italian government sought guidance in applying U.S. law to act as partners in gatekeeping, using the United States as a model for its own development in affairs of economics, international relations, and migration. While the role of the U.S. example in economic development and foreign affairs is well known, I argue the period before the emigration law of 1901 also shows how critically and carefully leaders in Rome examined U.S. immigration policy.[67]

On October 6, a month ahead of his departure for Rome, Stump wrote a personal letter to the ambassador. "My dear Baron," he began in an optimistic tone. "I trust that our efforts may result in much benefit to our respective Governments."[68] Stump summarized the views of his boss, the secretary of the Treasury, to capture the commissioner-general's understanding of his mission. As fall dawned in 1896 both leaders saw mutual benefits in cooperating to manage migration. But it is clear from the letter that the relationship between the two went beyond the professional and had entered into personal territory. The men had clearly spent time together and enjoyed each other's company. "I will be much pleased to look after and take care of the Baroness should she sail with Mrs. LeRoy and me on the 'Paris' to-morrow," Stump wrote. "Will call on you this evening." He signed off with "Very truly yours, Herman Stump." In September Fava had sent Stump a copy of his government's request for more information about U.S. immigration law. He asked for prompt attention to the letter but hadn't wanted to delay it by waiting for translation. "Please, let my letter be translated at once, and give me a full answer accordingly." For the task he recommended that Stump employ one of the bureau's "several very competent translators of Italian."[69] Letters like these demonstrate how the ambassador worked directly with the Bureau of Immigration in a remarkably personal and intimate manner. Fava and Stump facilitated a partnership between the two nations that certainly bent the rules of formal diplomacy. They acted as conduits of information behind the scenes and later brought this information forward in a more formal matter to their governments, and they watched as their work influenced migration policy.

Herman Stump could not wait to issue a report to Congress. The commissioner-general of immigration had just spent three weeks at sea returning from his second trip to Rome in the span of two years. He met with a number of government leaders, beginning with King Umberto I, seeking to better understand how immigration agents interpreted U.S. gatekeeping law. Stump argued to Congress that other governments may do what the Italians have done to facilitate the application of U.S. laws, if Italians saw fewer deportations result from their efforts. He concluded his Senate report: "I have reason to believe that other Governments would adopt like measures in order to lessen the deportation of their citizens should the action of the Italian Government find favor with your administration of the immigration laws." Appended to Stump's December congressional report is a translation of a directive sent out to the prefects in the kingdom from the prime minister responsible for issuing documents needed to emigrate, clarifying the definitions of labor contracts and excluded persons according to the U.S. government and offering guidance on how Italy should interpret the law in specific cases.[70] Ahead of the 1901 law that codified aspects of these roles, Stump's visit to Rome offered concrete evidence of the partnership between Italy and the United States, evidence of Italy's willingness to use "remote control" to do what U.S. law demanded.

## Closing the Office of Labor Information and Protection for Italians

In 1899, as the Chamber of Deputies in Rome debated changing emigration law, Chief Agent Egisto Rossi's annual report to the MAE emphasized how much the American government benefited from Italian cooperation in gatekeeping. "We may say right here that notwithstanding the number of so-called undesirable among the Italian immigrants, it would be far larger were it not for the process of selection or weeding out, which takes place on the other side in consequence of the continual information furnished to the Authorities there by this Bureau."[71] Despite their efforts, though, migrants had continued to find their way to the United States without the proper paperwork. In August 1898 the Italian government expressed its frustration with those who evaded the *certificato penale* requirement put in place after Stump's 1896 visit.[72] Like the related document the *nulla osta*, the *certificato penale* was a legal document issued by the local prefecture. It testified that a migrant did not have a criminal conviction that would bar them from entry into the United States under the terms of the 1891 and 1893 laws. Before passports were required by law the *certificato penale* could sometimes be used to enter the country or to secure employment. Almost two years after the Interior Ministry tightened the procedure for migrants to obtain it and required them to produce the *certificato penale* to depart, chargé d'affaires Count Vinci wrote to his counterpart at the American embassy in Rome to express the Italian government's concerns about new cases of evasion. Italian emigrants who departed for America from ports outside of Italian territory did not have to show the *certificato penale* required to exit at an official port. Vinci underscored the strict controls around the *certificato penale* exercised at Italian ports, and his frustration at the ability of migrants to evade this law.[73] Drawing on intelligence collected by the Office, Vinci's correspondence again emphasized how from 1894 to 1899 the Office of Labor Information and Protection for Italians was the most important conduit for information to the Italian government about U.S. border control practices.

On the evening of June 15, 1897, a massive fire broke out on Ellis Island. The flames destroyed almost all of the station's buildings, including the main arrivals hall. When the Office of Labor Information and Protection for Italians reopened it was near the temporary processing station set up at the Barge Office on Battery Park, at the old Castle Garden. The fire fundamentally disrupted the work of the Office. From Rome Luigi Bodio lamented the loss of carefully prepared records that he had used to analyze emigration to the United States.[74] At the temporary Barge Office quarters Egisto Rossi struggled to carry on, even after he received a new typewriter to replace the one that burned. Yet the American authorities themselves had suffered a massive disruption in order that would lead to a major shift in the status of the Office.[75]

In April 1898, ten months after the fire, American officials notified Chief Agent Rossi that the Bureau of Immigration would have to close the Office. Other national governments had complained, calling the Italians privileged, and "not wanting to show any spirit of partiality the U.S. authorities found themselves obliged to put Italy, regarding immigration, on the same footing as the other nations," explained Vinci.[76] Vinci had caught wind of the impending message when ten days earlier Rossi sent an urgent telegram describing his plan to demand space to reopen the Office once this "unexpected crisis" had passed. He believed this was temporary, pointing to his belief that Italy was a willing partner in gatekeeping that the Americans would want to retain. Rossi was brief and still hopeful as he dictated these lines: "Unexpected Crisis explained other governments insisting to have the same privilege I hope to continue the office demanding a nearby room."[77] Yet over the following months it became clear that the immigration authorities had come to see the Office as not an aid but an interference.

This was no temporary crisis as the conflict with Washington continued to deepen. Beginning in 1898 the Office had a new enemy in the commissioner of immigration in Washington. In the spring of 1898 President William McKinley appointed Terence Powderly, the former leader of the Knights of Labor, to the position of commissioner after Powderly had worked doggedly to help elect the Republican in 1896. Powderly faced strong opposition at his Senate confirmation hearing but ultimately prevailed and took up the office in March 1898. He quickly began an investigation into corruption at Ellis Island and fired Assistant Commissioner Edward McSweeney, whom Fava and Oldrini had seen as an unofficial ally. Powderly's crusade stirred up accusations of partisanship that eventually cost him his position when Theodore Roosevelt fired him on July 2, 1902.[78] President Roosevelt later acknowledged he had unfairly dismissed Powderly and reinstated him in 1906 to the position of special immigration investigator. He traveled to Great Britain and Europe, and on his return he advocated for the expansion of "remote control" gatekeeping. In his view this would consist of U.S. agents sent to Europe to prescreen immigrants before they left their homes, travel with them, and coordinate the better distribution of migrants throughout the country. Notably, these suggestions, which were not implemented, echoed the 1901 Italian law and Fava's efforts to establish Italian colonies in the rural South.

Powderly pushed to close the Office. He argued that helping Italians with an office at Ellis Island would be an incentive for Italians to come to the United States and that would mean their surplus labor would reduce wages.[79] The commissioner and his assistant commissioner, Thomas Fitchie, viewed Italian migrants with suspicion. In private correspondence with Powderly, Fitchie expressed his belief that hiring an Italian American inspector would give migrants a friendly advantage they could use to avoid exclusion. He leaned into anti-Italian stereotype when he fretted over the "large numbers of public charges [that] would not be discovered, much less the murderers and thieves."[80] Powderly, moreover, was at least partially motivated by his fear of anarchists and the steadily increasing numbers of Italian arrivals.[81] Powderly did not have faith in Italy's ability to serve as a partner in gatekeeping. Motivated by his own prejudices as well as what he observed over his time as commissioner since 1898, by 1899 the Office became a clear target. He doubted that the Italian government could control its emigration, adding to the pressure on Rome to refine its own regulations. Powderly was "convinced that in Italy it was not possible to avoid the departure of the 'undesirable.'"[82] Moreover, while Italian authorities quickly and effectively moved to police their own ports, they could not control migration out of foreign ports, the majority of which did not demand documentation required by American law.[83]

The Office was, after four years of operation, dismissed as a mere "experiment" by the commissioner of immigration, much to the surprise of the foreign minister.[84] In the period of chaotic international relations that followed Powderly's appointment, his attacks on the Office (which the minister of foreign affairs called a "surprise") also led the Americans to describe it as having an "experimental" character, an understanding that was decidedly absent from the original 1894 charter championed in the Senate by Fava's friend and ardent restrictionist Senator Chandler. "The 'experiment' character of the Office was repeatedly stressed by the American authorities," and Fava, who saw the office as his personal creation, decided to suspend his leave of absence from Washington to rush back to address these new threats.[85] Fava turned his attention to Senator Chandler, "who at the time had shown him solidarity and support" for the Office and whom Fava believed to be an ally in the fight against Powderly's attempts to close it. As a result of their protests and the support they received from the Italian government, U.S. authorities temporarily abandoned their crusade to dismantle the Office.

But back at the embassy Vinci and Fava were suspicious of the Americans' motives. Vinci suspected that the Office would have to agree to new restrictions in its work if it were to remain open. He lamented that "perhaps it would be a matter of returning to the past when our agents could only protect those who had already disembarked and not those who were disembarking."[86] He worried the Office would be forced to shed its unique governmental authority, only able to conduct what he saw as the limited work of the immigrant aid societies. The struggle over the Office laid bare the new constraints on Italian authority to intervene at the site of immigrants' arrival following a period of cooperation at Ellis Island.

In April 1898 Vinci held a meeting in New York with American officials. His efforts paid off, but just temporarily; neither he nor Fava could stem the tide of pressure to close the Office then cresting in Powderly's immigration commission. "If in March 1898 it was possible, with some difficulty, to revisit the decision to suppress the Italian Office at Ellis Island," Laura Pilotti argued in her institutional history of the Office, "when the problem reemerged in substantially similar terms one year later, it soon became clear that this time the intentions of the American authorities were much more determined and clear."[87] In testimony to the U.S. Industrial Commission in 1899 Powderly called Italians "less desirable" immigrants.[88] He was moved to close the Office by "reports made to me from inspectors there that agents of this Italian Bureau would prompt [immigrants] to evade our laws," and even that Fava and his officers actively encouraged the padrone system.[89] These salacious accusations seemed to come from a curious man, Cesare Celso Moreno, who three years earlier had been convicted in a Washington court of libeling Fava.[90] In 1894 Moreno published a vicious article in the *Colored American*, a Washington newspaper, that led to the libel charge in July 1895. He accused Fava, Oldrini, each consul stationed in the United States, and the foreign minister of conspiring to traffic in white slavery and pocketing the profits. Fava, Moreno wrote in the *Colored American*, kept "the lion's share of the spoils." Powderly testified that Moreno was wrong about the padrone connection but correct about other accusations against the Office. Where Powderly repeated Moreno's claims against Fava, Rossi, and the conduct of the Office, historian Teresa Fava Thomas's research confirmed that "these were Moreno's libels." William Draper, U.S. ambassador to Italy, tried to come to the Office's defense. Draper questioned why Powderly would, under oath, enter the views of a convicted libeler into official congressional testimony, and how dumbfounded the royal government was by this.[91]

Rossi, also called to testify in front of the Industrial Commission, was clearly under duress. Through the questioning "it was apparent that the Industrial Commission was gathering evidence to close it" permanently.[92] Question: "We do not see why you have any right to do any business in the Barge Office." Rossi's reply: "No other nation has it, but no other nation has an immigration of our kind." When the commission asked, "What good has your Bureau accomplished?" Rossi struggled to conceal his frustration. He demanded that the members of the commission "be called upon to furnish proof of their charges" for the evasion of U.S. immigration law and offering assistance to padrones.[93]

Finally, effective January 1, 1899, the U.S. government formally shut down the Office citing jealousy of other nations. The chargé d'affaires explained the decision thusly: "That the American government having been from the other European Governments repeatedly requested to have the same privilege conceded to their desire, and not wanting to show any spirit of partiality found itself obliged to put Italy, regarding immigration, on the same footing as the other nations."[94] By then leaders in the Treasury Department and the Bureau of Immigration had dragged the closing out for a year and a half.

Rossi accused the Americans of committing an act of self-sabotage by forcing the Office to close. The *New York Times* had reported breathlessly about the Office's failure to combat the padrone system. On November 26, 1899, the paper declared "Italian Agency to Close" because it failed to "break up the padrone system and protect Italian immigrants from the sharps who waylay them."[95] But the Office had served as quiet enforcers of contract labor law "more than the Federal Authorities have any idea of" with its intimate knowledge of illegal labor recruiting practices and Rome's decades-long focus on emigration agents. "Were it not for the existence of the Italian Bureau," Rossi added in a special addendum to what would become his final annual report, "the evils of the Padrone System would be far more felt and far more pernicious than they now are." While American newspapers blamed the Office's demise on its inability to rout the padrone system, the Immigration Bureau did not want other countries to request the same privileges of direct oversight of the gatekeeping system that Italians had enjoyed since 1894.

The fight over the Office had strained the unusually personal relationship with U.S. officials that Fava and Oldrini had cultivated in the aftermath of the New Orleans lynching. (Considering how far relations devolved between 1891 and 1893, it is notable how much Fava was able to rebuild from this nadir.) Rossi and chargé d'affaires Count Vinci moved their attention to strategies to centrally manage migration from Rome. Read through a transnational lens, the 1901 law emerged in part out of the work of the Office and the fight over its closure. In 1899 Egisto Rossi reported from Ellis Island on the law then pending passage. His observations are evidence of the reorientation of his government to the emigration question, and a recognition of the importance of the binational partnership.

> As a means of obviating many of the evils above indicated [notably, the padrone system, banking abuses] the Emigration Bill, now before the Italian Parliament, may be considered of prime importance. The Bill provides for the opening of a Labor Bureau in connection with the present Italian Emigration Bureau at New York [the Office], and its object will be to provide work without the exaction of any fee, as well as to protect the Italian Immigrant from abuses. It also provides for the establishment in New York or a branch of one of the largest Italian National Banks, with sub-branches in the cities where there is a sufficient Italian colony. By this means that the Italians will be able to send their money home at fair rates and in the safest and most economical way, as well as being a sure deposit for their savings. But to make all this really effective, *it is most necessary that there should be the full cooperation of the American Government*, or, at least, of the State authorities.[96]

Rossi took to heart his experiences at the Ellis Island office, a place his mentor Luigi Bodio had imbued with great significance from the beginning. In a letter to Foreign Minister Blanc written one month after Congress granted the Office its charter, Bodio praised the effort and framed it as a serious and unprecedented venture by the government in Rome. "It has been twenty years that the Italian government thinks to implement an effective protection for the emigrants in America," Bodio wrote in 1894, seven years before he would assume the title of first commissioner of emigration in Italy, "but now is the first time that the Ministry of Foreign Affairs thinks and really does serious work for this purpose. I would like the work to be stable and long-lasting." He highlighted "the work of two men," Oldrini and Rossi, "who dedicate to it all of their time, all of their thoughts."[97]

### Conclusion

The decades-long debate in Rome over how to protect emigrants without actively encouraging more emigration had reached a turning point. Through the struggle to keep the Office open following the disastrous fire at Ellis Island in June 1897, and the equally disastrous appointment of former leader of the Knights of Labor Terence Powderly as the commissioner of immigration, the Italian delegation and by extension the government in Rome became convinced that the best way to protect migrants was through revising their own emigration legislation. The culminating effort, the comprehensive emigration law ratified in 1901, emerged in part out of the unique gatekeeping partnership between the two countries, Fava's investment in the Office of Labor Information and Protection at Ellis Island, and his personal relationships with men like Senator Chandler and Commissioner Stump. The 1901 law codified an Italian approach to managing its migration. Between 1888 and 1901 the scale of Italian emigration had increased significantly, with more and more people choosing the United States as their destination. Now an "exodus," emigration needed more regulation.[98] This approach was distinctly influenced by American gatekeeping and evolved along with the steadily increasing stream of people moving between the two countries in the 1890s.

So why would the U.S. government move to close the Office after it had been so successful in broadening the impact of American gatekeeping? Had it been too successful—was it too powerful a conduit, too obvious a partner? The series of attacks on the Office and its eventual closure led Italy to expand its oversight of emigration. With the Office closed by January 1, 1901, the emigration law of 1901 took over its responsibilities, although in a much different way, for the *tutela* or protection of migrants. This expression of what historian Maddalena Marinari called "compromise and quiet diplomacy" at the close of the nineteenth century was exceptionally nuanced.[99] Even though the Americans dismissed it as an "experiment," the Office had a lasting impact on the evolving gatekeeping relationship. It included the creation of durable structures in the form of bureaucratic institutions to manage migration as well as reinforced ideas about the management of migratory people between the two nations, in particular where they should go and what they should do.

The intervention of American immigration authorities and their growing distrust of the Office's operations ended what could have been a fruitful partnership. It was from this Office that Fava tested his theory of immigrant colonization to alleviate migrant overcrowding; it was through this Office that the Italian government negotiated with American officials and learned how to navigate its growing immigration bureaucracy. It was through the experiences with the Office that Fava and the MAE became convinced of the need for clearer legislation and a gatekeeping system to mirror that of the Americans. While the dissolution of the physical Office left a void, it proved temporary. In the end, the Office of Labor Information and Protection for Italians led to an even more durable gatekeeping partnership in the form of the 1901 law.

# The Arc of Immigration Restriction in the United States

Turn on the news or pick up a newspaper today and you will find stories about how the federal government has unleashed its formidable powers to control the movement of migrants. Customs and Border Protection officers who may doubt that you have a right to enter the country can use the vague yet wide-reaching rules of their department at their disposal to exclude you. After selling everything you own and enduring a long and grueling trip to arrive at the U.S. border, an agent of the immigration service can decide to send you back or separate you from your family. Actions during the Trump administration generated a vast public outcry in the face of images and reports of terrible cruelty at the border, catch-22 legal proceedings, and government-imposed limits on refugees and asylum seekers, legal migrants, and the entry of people without official papers. Mass protests, legal briefs, and even subsequent elections have not been very effective in reversing these policies.

Beginning just days after Trump's inauguration in January 2017, marches and sit-ins erupted around the nation objecting to the supposedly unprecedented nature of forced separation and detention, yet historians of immigration policy have seen the immigration state act in arbitrary and capricious ways continuously since the promulgation of the first immigration laws in the United States at the turn of the nineteenth century. Fast-forward to the turn of the twenty-first century, when presidents of both parties from Reagan through Biden have been complicit in the criminalization of border crossers.[1]

Tensions over the extent of government power to control the borders have defined the debate over immigration restriction since the very beginning. I argue we must consider Italian migration, and the asymmetric partnership that emerged between the United States and Italy to manage that migration, as an essential piece in the history of how the United States became a gatekeeping nation. While stricter application of the law gave immigration agents of the U.S. government more power to exclude, the pressure to more control the borders only grew in tandem. In the first eight years of federal management from 1892, when Ellis Island opened, until 1900, 25,642 aliens were expelled from the country through formal deportation, exclusion, and removals by officers of the Bureau of Immigration. For the period 1901–1910, that number jumped to 119,769. The following decade it surged even higher to 206,021.[2] In the early twentieth century, a Congress emboldened by the plenary power doctrine designed increasingly sharp tools that border control agents then wielded against growing numbers of migrants. When measures of qualitative restriction proved inefficient by the early 1920s, quantitative restriction became the law. While racist national quotas were dismantled in 1965, an increasingly complex system of qualifications and new legal categories took their place. The bureaucracy required to manage the millions of yearly applicants has also grown, especially since the attacks of September 11, 2001, spurred the dissolution of the old Immigration and Naturalization Service and the creation of a Customs and Border Protection agency housed in the new, sprawling Department of Homeland Security. The fusion of immigration control with militarization of the line dividing the United States from Mexico has raised border enforcement to a central and deeply divisive position in American politics.

While the particular methods for the exclusion of immigrants have shifted over time, the essential foundations of gatekeeping were established in the 1890s. U.S. immigration law has long been used as a tool of repression far beyond the undesirable Chinese or Italian immigrants who were the initial target of restriction in the 1880s and 1890s.[3] The practice of extreme judicial deference to the executive and legislative branches that insulated immigration law from substantive judicial review continues largely unabated. The view of immigration officers as border control agents tasked with protecting the nation from a foreign threat emerged simultaneous to the creation of the federal immigration bureaucracy. This legacy has colored the practice of immigration control to the present day. The early history of immigration enforcement shows how deeply embedded this view is in the bureaucracy itself.

Looking back to the winter of 1892, the first superintendent of the newly created Office of Immigration warned a joint session of Congress, "We can not shut our eyes" to the negative social effects of unregulated immigration. As Herman Stump told the legislators assembled that day, while less than one-third of 1 percent of arrivals to the United States had been refused entry between April 1, 1891, and January 31, 1892, this figure was artificially—and dangerously—low.[4] Using the rhetoric of invasion to emphasize the threat, Stump implored Congress to pass amendments sponsored by the newly created Committee on Immigration and Naturalization as "there have been many undesirable immigrants permitted to land, who," in the superintendent's view, "under a reasonable and proper construction of the laws now in force should have been refused admission." He questioned whether a quick on-site inspection at Ellis Island could reliably determine whether a migrant should be admitted as "the examination of from two to four thousand immigrants a day between the hours of 8:30 and 3 o'clock must be of the most superficial character, unreliable, and of little value." Not only was the existing law too weak, but inspectors struggled to apply purposefully vague clauses that demanded close judgment. Stump warned that under America's existing policies Europe was "thereby dumping thousands of the worst classes of European population upon our shores, to become a burden upon our country, a source of menace to honest labor, and an incubus upon society."[5] Even though the percentage of migrants excluded grew despite a temporary decline in overall immigration between 1894 and 1895, by 1896 increasing numbers of new arrivals seemed to give proof that Stump's warnings were coming true.[6] Italians made up the majority of the rejected.

In 1895 the writer Thomas Bailey Aldrich asked, "O Liberty! white goddess. Is it well / to leave the gates unguarded?"[7] Aldrich's poem captured an important question on the minds of legislators that also hung over the work of the agents of the new federal immigration service. The interplay between Congress, with its sovereign power to regulate who could enter upheld by the Supreme Court in 1893 in *Fong Yue Ting*, and the agents tasked with applying the law was an essential and evolving part of border control. By the mid-1890s immigration officers became more adept at identifying questionable cases as they fine-tuned their sense of the parameters of the statute. Still, their decisions were challenged for being either too strict or not strict enough.

As interest groups and foreign governments attempted to influence the shape and the application of gatekeeping policy, the leaders of the immigration service resisted the critiques of their work. In April 1894 Ellis Island commissioner Joseph Senner took to the pages of *North American Review*, the unofficial organ of the Boston Brahmins then leading the restrictionist movement, to praise his inspectors' ability to exclude the undesirable.[8] He highlighted "a notable and most beneficial improvement in the methods provided for their detection." Senner focused on the impact of Boards of Special Inquiry created by the 1893 Immigration Act as key to enforcement. Their results pointed to an effectively working gatekeeping system, Senner emphasized, as the boards offered a method by which persons suspected of violating the law could be more closely and carefully considered.

Yet despite these efforts to patrol the gates from the very beginning, powerful groups like the Immigration Restriction League in Boston and even officers within the system itself questioned its strength and efficiency in keeping undesirable people out. Between the superintendent of immigration and the Ellis Island commissioner, and from Ambassador Fava to the Office of Labor Information and Protection's chief agents, a bitter consensus emerged. The inspection system was too unpredictable. This had been Stump's concern in January 1892 when he testified for the first time in front of the newly formed Senate Committee on Immigration and Naturalization, less than a year after the assumption of federal control of American borders.

In 1896 the Immigration Restriction League amplified the concern first expressed by Stump in 1892 that "the present law places in the hands of one person too much power and responsibility."[9] His statement gets to the heart of the tension inherent in the structure of immigration law: the power deemed essential for agents of the system to carry out their work also hides their use of the tools of exclusion. From its origins the federal system of gatekeeping relied on the independence of immigration officers embedded within a bureaucracy endowed with a remarkably large degree of discretionary power. Inconsistencies in the formerly state-managed procedures (with variable levels of discretion) were initially carried over. Within only a few years new practices of the Bureau of Immigration became entrenched, and with them so did the language of containment and invasion that reinforced the need for even more discretionary power on the part of officials to limit increasing numbers of new arrivals. Superintendent Stump's descriptions of immigrants as a threat that needed to be controlled tied effective gatekeeping to the health of the nation at large using language that points to how, as Julia Rose Kraut has argued, immigration law could be used as a tool to contain perceived political threats. Stump's rhetoric is an example of how xenophobia has functioned in American history.[10] Fear of an invasion of undesirable foreigners, latent in the construction of the immigration system, expanded within an organization that often seemed strained to contain the threat it described amassing at the borders.

While the growing American practice of border control had its critics, these critiques still respected key aspects of the evolving system. After *Fong Yue Ting* upheld the right of Congress to create and carry out immigration law as a natural extension of national sovereignty, Italy never questioned the underlying rationale of federal management of immigration and its growing concentration of power in the hands of a small number of bureaucrats even as the Ministry of Foreign Affairs challenged the enforcement of the law. The plenary power doctrine had established a foundation for an increasingly powerful border control regime whose tactics remained largely isolated from judicial review. While Congress explicitly determines American immigration policy, foreign actors have long had a role in shaping U.S. gatekeeping.[11] The resistance that representatives of a foreign government mounted to gatekeeping policy had a discernible impact. Enacted through a binational partnership in gatekeeping, Italy's practice of anticipatory remote control illuminates the construction of the American immigration system.

The careful reports and frequent correspondence collected by the Italian ambassador reveal how Americans defined essential elements of their enforcement regime in the critical years after the courts upheld the principle of administrative authority in immigration enforcement. Instead of fighting restriction head on, the Italian government initially took the strategy of cooperation with U.S. policy with the intention to prevent further restriction, setting the stage for the expansion of "remote control" in the next century. An American newspaper praised Chief Agent Alessandro Oldrini in 1895 for his ability "to unravel many complications that might be insoluble without him and more thoroughly to protect the newly arrived Italian immigrants more than they have ever before been protected." The article then emphasized how Italian support for gatekeeping laws formed a fundamental part of this work. "He is as anxious to see the restrictive laws carried out as any of the United States authorities, for the simple reason that he realizes that in that way only can those Italian immigrants legally entitled to land reap to the full the advantages of residence in the new world."[12]

The discretionary power that the Immigration Restriction League saw concentrated in the hands of federal immigration agents in the 1890s has remained an essential part of the system of border controls since its founding. In the early 1890s an immigrant landing without enough money to pass inspection could provide evidence of an arrangement or solid promise of work through family members or friends. This promise was usually enough to gain entry. By the end of the decade, however, inspectors were rejecting such applicants under the grounds that their promised work violated the Alien Contract Labor Law of 1885, which barred the entry of immigrants with prenegotiated labor contracts. The second chief agent of the Office of Labor Information, Egisto Rossi, reported on shifting application of exclusionary law in November 1899. By this time inspectors sometimes combined two essentially contradictory immigration laws, LPC and contract labor, to increase the rate of rejection. "With these two conflicting clauses, the poor immigrant is very often placed between Scylla and Charybdis, notwithstanding the information sent out by this office as to the requirement of the immigration laws," Rossi lamented, alluding to his government's efforts to coach migrants through the changing American system.[13]

The Italian government "desire[d] to cooperate most heartily in preventing the departure for the United States of all persons inimical to its interests," Rossi emphasized as he struggled to help emigrants navigate the changing rules of gatekeeping.[14] One key tool had been the Office of Labor Information and Protection for Italians at Ellis Island, which even the head of the immigration service had praised in a report to Congress. In a sudden reversal just a few years later in 1899, U.S. immigration authorities ordered it closed even as Rossi carefully highlighted its effectiveness in enforcing U.S. law. "The co-operation of the Italian Bureau toward ensuring the strict observance of the immigration laws," a demonstration of Italy's efforts to partner with the United States in its gatekeeping in what Rossi called "the joint endeavors of the respective governments," had been enthusiastically praised by Stump in his report to the Immigration Investigating Commission as having "resulted in bringing to the United States a far better class of Italian immigrants."[15] While Italy had capitulated in part to the interests of the United States in managing migration, the U.S. government continued to act in arbitrary and capricious ways as it policed its borders, reinforcing federal power while also demanding the partnership of sending states on the United States' own terms.

The aftermath of the 1891 lynching strained relations between Rome and Washington to a breaking point that compromised the principle of reciprocity, yet within a few years the Italian government had assumed a new and unique position within the expanding federal immigration system.[16] Once the Office began operations on Ellis Island in the summer of 1894, and for the remainder of the decade, the partnership in gatekeeping offered an avenue to reshape the dynamic between the two countries at the same time as the United States moved to systematically exclude those deemed undesirable. "Much more can be said in demonstration of the usefulness and good work done by our Office, both as regards the immigrants and the Federal Authorities, with whom the Bureau has always been in most friendly relations," Rossi emphasized in 1899. "I will only say in conclusion that since I have been in charge of this Bureau, it has been my most earnest desire to accomplish, as far as the circumstances would permit, the objects, for which it was established, and to do all in my power to improve the character of our immigration, making the Bureau useful and necessary to both countries and particularly worthy of the protection and hospitality of the United States."[17]

Rossi's final words captured the essence of anticipatory remote control. Beginning in the mid-twentieth century Mexico also sought to cooperate with and navigate American immigration policy as a way to protect its vulnerable migratory citizens, and the power dynamics of Italy's relationship with the United States have shaped Mexico's attempts to negotiate with its powerful neighbor the terms over which it will accept migrants, and how those citizens will be treated. [18] The unpredicted effect of U.S. restrictionist law for Italians, also later observed among Mexicans, led migrants to root themselves in the United States and in this way acted as a restraining force as much on exit as on entry.[19]

Over time gatekeeping power would expand in ways frightening even to the original architects of the system in the 1890s. The 1934 case of an Italian man ordered deported on his return home from a vacation in Canada with his wife and three children for a crime of "moral turpitude" he was convicted of in his youth—stealing a small amount of coal to heat his family's home—pointed to a growing public frustration with the application of an arbitrary and punitive system of immigration control to groups beyond the Chinese laborers it was originally designed to exclude. The governor of New York pardoned the man, Nicholas Grisanti, for what the governor dismissed as a "little offense." "In a sense," historian Mae Ngai wrote about the case, "the protest against unjust deportations stemmed from the fact that European and Canadian immigrants had [by the 1930s] come face-to-face with a system that had historically evolved to justify arbitrary and summary treatment of Chinese and other Asian immigrants." But Italians had been the target of these arbitrary and capricious exclusions for decades by the time INS ordered Grisanti deported. "It seemed that the warning sounded by Supreme Court Justice Brewer's dissent in *Fong Yue Ting* had come true," Ngai mused. The case that established the state's authority to deport, Brewer worried, could be, in his words, "directed not only against the obnoxious Chinese, but, if the power exists, who shall say it will not be exercised tomorrow against other classes and other people?"[20] Long before this 1934 case the experiences of Italians at the U.S. gates illuminate the transition from Chinese to European exclusion.

From 1891 to 1901 the foundation of a modern system of gatekeeping was laid. Italy's 1901 emigration law further codified a particular relationship between sending states and the U.S. government, affecting foreign citizens who wish to enter, live and work in, and naturalize into this country. Since the late nineteenth century, sending states have consistently played an essential role in the tug-of-war between cooperation with and resistance to American border controls. Italy set a precedent for other countries to assume the enforcement of U.S. law through "remote control."[21] Yet what does it mean to be partners in gatekeeping, when ultimately the United States holds the power? From its very first days the American system of immigration control has been criticized from outside as sending states pass laws, change policy, and craft diplomacy in reaction. Indeed, changes in the law of one country have profound effects on the population of the other.

In one powerful recent example, in the 1990s Congress passed a series of laws designed to militarize the border with Mexico in response to increased crossings that stirred up a reactionary politics of fears. Operation Gatekeeper, which began in 1994, targeted the two largest crossing points, San Diego and El Paso, where 70 percent of migrants entered. That year Congress authorized a budget that doubled the number of border patrol agents at the southern border and appropriated millions of dollars to build secondary fencing along fourteen miles in the San Diego sector, which includes the busiest land crossing in the Western Hemisphere at San Ysidro, California.[22] In the summer of 2015 I walked this land with a group of migration scholars and Customs and Border Patrol agents.[23] We saw firsthand the legacy of Operation Gatekeeper, from the miles of fencing that continues into the ocean, to the massive complex funneling vehicular and pedestrian traffic into a series of checkpoints with, at that time, twenty-seven lanes for U.S.-bound cars and trucks and fifteen for pedestrians, more than I had ever seen anywhere else in the world. The U.S. and Mexican governments recently expanded pedestrian and vehicular crossing capacity even more. Customs and Border Protection built eight more vehicular lanes, and Mexico expanded southbound traffic capacity.[24] We saw logbooks tracking the mostly male migrants apprehended while crossing in the 1970s, and how this traffic changed as a direct result of the new 1990s policy that made migration more dangerous, difficult, and expensive. CBP agents described their work in paramilitary terms as they drove and walked us through miles of the no-man's-land between Tijuana and the rows of identical pastel stucco townhomes, massive gray warehouses, and big-box store parking lots that now occupy the southernmost swath of U.S. territory.

The most significant effect of Operation Gatekeeper was that it did not slow the flow of migration. Instead it diverted movement across the border with Mexico, reshaped the migrant stream away from single men to include women, children, and families, and inadvertently encouraged Mexicans to root themselves in the United States and cease what had been a seasonal migration, effectively creating a new generation of Mexican Americans and changing our relationship with Mexico.[25] We saw the results of this policy hundreds of miles away, where we held our seminar on the campus of UCLA, a setting that reflected the contemporary demographics of the city of Los Angeles. Beginning in the 1990s, "Mexican" became a byword for "illegal immigrant," an association that Donald Trump used to elevate himself to the White House in 2016. As president he pushed Mexico to take on enforcement and even detention of citizens of other countries seeking to enter the United States, a policy known as "Remain in Mexico" that the Biden administration has yet to unravel.

The militarization of the southern border beginning in the 1920s and accelerated in bursts in the 1990s and the 2010s actually increased illegal migration and the population of persons without authorization in the United States. At the same time, increasingly punitive border controls amplified fears of an immigrant "invasion," which has further warped the national debate over the law.[26] The long-term effect of Operation Gatekeeper has been to turn what had been a circular flow of men to three states into a permanent settlement of families across many states. A border mythology steeped in a need for gatekeeping remains acutely powerful despite the fact that most migrants are stopped today in airports.

What began as anticipatory remote control in the 1890s has evolved into a "cage of the rejected" far outside U.S. borders. Wide-reaching administrative power surely characterizes our current moment as the federal government has thrown up ever-increasing and confusing obstacles to stymie immigrants seeking lawful entry to the United States.[27] The roots of this strategy and its remarkable power stretch back into the 1890s. The history of gatekeeping viewed through the experiences of Italian migrants and U.S.–Italian relations between 1891 and 1901—from the New Orleans lynching and the establishment of a federal immigration bureaucracy to the passage of the 1901 emigration law—shows how this mythological "nation of immigrants" created a transnational system of immigration enforcement that continues to restrict the freedom to move.

# A NOTE ON SOURCES

Italian migration informed the practice of immigration enforcement in the United States at the same time Italy was building its own systems to manage a growing diaspora, as mass migration picked up dramatically in the 1890s with arrivals to United States peaking in 1907. Despite these critical connections, the literature on U.S. immigration enforcement largely skips over these binational nineteenth-century origins in part because of the limits of American archival records. A robust historiography on Asian exclusion has established the legal precedents that would shape Italians' experiences with immigration enforcement. *Partners in Gatekeeping* fills out this history that explains a common epithet at the time labeling Italians the "Chinese of Europe." This book fleshes out the transformation of the United States into a gatekeeping nation. Before the era of European exclusion, the United States began "sifting" new arrivals into desirable and undesirable categories. In order to do this, new systems had to be established, and Italian records tell us how. This evidence forces a reenvisioning of key concepts of gatekeeping and the practices of border control.

The origin story of the parallel development of migration controls in Italy and the United States has yet to be fully told largely because the sources detailing this relationship have remained buried in relative obscurity in the complicated archives of the Ministry of Foreign Affairs. The ASDMAE, as an archive of diplomacy focused on maintaining an official record, offers glimpses of the ordinary people who, by virtue of their appointed positions, had an extraordinary impact on the lives of migrants. In this archive I occasionally got glimpses into how diplomats in the period I study, and archivists in later decades, decided what was and what was not worthy of inclusion in the official record. Yet reconstructing the history of marginalized people through the records of those with power is a difficult, and worthwhile, exercise. This book is not a social history of migrants' experiences because so few of these documents survived. Further, the class dynamics between mostly poor migrants and the elite men who represented the Italian state shaped the evidence of their interactions. Seeing handwritten topics and words emphasized in Ambassador Fava's own hand felt like a window into his otherwise obscured thoughts. Fava's personnel record was lost, and he left behind no memoirs and few accounts I could use to reconstruct his life. The years I have spent reading the record of his work in Washington have given me the ability to discern meaning out of his one- or two-word notes or emphatic pencil strokes on the pages of a newspaper clipping.

Since 2004 the bulk of my research in Rome has been deciphering handwritten documents collected over Fava's term in Washington and figuring out the meaning in these piles of clippings and scratched-out report drafts, in the gaps and omissions. The haphazard nature of the record—few formal signposts exist in the record or archive organization—turned me into a detective. The arguments in this book are the result of more than nineteen years of critical reading in this archive. This book is not a definitive account of Italian migration history, or of the totality of U.S. gatekeeping in the 1890s. Rather, *Partners in Gatekeeping* is the first to use a rich and largely unexplored set of records to illuminate the history of the origins of U.S. border controls, expand our time line of remote control, and broaden our definition of gatekeeping.

# Italian Immigrants Admitted and Rejected at Ellis Island, April–May 1896

| Ship | Line | Arrived from | Total number of immigrants on board | Number detained on Ellis Island | Released after special exam | Returned to Italy | | Total rejected | Percentage of passengers rejected out of total | Percentage of detained ultimately rejected | Percentage rejected for LPC |
| | | | | | | For insufficient money (?) or lacking family [LPC] | For arriving under contract [violating Alien Contract Labor Law] | | | | |
|---|---|---|---|---|---|---|---|---|---|---|---|
| **ANNUAL TOTAL+** | | | | | | | | | | | |
| Fiscal year 1894–95 | | | 33,902 | | | | | | | unknown | 77.72 |
| Fiscal year 1895–96 | | | 66,425 | | | 977 | 280 | 1257 | 1.89 | unknown | 77.72 |
| **APRIL 1896** | | | | | | | | | | | |
| Scotia | Hamburg America | Havre | 60 | 36 | 30 | 6 | 0 | 6 | 10.00 | 16.67 | 100.00 |
| Caledonia | Anchor | Naples | 499 | 240 | 225 | 14 | 1 | 15 | 3.01 | 6.25 | 93.33 |
| Fuerst Bismarck | Hamburg America | Naples | 909 | 312 | 284 | 21 | 8 | 29 | 3.19 | 9.29 | 72.41 |
| La Bourgogne | General Transatlantic Company | Havre | 207 | 79 | 75 | 3 | 1 | 4 | 1.93 | 5.06 | 75.00 |
| Kaiser Wilhelm II | North German Lloyd | Genova-Naples | 806 | 246 | 229 | 14 | 3 | 17 | 2.11 | 6.91 | 82.35 |
| Bolivia* | Anchor | Naples | 1,376 | 593 | 525 | 63 | 5 | 68 | 4.94 | 11.47 | 92.65 |
| La Touraine | General Transatlantic Company | Havre | 157 | 50 | 46 | 4 | 0 | 4 | 2.55 | 8.00 | 100.00 |
| Alesia* | Fabre | Naples | 1,065 | 524 | 462 | 59 | 3 | 62 | 5.82 | 11.83 | 95.16 |
| Werra | North German Lloyd | Genova-Naples | 756 | 193 | 164 | 27 | 2 | 29 | 3.84 | 15.03 | 93.10 |
| Britannia | Fabre | Naples | 1,012 | 349 | 321 | 24 | 4 | 28 | 2.77 | 8.02 | 85.71 |
| La Gascogne | General Transatlantic Company | Havre | 222 | 89 | 83 | 6 | 0 | 6 | 2.70 | 6.74 | 100.00 |
| Elysia | Anchor | Naples | 972 | 253 | 326 | 24 | 3 | 27 | 2.78 | 10.67 | 88.89 |
| Fielda | North German Lloyd | Genova-Naples | 848 | 68 | 59 | 9 | 0 | 9 | 1.06 | 13.24 | 100.00 |

| Ship | Company | Port | | | | | | | | | |
|---|---|---|---|---|---|---|---|---|---|---|---|
| | General Transatlantic Company | Havre | 219 | 30 | 24 | 5 | 1 | 6 | 2.74 | 20.00 | 83.33 |
| *Neustria* | Fabre | Naples | 916 | 427 | 400 | 21 | 6 | 27 | 2.95 | 6.32 | 77.78 |
| *Ems* | North German Lloyd | Genova-Naples | 707 | 200 | 181 | 11 | 8 | 19 | 2.69 | 9.50 | 57.89 |
| *Belgravia* | Anchor | Naples | 1,547 | 598 | 558 | 25 | 15 | 40 | 2.59 | 6.69 | 62.50 |
| **MAY 1896** | | | | | | | | | | | |
| *Sergovia* | Fabre | Naples | 785 | 355 | 339 | 15 | 1 | 16 | 2.04 | 4.51 | 93.75 |
| *Braunschweig* | North German Lloyd | Naples | 845 | 256 | 239 | 17 | 0 | 17 | 2.01 | 6.64 | 100.00 |
| *Hesperia* | Anchor | Naples | 308 | 115 | 110 | 4 | 1 | 5 | 1.62 | 4.35 | 80.00 |
| *La Bourgogne* | Transatlantic General Company | Havre | 225 | 103 | 101 | 2 | 0 | 2 | 0.89 | 1.94 | 100.00 |
| *Italia‡* | Hamburg America | Naples | 1,099 | 312 | 284 | 24 | 4 | 28 | 2.55 | 8.97 | 85.71 |
| *Patria* | Fabre | Naples | 993 | 367 | 342 | 18 | 7 | 25 | 2.52 | 6.81 | 72.00 |
| *Chandernagor* | Co. F. Nazionale | Naples | 969 | 311 | 288 | 18 | 5 | 23 | 2.37 | 7.40 | 78.26 |
| *La Touraine* | Transatlantic General Company | Havre | 190 | 39 | 37 | 2 | 0 | 2 | 1.05 | 5.13 | 100.00 |
| *Alsatia* | Anchor | Naples | 963 | 377 | 363 | 8 | 6 | 14 | 1.45 | 3.71 | 57.14 |
| *Kaiser Wilhelm II* | North German Lloyd | Genoa-Naples | 921 | 206 | 191 | 6 | 9 | 15 | 1.63 | 7.28 | 40.00 |
| *La Normandie* | Transatlantic General Company | Havre | 164 | 7 | 7 | 0 | 0 | 0 | 0.00 | 0.00 | |
| *Burgundia* | Fabre | Naples | 954 | 416 | 401 | 8 | 7 | 15 | 1.57 | 3.61 | 53.33 |
| *Olympia* | Anchor | Naples | 698 | 153 | 146 | 3 | 4 | 7 | 1.00 | 4.58 | 42.86 |
| *Scindia* | Anchor | Naples | 1,010 | 264 | 254 | 1 | 9 | 10 | 0.99 | 3.79 | 10.00 |
| *Nerra* | North German Lloyd | Genoa-Naples | 833 | 172 | 166 | 4 | 2 | 6 | 0.72 | 3.49 | 66.67 |
| *La Bretagne* | Transatlantic General Company | Havre | 108 | 37 | 35 | 0 | 2 | 2 | 1.85 | 5.41 | 0.00 |
| *Massilia* | Fabre | Naples | 669 | 205 | 197 | 7 | 1 | 8 | 1.20 | 3.90 | 87.50 |
| *Chateau Yquem§* | Co. Gen. F. | Naples | 1,128 | 305 | 294 | 8 | 3 | 11 | 0.98 | 3.61 | 72.73 |

| Ship | Line | Arrived from | Total number of immigrants on board | Number detained on Ellis Island | Released after special exam | Returned to Italy | | | Percentage of passengers rejected out of total | Percentage of detained ultimately rejected | Percentage rejected for LPC |
|---|---|---|---|---|---|---|---|---|---|---|---|
| | | | | | | For insufficient money (?) or lacking family [LPC] | For arriving under contract [violating Alien Contract Labor Law] | Total rejected | | | |
| AVERAGE OR MEAN | | | | 33.32 | | | | | | | |
| TOTALS | | | 25,865 | 8,619 | | | | | 2.24 | 6.72 | |

Anglicized names and spellings: General Transatlantic Company (French), in record as Co. Gen.le Trans.c. Hamburg America Line (German) in record as Ambg. Am.

* Detained Italians aboard these ships described in detail in Thomas M. Pitkin, *Keepers of the Gate: A History of Ellis Island* (New York: New York University Press, 1975), 25.

† Rossi 2nd Annual Report, 2–4; returned figs. from pp. 9–12.

‡ *Italia*'s Manifest Identification Number was 58,121, and it arrived in port May 7, 1896. NARA code for passenger lists in AAD (Access to Archival Databases).

§ *Chateau Yquem* Manifest Identification Number was 82,778, and it arrived in port May 26, 1896. NARA code for passenger lists in AAD.

# NOTES

## Introduction

1. On March 17, 1861, Italy officially came into existence as a unified kingdom under King Vittorio Emmanuele II of Piedmont-Sardinia.

2. Alessandra Cavaterra, "FAVA, Francesco Saverio," in *Dizionario biografico degli italiani*, vol. 45 (Treccani, 1995), http://www.treccani.it//enciclopedia/francesco-saverio -fava_(Dizionario-Biografico). Unfortunately, Fava's personnel file is reported as lost. Inventario archivio del personale serie i diplomatici e consolari, Archivio storico diplomatico degli Affari Esteri, Rome (hereafter ASDMAE).

3. Francesca Loverci, "Il Primo Ambasciatore Italiano a Washington: Saverio Fava," *Estratto dalla rivista CLIO Anno* 13, no. 3 (July–September 1977): 241, extract in the library of the Centro Studi Americani, Rome.

4. Cinzia Maria Aicardi and Alessandra Cavaterra, eds., *I Fondi archivistici della legazione sarda e delle rappresentanze diplomatiche italiane negli U.S.A. (1848–1901)*, vol. 3, *Fonti per la storia dell'emigrazione* (Rome: Istituto poligrafico e zecca dello stato, 1988), xvi.

5. The American delegation in Rome likewise elevated its designation when Ambassador A. J. Porter reassumed his post that same year. On relations between the two countries during this period, see Daniele Fiorentino, "Gli Stati Uniti e l'Italia dal Risorgimento all'immigrazione," in *Gli Stati Uniti e l'Italia alla fine del xix secolo* (Rome: Gangemi Editore, 2010), 55–56.

6. See, among other works, Elliott Young, *Alien Nation: Chinese Migration in the Americas from the Coolie Era through World War II* (Chapel Hill: University of North Carolina Press, 2014); Erika Lee, *At America's Gates: Chinese Immigration during the Exclusion Era, 1882–1943* (Chapel Hill: University of North Carolina Press, 2003); Lucy Salyer, *Laws Harsh as Tigers: Chinese Immigrants and the Shaping of Modern Immigration Law* (Chapel Hill: University of North Carolina Press, 1995).

7. Aristide Zolberg, *A Nation by Design: Immigration Policy in the Fashioning of America* (Cambridge, Mass.: Harvard University Press, 2006), 9.

8. Aristide Zolberg, "The Archaeology of Remote Control," in *Migration Control in the North Atlantic World: The Evolution of State Practices in Europe and the United States from the French Revolution to the Inter-War Period*, ed. Andreas Fahrmeir, Olivier Faron, and Patrick Weil (New York: Berghahn, 2003), 195–222.

9. "The bureaucracy that had been developed to exclude Chinese," historian Elliott Young has written, "had by the early twentieth century become a much larger and more expensive bureaucracy whose mandate had expanded far beyond the Chinese." According to Young, "in the nineteenth century, almost all of the costs of the immigration bureaucracy came from enforcing Chinese exclusion, but by the early twentieth century the amount dedicated to excluding Chinese became a smaller and smaller portion of the total budget as the bureau began inspections for Europeans and others." *Alien Nation*, 132.

10. The status of "Remain in Mexico," officially called Migrant Protection Protocols, remains unclear. Priscilla Alvarez and Dan Berman, "Biden Administration Asks Supreme Court to Let It End Trump-Era 'Remain in Mexico' Immigration Policy," CNN, 30 December 2021, https://www.cnn.com/2021/12/30/politics/remain-in-mexico-policy -supreme-court-biden-administration/index.html. On Haitian detention in Cuba, see Carl Lindskoog, *Detain and Punish: Haitian Refugees and the Rise of the World's Largest Immigration Detention System* (Gainesville: University Press of Florida, 2018); quotation from Elliott Young, "Beyond Borders: Remote Control and the Continuing Legacy of Racism in Immigration Legislation," in *A Nation of Immigrants Reconsidered: U.S. Society in an Age of Restriction, 1924–1965,* ed. Maddalena Marinari, Madeline Y. Hsu, and Maria Cristina Garcia (Urbana: University of Illinois Press, 2019), 36. Young notes that in the four years following the passage of the Quota Act of 1924, 0.02 percent of immigrant arrivals bearing visas were rejected at the border. "By the 1920s, inspections and visa denials became the principal mechanism for exclusion, but after 1924 this process became institutionalized, and the Department of State officially assumed the role of gatekeeper" (38).

11. On the 1901 law, see Dolores Freda, *Governare i migranti. La Legge sull'emigrazione del 1901 e la giurisprudenza del Tribunale di Napoli* (Rome: Giappichelli, 2017); Maria Rosaria Ostuni, "Leggi e politiche di governo nell'Italia liberale e fascista," in *Storia dell'emigrazione italiana: Partenze,* ed. Piero Bevilacqua, Andreina De Clementi, and Emilio Franzina (Rome: Donzelli Editore, 2001): 309–19; Giula di Giacomo, "Dalla tutela alla disciplina dei migranti: la libertà di emigrazione alla prova della grande guerra," *Italian Review of Legal History* 6 (28 December 2020): 111–43; Corrado Bonifazi, *L'Italia delle migrazioni* (Bologna: il Mulino, 2013), 101–6.

12. Eiichiro Azuma, *Between Two Empires: Race, History, and Transnationalism in Japanese America* (New York: Oxford, 2005).

13. "Immigration as foreign relations" is the central premise of Donna Gabaccia, *Foreign Relations: American Immigration in Global Perspective* (Princeton, N.J.: Princeton University Press, 2012).

14. See Donna Gabaccia, *Italy's Many Diasporas* (Seattle: University of Washington Press, 2000). The scope of the Italian diaspora is immense. Twenty-nine million Italians left Italy between 1860 and 2011, according to Maddalena Tirabassi, "Why Italians Left Italy: The Physics and Politics of Migration, 1870–1920," in *The Routledge History of Italian-Americans,* ed. Stanislao Pugliese and William Connell (New York: Taylor & Francis, 2018), 117.

15. Campbell Gibson and Emily Lennon, "Historical Census Statistics of the Foreign Born in the United States 1850 to 1930," table 4, Region and Country or Area of Birth of the Foreign-Born Population, with Geographic Detail Shown in Decennial Census Publications of 1930 or Earlier: 1850 to 1930 and 1960 to 1990, https://www.census.gov/library /working-papers/1999/demo/POP-twps0029.html. In comparison, the population of Chinese in the United States in 1880, two years before Congress passed the exclusion law, was 105,465 with 99 percent living in western states and territories. By 1890 the census counted 107,488 persons with 90 percent living in the West; in 1900 the population decreased to 89,863 but became more distributed around the country with 75 percent of this number concentrated in western states and territories as some Chinese headed east or left the United States entirely. The effect on the population of the Geary Act, which was renewed in 1892 and became permanent in 1902, is clear from these figures. In 1910 the

Chinese population shrank even more, numbering 71,531 with a slightly smaller percentage, 73 percent, counted as living in the West. As historian Beth Lew-Williams explained, "For the Chinese, there was safety to be found in large numbers or in near-isolation, which explains why the Chinese in the United States emerged from the nineteenth century more isolated and segregated than they had ever been before." *The Chinese Must Go: Violence, Exclusion, and the Making of the Alien in America* (Cambridge, Mass.: Harvard University Press, 2018), figures and quotation, 224.

16. William Lerner and U.S. Bureau of the Census, "Series C 228–295: Population of Foreign Born by Country of Birth: 1850–1970," in *Historical Statistics of the United States: Colonial Times to 1970*, Bicentennial ed. (Washington, D.C.: U.S. Department of Commerce, Bureau of the Census, 1975), 118.

17. Rough calculation based on Tirabassi, "Why Italians Left Italy," table 6.4, 124.

18. Tirabassi, "Why Italians Left Italy," tables 6.5 and 6.6, 124, quotation on 129. Emigration within Europe, when compared to traffic to the United States, is similar. For the period 1896–1905, using official statistics compiled by Tirabassi, 1,890,943 persons left Italy for other countries in Europe (including Great Britain) while 1,306,083 departed for the United States. See tables 6.4 and 6.5.

19. Prejudice, fears, and stereotypes about the "padrone" system confined many Italians to "little Italies" and labor camps where their relative isolation played a significant role in fostering labor radicalism, which was often transnational in nature. See, for example, Marcella Bencivenni, *Italian Immigrant Radical Culture: The Idealism of the Sovversi in the United States, 1890–1940* (New York: New York University Press, 2014); Donna Gabaccia and Fraser Ottanelli, eds., *Italian Workers of the World: Labor Migration and the Formation of Multiethnic States* (Champaign: University of Illinois Press, 2005).

20. In the sixty-two years that Ellis Island screened immigrant arrivals, 2,503,310 Italians landed there. The second-largest group, migrants from Russia, numbered 1,893,542 persons, and the third-largest group were 859,559 Hungarians. Figures in Barry Moreno and Michael C. LeMay, "The Ellis Island Station," in *Transforming America: Perspectives on U.S. Immigration*, vol. 2, ed. Michael C. LeMay (Santa Barbara, Calif.: Praeger, 2013), 199.

21. "When we write transnational narratives of modern migration," Donna Gabaccia argued in 1999, "we produce a world history in which nations and nation states continue to be important constituent elements and explanatory forces." Gabaccia, "Is Everywhere Nowhere? Nomads, Nations, and the Immigrant Paradigm of United States History," *Journal of American History* 86, no. 3 (1999): 1117.

22. Ministero degli Affari Esteri, *Documenti diplomatici: Incidente di Nuova Orleans*, serie XCVIII (Rome: Ministero degli Affari Esteri, 1891–1902).

23. Marilyn Lake and Henry Reynolds, *Drawing the Global Colour Line: White Men's Countries and the International Challenge of Racial Equality* (London: Cambridge University Press, 2008).

24. Marian L. Smith, "Overview of INS History to 1998," U.S. Customs and Immigration Service, https://www.uscis.gov/history-and-genealogy/our-history/overview-ins-history/overview-ins-history-1998 (accessed 29 April 2020).

25. Salyer, *Laws Harsh as Tigers*.

26. Torrie Hester, "'Protection, not Punishment': Legislative and Judicial Formation of U.S. Deportation Policy, 1882–1904," *Journal of American Ethnic History* 30, no. 1 (Fall 2010): 11–36.

27. See Brian Balogh, *The Associational State: American Governance in the Twentieth Century* (Philadelphia: University of Pennsylvania Press, 2018).

28. Daniel Kanstroom, *Deportation Nation: Outsiders in American History* (Cambridge, Mass.: Harvard University Press, 2007).

29. See Azuma, *Between Two Empires*; Lew-Williams, *Chinese Must Go*; Madeline Hsu, *Dreaming of Gold, Dreaming of Home: Transnationalism and Migration between the United States and South China, 1882–1943* (Stanford, Calif.: Stanford University Press, 2002).

30. One exception is the work of Hidetaka Hirota in *Expelling the Poor: Atlantic Seaboard States and the Nineteenth-Century Origins of American Immigration Policy* (New York: Oxford University Press, 2017), which focuses on European exclusion based on poverty in the mid- to late nineteenth century.

31. Erika Lee, "The Chinese Exclusion Example: Race, Immigration, and American Gatekeeping, 1882–1924," *Journal of American Ethnic History* 21, no. 3 (2002): 37.

32. Freda, *Governare i migranti*, 5.

33. Zolberg, "Archaeology of Remote Control"; Young, "Beyond Borders."

34. See the essays by Dolores Freda, Lorenzo Prencipe and Matteo Sanfilippo, Giovanni Terragni, and Corrado Bonifazi in *Studi Emigrazione* 215 (2019).

35. See Betty Boyd Caroli, table X, Immigration to the United States, 1861–1899, and table XII, Italian Emigration, 1900 to 1914, in *Italian Repatriation from the United States, 1900–1914* (New York: Center for Migration Studies, 1973), 33, 38.

36. For more on this transformation, see Katherine Benton-Cohen, *Inventing the Immigration Problem: The Dillingham Commission and Its Legacy* (Cambridge, Mass.: Harvard University Press, 2018); Mae Ngai, *Impossible Subjects: Illegal Aliens and the Making of Modern America* (Princeton, N.J.: Princeton University Press, 2004), 11, 17–20.

37. Hirota, *Expelling the Poor*.

38. By 1901 Italy's cooperation with U.S. officials exemplified what Elliott Young defined as the "extraterritorial enforcement of immigration restrictions," a phenomenon that has only expanded in the twentieth and twenty-first centuries, where today exclusion happens more frequently in home or transit countries. Young, "Beyond Borders," 26.

39. See work by Elliott Young, Erika Lee, Lucy Salyer, and Beth Lew-Williams.

40. Kathleen López, "Gatekeeping in the Tropics: U.S. Immigration Policy and the Cuban Connection," in Marinari et al., *Nation of Immigrants Reconsidered*, 48; Grace Delgado, *Making the Chinese Mexican: Global Migration, Localism, and Exclusion in United States–Mexico Borderlands* (Stanford, Calif.: Stanford University Press, 2013).

41. Peter D'Agostino, "Craniums, Criminals, and the 'Cursed Race': Italian Anthropology in American Racial Thought, 1861–1924," *Comparative Studies in Society and History* 44, no. 2 (2002): 319. Beginning in 1899 the Bureau of Immigration began categorizing southern and northern Italians differently in its record keeping.

42. D'Agostino, "Craniums, Criminals, and the 'Cursed Race,'" 328–30.

43. D'Agostino, 320–21. See also Aliza Wong, *Race and the Nation in Liberal Italy, 1861–1911* (London: Palgrave Macmillan, 2006); Gian Carlo Jocteau, *L'armonia perturbata: Classi dirigenti e percezione degli scioperi nell'Italia liberale* (Rome: Laterza, 1988).

44. General James Rusling, "Interview with President William McKinley," *Christian Advocate*, 22 January 1903, 17, http://historymatters.gmu.edu/d/5575/.

45. Benton-Cohen, *Inventing the Immigration Problem*, 9.

46. See in particular the primary and secondary literature examining the views of Senator LeRoy Percy of Mississippi on race. Benton-Cohen explores Percy's role on Dillingham in chap. 5 of *Inventing the Immigration Problem*. On the race theory of the Lombrosians, see D'Agostino, "Craniums, Criminals, and the 'Cursed Race,'" 326, quoting Giuseppe Sergi's *Arii e Italici* published in 1898.

47. Ambassador Edmondo Mayor des Planches to Ministry of Foreign Affairs, "Ogg: Immigrazione," 12 April 1905, box 144, fasc. 3167, Ambasciata Washington 1901–1909, ASDMAE.

48. Giovanni Battista Scalabrini, *Il Disegno di legge sull'emigrazione italiana. Osservazioni e proposte* (Piacenza: Tipografia dell'amico del popolo, 1888), 49.

49. As the Italian case shows, "in order for the United States to consolidate its regime of immigration restriction, it had to rely on the collaboration of sending and transit countries," as Maddalena Marinari, Madeline Hsu, and Maria Cristina Garcia explained in the introduction to their anthology *A Nation of Immigrants Reconsidered* (13). The methods and results of anticipatory remote control described in *Partners in Gatekeeping* illustrate how "this interdependency highlighted the reach but also the limitations of U.S. influence."

50. Even during the supposed era of exclusion, from 1924 to 1965, Uzma Quraishi has shown how middle-class Indians and Pakistanis began to envision migrating to the United States after learning about educational opportunities from State Department–sponsored information centers and speaking tours, both Cold War tools of public diplomacy. Quraishi's research in Houston's South Asian community shows how, as selective processes, gatekeeping and migration control decisions reverberated through immigrants' lives for decades after their arrival. This is a reminder of how important it is for historians to pay close attention to the mechanisms for selection unfolding through foreign policy across national borders. Uzma Quraishi, *Redefining the Immigrant South: Indian and Pakistani Immigration to Houston during the Cold War* (Chapel Hill: University of North Carolina Press, 2020).

51. Since the publication of Mae Ngai's *Impossible Subjects* in 2004, a distinct subfield dedicated to the study of immigration policy has emerged, and as of late much work has focused on the ideological paradox of restriction in a country seen as welcoming to immigrants. Recent scholarship has examined the complex ways groups subject to restriction responded both domestically and diplomatically. Books by Maddalena Marinari, Danielle Battisti, and Jane Hong reexamine the so-called era of exclusion to find evidence in the mid-twentieth century of how targeted groups, particularly Italian, Jewish, and Asian Americans, lobbied against restrictive law, although, as Marinari has shown, their efforts were shaped by the hierarchies imposed by earlier prohibitions on naturalization. Jane Hong, *Opening the Gates to Asia: A Transpacific History of How America Repealed Asian Exclusion* (Chapel Hill: University of North Carolina Press, 2020); Maddalena Marinari, *Unwanted: Italian and Jewish Mobilization against Restrictive Immigration Laws, 1882–1965* (Chapel Hill: University of North Carolina, 2019); Danielle Battisti, *Whom Shall We Welcome: Italian Americans and Immigration Reform, 1945–1965* (New York: Fordham University Press, 2019).

52. Alessandro Oldrini to Baron Saverio Fava, report no. 80, "Relazione dell'ufficio ital. colle autorità Americane e l'emigrazione," 1 December 1894, p. 3, box 113, Rappresentanze diplomatiche italiane negli USA (1848–1901), ASDMAE (hereafter cited as RDI).

53. The U.S.–Italian relationship establishes another important antecedent, setting up a pathway to the United States of lobbying to influence immigration policy that will come to full fruition in the mid-twentieth century. See Marinari, *Unwanted*; Battisti, *Whom Shall We Welcome*.

54. Egisto Rossi, "2.0 Rapporto annuale, dal 30 giugno 1895 al 30 giugno 1896 [2nd Annual Report from the Office of Labor Information and Protection, from 30 June 1895 to 30 June 1896]," 10 September 1896, p. 7, box 111, RDI (hereafter "2nd Annual Report").

55. In this period the prime minister also served as minister of the interior.

56. "The Detained Immigrant," *Harper's Weekly*, 26 August 1893.

57. First introduced in 1896, a literacy test was finally adopted in 1917 over President Wilson's veto. For more on the literacy test debate in Congress, see Benton-Cohen, *Inventing the Immigration Problem*. For more on the history of poverty as a reason for exclusion, see Hirota, *Expelling the Poor*.

58. Jessica Barbata Jackson examines the history of people she calls "Sicilians and other Italians" who migrated voluntarily to the nearby Gulf South region. While scattered histories of Italians in the South exist, the vast majority of the literature focuses on the experiences of Italians elsewhere in the United States. Jessica Barbata Jackson, *Dixie's Italians: Sicilians, Race, and Citizenship in the Jim Crow South* (Baton Rouge: Louisiana State University Press, 2020).

59. Sociologist of migration David Fitzgerald defined the nation-state as "the organizational fusion of a territory, a government, and a people," in *A Nation of Emigrants: How Mexico Manages its Migration* (Berkeley: University of California Press, 2009), 15. Caroline Douki discussed how the Italian state created and then exercised its official power to study its migratory population as a tool to legitimize that state in "The Italian State and Mass Emigration: 1860–1914," in *Citizenship and Those Who Leave*, ed. Nancy L. Green and François Weil (Urbana: University of Illinois Press, 2007), 91–113, esp. 92–95.

60. Benton-Cohen, *Inventing the Immigration Problem*, 200. This perception traces back to the Dillingham era. Commission experts Jeremiah Jenks and W. Jett Lauck's 1913 book based on their research, which they called "the Immigration Problem," called Italian immigration to the South "relatively numerically unimportant." Jenks and Lauck, *The Immigration Problem: A Study of American Immigration Conditions and Needs* (New York: Funk & Wagnalls, 1913), 85.

61. Fitzgerald, *Nation of Emigrants*, 15.

62. Nancy Green and François Weil, "Introduction," in *Citizenship and Those Who Leave*, 8.

63. Rossi, "2nd Annual Report," 4, 6, quotation on 7.

64. See Ostuni, "Leggi e politiche di governo," 314–15.

65. See Freda, *Governare i migranti*; Bonifazi, *L'Italia delle migrazioni*. The "social law" of 1901 shifted the government's role in allowing what Dolores Freda has called the "freedom to emigrate" to "the freedom of letting people emigrate."

66. Daniele Fiorentino, *Gli Stati Uniti e il Risorgimento d'Italia 1848–1901* (Rome: Gangemi Editore, 2013), characterizing the relationship between the nations in this period. Notably, the management of migration became a tool in this effort.

67. This book builds on the transnational work of scholars like Elliott Young and Kelly Lytle Hernandez to uncover the functions of border and remote control. Kelly Lytle Hernandez, *Migra!: A History of the U.S. Border Patrol* (Berkeley: University of California Press, 2010); Young, *Alien Nation*.

## Chapter 1. The Murder of David Hennessy and Its Aftermath

1. Throughout this chapter I will refer to Sicilians and Italians using these terms as they were used by English-language sources who collapsed the significant differences of identity and language between Sicilian dialect speakers from the island and Italian speakers in the decades just following unification, between 1861 and 1871. While this chapter does not seek to examine Italian identity explicitly, it considers the relationship between the project to create a unified Italy and the related racialized stereotypes that the lynching and newspaper coverage promulgated in the early 1890s.

2. Quoted in Tom Smith, *The Crescent City Lynchings: The Murder of Chief Hennessy, the New Orleans "Mafia" Trials, and the Parish Prison Mob* (Guilford, Conn.: Lyons, 2007), 99.

3. Patrizia Salvetti, *Corda e sapone: Storie di linciaggi degli italiani negli Stati Uniti* (Rome: Donzelli Editore, 2003), 12, published in English as *Rope and Soap: Lynchings of Italians in the United States*, trans. Fabio Girelli-Carasi (New York: Bordighera Press, 2017); Daniele Fiorentino, *Gli Stati Uniti e il Risorgimento d'Italia 1848–1901* (Rome: Gangemi Editore, 2013), 296.

4. Smith's *Crescent City Lynchings* offers the most detailed version of the trial.

5. Letter from U.S. Attorney Grant to Attorney General Miller, 27 April 1891, reproduced in *Correspondence in Relation to the Killing of Prisoners in New Orleans on March 14, 1891* (Washington, D.C.: Department of State, 1891).

6. Charles Mantranga, Bastian Incardona, and Gaspare Marchese, age fourteen and tried alongside his father Antonio, were acquitted but escaped the lynch mob by hiding within the jail.

7. The acquitted victims were Antonio Marchese (pseudonym for Antonio Grimando), Joseph Macheca, and Antonio Abbagnato. Lynched men Pietro Monastero, Emanuele Polizzi, and Antonio Scalfidi had their cases declared a mistrial. The remaining five victims were still awaiting trial: Girolamo (James) Caruso, Loreto Comitis, Rocco Geraci, Frank Romero, and Vincenzo (Charles) Traina. Note that errors in the spelling of the victims' names, some of which are egregious (for instance, *Smith's Crescent City* Lynchings [2007] lists Antonio Abbagnato as Antonio Bagnetto), have carried over across various English-language sources. For more on the presence or absence of criminal records for the nine already tried, see Salvetti, *Corda e sapone*, 13.

8. The Committee of Fifty (or the Committee of the Fifty) was organized by Mayor Joseph Shakspeare to investigate the murder of Chief of Police David Hennessy. Telegram, Consul Pasquale Corte to Ambassador Fava, 14 March 1891, translated and reproduced in *Correspondence in Relation to the Killing of Prisoners*, 14.

9. The next day Corte described this scene to Fava: "I saw many dead bodies on the trees, [signaling] that the massacre was over and the crowd was returning. Coming to the consulate, at the door three Black men rushed against me and, to keep them off, I had to draw my revolver. A moment later came Mr. Papini, secretary of the consulate, all pale and frightened, and told me that, having heard in the crowd cries of *kill the Italian* directed at him, he had to take refuge inside a store." Corte to Fava, 15 March 1891, *Documenti diplomatici serie XCVIII incidente di Nuova Orleans 1891–1902, confidenziale* (Rome: Tipografia del Ministero degli Affari Esteri, n.d.), 5–6, ASDMAE. All translations from Italian are by the author unless otherwise noted.

10. "A Nation of Murderers," *Washington Post*, 18 April 1891.

11. Henry Cabot Lodge (R) represented Massachusetts in the House of Representatives from 1889 to 1893, when he ascended to the Senate. He later became a member of the Immigration Restriction League.

12. Henry Cabot Lodge, "Lynch Law and Unrestricted Immigration," *North American Review*, May 1891, 602–4.

13. U.S. Congress, House, Select Committee on Immigration and Naturalization, *Report*, 51st Congress, 2d session (1891), ii, quoted in Lucy Salyer, *Laws Harsh as Tigers: Chinese Immigrants and the Shaping of Modern Immigration Law* (Chapel Hill: University of North Carolina Press, 1995), 26.

14. Hidetaka Hirota, *Expelling the Poor: Atlantic Seaboard States and the Nineteenth-Century Origins of American Immigration Policy* (New York: Oxford University Press, 2017); Torrie Hester, *Deportation: The Origins of U.S. Policy* (Philadelphia: University of Pennsylvania Press, 2017); Salyer, *Laws Harsh as Tigers*.

15. *Chap. 551: An Act in Amendment to the Various Acts Relative to Immigration and the Importation of Aliens under Contract or Agreement to Perform Labor, U.S. Statutes at Large* 26 (1891): 1084–86.

16. The Supreme Court upheld the constitutionality of the law in 1893. Salyer, *Laws Harsh as Tigers*, 26. Historian Patricia Russell Evans, in her comprehensive dissertation on the application of early immigration law to those deemed "likely to become a public charge," gives a useful definition of administrative authority in this context. Evans cites Kenneth Culp Davis, *Administrative Law Treatise*, 2nd ed., 5 vols. (San Diego: K. C. Davis, 1978), 1:1, as a foundation of her definition. What she describes as "the disproportionate influence of agency officials" had a profound effect on immigration law enforcement. "Administrative law is the law concerning the powers and procedures of administrative agencies, including especially the law governing judicial review of administrative action. . . . More simply, it is the law governing those who administer governmental activities. It excludes the mass of substantive law that agencies produce. . . . It is concerned with the machinery of government." Patricia Russell Evans, "'Likely to Become a Public Charge': Immigration in the Backwaters of Administrative Law, 1882–1933" (PhD diss., George Washington University, 1987), 239–40.

17. Fiorentino, *Gli Stati Uniti e il Risorgimento d'Italia*, 293–300.

18. "Nation of Murderers," *Washington Post*. This kind of language echoed in Donald Trump's presidential announcement speech, delivered 16 June 2015, when he broadly described Mexicans as rapists and murderers.

19. Lodge, "Lynch Law and Unrestricted Immigration," 604.

20. See also Jessica Barbata Jackson, *Dixie's Italians: Sicilians, Race, and Citizenship in the Jim Crow South* (Baton Rouge: Louisiana State University Press, 2020). For more on newspapers' role in responding to these challenges, see Peter Vellon, *A Great Conspiracy against Our Race: Italian Immigrant Newspapers and the Construction of Whiteness in the Early Twentieth Century* (New York: New York University Press, 2014). For an analysis of 1891 lynching coverage that draws different conclusions, see Charles Seguin and Sabrina Nardin, "The Lynching of Italians and the Rise of Antilynching Politics in the United States," *Social Science History* 46 (Spring 2022): 65–91. Their keyword-based quantitative study attempted in part to uncover what they call "civilization discourse." They looked at three papers outside of the Southeast and language used by "political elites," such as State of the Union addresses and diplomatic correspondence. Although it is discussed as examined, little is actually cited from ASDMAE. "This language, which we call 'civilization

discourse,' drew from imperialist themes, casting the violence of lynching as indicative of 'lower civilization' or 'savagery,' as opposed to the 'higher [White] civilization' to which most of the United States supposedly belonged." In their study, Seguin and Nardin sought out instances of this language when it was applied to the lynch mobs and not to the victims (69–70).

21. "The New-Orleans Affair," *New York Times*, 16 March 1891; "Mafia Murderers Slain," *Chicago Daily Tribune*, 15 March 1891.

22. Cartoon described in Salvetti, *Rope and Soap*, 60. The years after the lynching, following what Daniele Fiorentino called the "partial resolution" of the New Orleans crisis, as well as the Panic of 1893, revealed for Italy the stark "differences between them that had always marked the two aspiring powers." Italy was focused on its imperial ambitions on Africa, where it met with little success, while the United States expanded its sphere of influence in the Caribbean and Asia Pacific through the acquisition of formerly Spanish colonial territories. Fiorentino, *Gli Stati Uniti e il Risorgimento d'Italia*, 295.

23. Fiorentino, *Gli Stati Uniti e il Risorgimento d'Italia*, 299–300.

24. This strategy would be used to greater effect to try to control the movement of men of draft age during World War I. See the essay by Matteo Pretelli in *Managing Migration in Italy and the United States*, ed. Lauren Braun-Strumfels, Maddalena Marinari, and Daniele Fiorentino (forthcoming, DeGruyter).

25. On Italy and the United States emerging on the world stage, see Fiorentino, *Gli Stati Uniti e il Risorgimento d'Italia*, 239–44; Giampaolo Ferraioli, *L'Italia e l'ascesa degli Stati Uniti a rango di potenza mondiale* (Napoli: Edizioni Scientifiche Italiane, 2013), 101–19.

26. Salyer, *Laws Harsh as Tigers*, 27.

27. Saverio Fava, "Rapporto Bill Dolph," 20 August 1892, box 109, pos. 152, fasc. II Q, RDI.

28. Hirota's *Expelling the Poor* focuses on two examples of state-level management of poor immigrants in the era before 1891.

29. Republican and Democratic Party planks quoted in Senator William P. Dillingham, *Reports of the Immigration Commission: Immigration Legislation*, 61st Congress, 3rd session (Washington, D.C.: Government Printing Office, 1911), 41. The Democrats made a more careful distinction designed to protect organized labor. Their plank continued: "We demand the rigid enforcement of the laws against Chinese immigration, or the importation of foreign workmen [*sic*] under contract, to degrade American labor and lessen its wages, but we condemn and denounce any and all attempts to restrict the immigration of the industrious and worthy of foreign lands."

30. See Marilyn Lake and Henry Reynolds, *Drawing the Global Colour Line: White Men's Countries and the International Challenge of Racial Equality* (London: Cambridge University Press, 2008); David Fitzgerald and David Cook-Martin, *Culling the Masses: The Democratic Origins of Racist Immigration Policy in the Americas* (Cambridge, Mass.: Harvard University Press, 2014).

31. Yet the lynching has been examined in a way that misses this profound connection to immigration policy. Jessica Barbata Jackson, in *Dixie's Italians*, uses the lynching as a way to examine race politics and the racialization of "Sicilians and other Italians" at the turn of the century in the states she calls the Gulf South: Louisiana, Mississippi, and Alabama. She looks at U.S.-Italian relations through the lens of lynchings in these states from 1891 through 1910 using the State Department's official record of Italian correspondence in English, missing the rich context of diplomats' backchannel and internal com-

munications with Rome. Patrizia Salvetti's *Corda e Sapone*, published in English as *Rope and Soap*, frames New Orleans in comparison to other U.S. locations of Italian lynchings or near-lynchings. The essays in *The 1891 Lynching and U.S.–Italian Relations: A Look Back* remember the lynching through alternative forms such as memoir in addition to archivally based research. These two books rely at least in part on diplomatic documents to construct a history of the lynching. See Salvetti, *Corda e Sapone*, and Marco Rimanelli and Sheryl Postman, eds., *The 1891 Lynching and U.S.–Italian Relations: A Look Back* (New York: Peter Lang, 1992).

Outside of a few short pieces, most of the literature on the lynching is problematic and sensationalized. An encyclopedia article by historian Justin Nystrom offers a summary of the known facts of the case but is limited in scope. Justin Nystrom, "Sicilian Lynchings in New Orleans," in *Know Louisiana: The Digital Encyclopedia of Louisiana* (Louisiana Endowment for the Humanities, 2013), http://www.knowlouisiana.org/entry/sicilian -lynchings-in-new-orleans (accessed 12 March 2018). The lynching receives some treatment in Nystrom's history of New Orleans, but his book on Sicilian foodways in the city makes a case for not examining it. Nystrom, *New Orleans after the Civil War: Race, Politics, and a New Birth of Freedom* (Baltimore: Johns Hopkins University Press, 2010), esp. 220–24; Nystrom, *Creole Italian: Sicilian Immigrants and the Shaping of New Orleans Food Culture* (Athens: University of Georgia Press, 2018).

Two of the most cited works are Richard Gambino, *Vendetta: A True Story of the Worst Lynching in America, the Mass Murder of Italian-Americans in New Orleans in 1891, the Vicious Motivations behind It, and the Tragic Repercussions That Linger to This Day (Garden City, NY: Doubleday)*, published in 1977 and the basis for a 1999 HBO movie, and Tom Smith's *Crescent City Lynchings*. Both include bibliographies but lack footnotes, in addition to other problems, yet are still widely cited. Smith's book describes conversations with the Italian consul that I have found impossible to verify with extant sources, despite a note on the copyright page stating, "All dialogue appearing in this book is taken from accounts contemporary with the events." Two articles published in *Louisiana History* in the 1930s argued Sicilian Mafia wars were to blame for Hennessy's murder: John S. Kendall, "'Who Killa Da Chief?'" *Louisiana Historical Quarterly* 22 (1939): 492–530; John E. Coxe, "The New Orleans Mafia Incident," *Louisiana Historical Quarterly* 20 (1937): 1067– 110. This explanation has been reexamined by contemporary scholars and authors who have found scant evidence to support this claim, although the original articles are still cited without qualifiers by some more recent accounts, notwithstanding legal scholar John Baiamonte Jr.'s explicit revision published in 1992, "'Who Killa de Chief' Revisited: The Hennessey Assassination and Its Aftermath, 1890–1991," *Louisiana History* 33, no. 2 (Spring 1992): 117–46.

Beyond Barbata Jackson's examination of debates over Italians in miscegenation and voting law, other recent scholarly work frames the lynching in the context of southern U.S. and, more unusually, Central and South American history, and also places the lynching as the inflection point in an emerging international anti-lynching campaign. While the effects on diplomacy and the role of international relations are elements of Seguin and Nardin's analysis, ultimately their view of these aspects is tightly woven into their research focus on what they call "lynching politics." See Seguin and Nardin's 2022 article, "The Lynching of Italians and the Rise of Antilynching Politics," in *Social Science History*. In 2017 historian Sarah Fouts examined coverage of the lynching in the international

Spanish-language press in an article that focused largely on transnational patterns of racialization and critiques of U.S. imperialism stemming from the murders in "The Mafia, La Raza, and the Spanish-Language Press Coverage of the 1891 Lynchings in New Orleans," *Journal of Southern History* 83, no. 3 (August 2017): 509–31. Building on the transnational focus of Fouts, and expanding on Barbata Jackson's domestic lens, this chapter offers a corrective to the literature on the lynching, which tends to focus on the crime's local causes and cultural impact and leaves out the powerful repercussions in Italian diplomatic relations that shaped U.S. immigration policy on the eve of mass restriction.

32. Most historians and popular authors have placed the blame for the murder on openly warring factions within the Democratic Party that Chief Hennessy had been stoking in the years prior to his death.

33. "Exterminating the Mafia. Pictorial Account of the Work of Judge Lynch in New Orleans," *Illustrated American*, 4 April 1891, listed E. H. Farrar, "President, committee of Law and Order," as author of the notice quoted above.

34. Salvetti, *Rope and Soap*, 51.

35. According to the NAACP, 73 percent of victims were Black while 27 percent were white. https://www.naacp.org/history-of-lynchings/ (accessed 6 December 2018). A ratio of seventy-five Black victims to one white was cited in Fouts, "Mafia," 517.

36. U.S. Census Bureau, table 12: Population of the 100 Largest Urban Centers: 1890, https://www.census.gov/population/www/documentation/twps0027/tab12.txt.

Mob size figures from Smith, *Crescent City Lynchings*, 241. In 1890 New Orleans was the twelfth largest city in America.

37. Marco Rimanelli, "The 1891 New Orleans Lynching: Southern Politics, Mafia, Immigration, and the American Press," in Rimanelli and Postman, *The 1891 Lynching*. See also the drawing in "Exterminating the Mafia," *Illustrated American*, as an example of the phenomenon described.

38. "Exterminating the Mafia."

39. Smith, *Crescent City Lynchings*, 228.

40. "Exterminating the Mafia."

41. Nystrom, "Sicilian Lynchings in New Orleans." For the longer history of politics and the fight for Italian votes, see Nystrom, *New Orleans after the Civil War*, chap. 9. The Young Men's Democratic Association or YMDA was a local political club made up of prominent Democrats in New Orleans.

42. Salvetti, *Rope and Soap*, 49–50. "Among the eleven victims, some were hardly model citizens, not unlike many other Italian residents in New Orleans," she wrote.

43. "What Do the Italians Want?" *New York Times*, 18 March 1891.

44. John Higham, *Strangers in the Land: Patterns of American Nativism*, 2nd ed. (New Brunswick, N.J.: Rutgers University Press, 1992), 90–92. Erika Lee's *America for Americans: A History of Xenophobia in the United States* (New York: Basic Books, 2019) is a significant update of the history of xenophobia and the first major critical reexamination of Higham's thesis.

45. "There was still a suspicion, *rather justified*, that the acquittal of the Italians charged with the Hennessy murder had resulted from the corruption of the jurors, a suspicion that was not erased for years and that resurfaced from time to time in similar circumstances." Salvetti, *Rope and Soap*, 72, emphasis added.

46. "What Do the Italians Want?"

47. For eleven months these statistics were collected at the Castle Garden station. Ellis Island opened January 1, 1892. "First. As to the working of the various laws relating to immigration and the importation of contract laborers. The committee submit the following table: (shows 476,658 total immigrants arrived in the U.S. between April 1, 1891 and January 31, 1892. 376,785 landed at Port of New York. "Percentage rejected: Less than one-third of 1 per cent." House Committee on Immigration and Naturalization, 52d Congress, 1st session, *"Report from the House Committee on immigration and naturalization under the resolution of Jan. 29, 1892 [Affairs on Ellis Island.]*," 28 July 1892, i.

48. *Report from the House Committee . . . Affairs on Ellis Island*, iii, iv.

49. Thomas Guglielmo, "'No Color Barrier': Italians, Race and Power in the United States," in *Are Italians White? How Race Is Made in America*, ed. Jennifer Guglielmo (New York: Routledge, 2003), 32–36.

50. See Aliza Wong, *Race and the Nation in Liberal Italy, 1861–1911* (London: Palgrave Macmillan, 2006).

51. Peter D'Agostino, "Craniums, Criminals, and the 'Cursed Race': Italian Anthropology in American Racial Thought, 1861–1924," *Comparative Studies in History and Society* 44, no. 2 (2002): 323, quoting Lombroso in 1900 following a visit to Calabria.

52. D'Agostino, 330. See also the entries on northern Italians and southern Italians in the Dillingham Commission's report, also published as Daniel Folkmar and Elnora Folkmar, *The Dictionary of Races or Peoples* (Washington, D.C.: Government Printing Office, 1911), 81–82 (quoting Niceforo and fellow criminologist Giuseppe Sergi). For more on race and the Dillingham Commission, see Katherine Benton-Cohen, *Inventing the Immigration Problem* (Cambridge, Mass.: Harvard University Press, 2018).

53. D'Agostino, "Craniums, Criminals, and the 'Cursed Race,'" 326, quoting Niceforo.

54. "Exterminating the Mafia."

55. "Nation of Murderers."

56. 12 April 1891. See note 22 above.

57. Vellon, "Italian Americans and Race," 213–15.

58. Vellon, 35; see also 15.

59. Barbata Jackson, *Dixie's Italians*, 38–42.

60. Lombrosian academic Giuseppe Sergi published *The Mediterranean Race* in Italy in 1900; in 1905 the Immigration Bureau began categorizing northern and southern Italians separately in its statistics. Vellon, "Italian Americans and Race," 17.

61. Salvetti, *Rope and Soap*, 75.

62. Quoted in Vellon, "Italian Americans and Race," 83.

63. Report by Luigi Scala, "Juridical and Social Considerations on Italian Emigration to the United States and in Particular to Louisiana," quoted in Salvetti, *Rope and Soap*, 75. Salvetti says this report was commissioned by a committee created in New Orleans for the Second Convention of Italians Abroad, which met in Rome in 1911. Scala was stationed in Independence, Louisiana, from 1913 to 1917 and Hammond, Louisiana, after 1917, according to *Register of the Department of State December 23, 1918* (Washington, D.C.: Government Printing Office, 1919), 238.

64. Vellon writes, "Fueling this fear of a racial alliance between Italians and African Americans was the perceived indiscriminate manner in which Italian shopkeepers, merchants, and peddlers engaged in business transactions and sold to African American customers." "Italian Americans and Race," 84.

65. "The Lynching Justifiable," *New York Times*, 17 March 1891.

66. For more on Italians and voting in Louisiana, see Barbata Jackson, *Dixie's Italians*, chap. 3; on the Ring and the lynching, see Nystrom, *New Orleans after the Civil War*, 216–24.

67. See W. Fitzhugh Brundage, *Lynching in the New South* (Champaign: University of Illinois Press, 1993).

68. "Blaine Acts," *Daily Picayune*, 16 March 1891.

69. "A Day of Blood in New Orleans," *San Francisco Chronicle*, 15 March 1891.

70. *Documenti diplomatici . . . confidenziale.*

71. "Quiet in New Orleans: Funeral of All the Victims of the Mob's Summary Vengeance," *Philadelphia Inquirer*, 16 March 1891.

72. "The New Orleans Affair," *New York Times*, 16 March 1891.

73. See Erika Lee, *America for Americans: A History of Xenophobia in the United States* (New York: Basic Books, 2019).

74. By the mid-1890s "[Prescott] Hall and the IRL effectively used the tactic of linking the new 'Italian problem' with the old 'Chinese problem' to expand the organization's influence and secure support from white workers—they drew on fears that were already activated in Americans to animate new ones." Lee, *America for Americans*, 125–26.

75. Donna Gabaccia, "The 'Yellow Peril' and the 'Chinese of Europe': Global Perspectives on Race and Labor, 1815–1930," in *Migration, Migration History, History: Old Paradigms and New Perspectives*, ed. Jan Lucassen and Leo Lucassen (Bern: Peter Lang, 1999), 177–96. On Chinese exclusion and its role in creating a gatekeeping nation, see Elliott Young, *Alien Nation: Chinese Migration in the Americas from the Coolie Era through World War II* (Chapel Hill: University of North Carolina Press, 2014); Torrie Hester, "'Protection, not Punishment': Legislative and Judicial Formation of U.S. Deportation Policy, 1882–1904," *Journal of American Ethnic History* 30, no. 1 (Fall 2010): 11–36; Mae M. Ngai, "The Architecture of Race in American Immigration Law: A Reexamination of the Immigration Act of 1924," *Journal of American History* 86, no. 1 (June 1999): 67–92.

76. Roger Daniels, *Guarding the Golden Door: American Immigration Policy and Immigrants since 1882* (New York: Hill & Wang, 2004), 19.

77. Salyer describes the three essential cases: *Chae Chan Ping* (1888), *Nishimura Ekiu* (1892), and *Fong Yue Ting* (1893). See Salyer, *Laws Harsh as Tigers*, chap. 1 and 2.

78. *Report from the House Committee . . . Affairs on Ellis Island*, iv.

79. Stump elaborated: "The building of the immigrant station at Ellis Island and the employment of a large force of inspectors and others at a great cost and expense certainly justified the expectation that the work of inspection done there should be more thoroughly and effectually conducted than that done at the other ports of entry, where it is made on shipboard or upon the wharf." *Report from the House Committee . . . Affairs on Ellis Island*, iv.

80. *Report from the House Committee . . . Affairs on Ellis Island*, iii–iv.

81. Lee, *America for Americans*, expands significantly on the theme of invasion in the history of American xenophobia.

82. See chapter 2 for more on the Board of Special Inquiry in its earliest years of operation.

83. 52nd Congress, 2nd Session, *Chap. 206, An Act to Facilitate the Enforcement of the Immigration and Contract-Labor Laws of the United States*, U.S. *Statutes at Large* (1893).

84. *Report from the House Committee . . . Affairs on Ellis Island*, iv.

85. By the end of the decade, Ambassador Fava had come to a frustrating conclusion. As historian Giampaolo Ferraioli writes, "It was necessary to eliminate and overcome those doubts supported by Fava, about the fact that the United States had become a world power." Ferraioli, *L'Italia e l'ascesa degli Stati Uniti a rango di potenza mondiale*, 101–2.

86. Salvetti, *Rope and Soap*, 68.

87. Imperiali to Ministero degli Affari Esteri, 21 March 1891, quoted in Salvetti, *Rope and Soap*, 68–69.

88. Imperiali to Ministero degli Affari Esteri, 15 June 1891, quoted in Salvetti, *Rope and Soap*, 68–69.

89. Sociologists Charles Seguin and Sabrina Nardin used keyword search to plot the volume of lynching coverage in a dataset of two Italian newspapers, *Corriere della Sera* of Milan and *La Stampa* of Turin; three major U.S. newspapers (*New York Times, Chicago Tribune*, and *Los Angeles Times*); and one British newspaper, the *Manchester Guardian*. Their quantitative analysis concluded that coverage of the lynching of Italians influenced what they call "lynching politics" because of the pressure the Italian government brought to bear on the United States following the 1891 New Orleans lynching, which was a turning point that internationalized the U.S. anti-lynching campaign. However, their analysis consciously examines only U.S. newspapers outside of the South. Seguin and Nardin, "Lynching of Italians," 65–91.

90. Vellon, "Italian Americans and Race," 89.

91. "Made a Big Blunder," *Weekly Nebraska State Journal*, 3 April 1891; "Baron Fava Is Recalled," *New York Times*, 1 April 1891.

92. Pietro Nocito, "La Legge di lynch ed il conflitto italo-americano," *Nuova Antologia*, 1 June 1891, xxxvi.

93. "Blaine Acts."

94. Editor Carlo Barsotti had raised $500 through his newspaper to fund the defense of the men accused of Hennessy's murder. For more on the defense of the race in the face of the 1891 lynching and others, see Vellon, *Great Conspiracy against Our Race*, chap. 1 and 4, quotation on 31.

95. Letter from Theodore Roosevelt to Anna Roosevelt, 21 March 1891, Theodore Roosevelt Collection, MS Am 1834 (307), Harvard College Library Collection, available at Theodore Roosevelt Digital Library, Dickinson State University. https://www.theodore rooseveltcenter.org/Research/Digital-Library/Record?libID=o280928 (accessed 16 December 2022).

96. Roosevelt shifted his public position between 1903 and 1906, although not in direct regard to Italian victims. According to Seguin and Nardin, "international condemnation of the lynching of Blacks reached a peak when it was juxtaposed with the Kishinev pogrom in 1903, prompting Theodore Roosevelt to denounce lynching." See "Lynching of Italians," 86.

97. For an overview of the remittance economy, see Gino Massullo, "Economia delle rimesse," in *Storia dell'emigrazione italiana*, vol. 1, *Partenze*, ed. Piero Bevilacqua, Andreina De Clementi, and Emilio Franzina (Rome: Donzelli Editore, 2001), 161–83; Mark Choate, "Sending States' Transnational Interventions in Politics, Culture, and Economics: The Historical Example of Italy," *International Migration Review* 41, no. 3 (2007): 728–68. Donna Gabaccia noted that "Italy's migrants sent home so much cash—peaking at 981

million lire in 1906—that Italians too began to speak of migrants as the country's most valuable 'export.'" *Foreign Relations: American Immigration in Global Perspective* (Princeton, N.J.: Princeton University Press, 2012), 103.

98. Fiorentino, *Gli Stati Uniti ed il Risorgimento d'Italia*, 239–44.

99. *Washington Post*, 14 April 1892.

100. Corte to Ministero degli Affari Esteri (MAE), 10 May 1891, quoted in Salvetti, *Rope and Soap*, 63.

101. MAE to Italian Embassy, 28 May 1891, quoted in Salvetti, *Rope and Soap*, 64.

102. Avvocato Generale Erariale [likely Giacomo Giuseppe Costa] to the Minister of Foreign Affairs, "Ogg: Ripartizione della indennità dal governo nord-americano alle famiglie dei linciati di Nuova Orleans," 4 January 1893, document no. 54, *Documenti diplomatici . . . confidenziale*. For an explanation of the origins and duties of the role of the *avvocato generale erariale* (a title without a direct English translation) and its equivalent in the Italian Republic, see http://www.avvocaturastato.it/node/595#I_2 (accessed December 28, 2018).

103. Document no. 54, *Documenti diplomatici . . . confidenziale*. The issue of citizenship was an ongoing problem the Italian government confronted in the age of mass migration because of the conflicting definitions of citizenship—*jus sanguinis* in Italy versus *jus solis* in the United States, Canada, and South America. Citizenship by blood meant that the government in Rome saw not only migrants as citizens but their descendants born abroad as well, while receiving nations had much more lax processes for Europeans to naturalize in this period, "tending to give entrance to new arrivals and, above all, their descendants to join the national community in relatively short time." See Corrado Bonifazi, *L'Italia delle migrazioni* (Bologna: il Mulino, 2013), 94. More recently, a broad citizenship law has enacted a process for persons born and residing outside of Italy to gain Italian citizenship if they can establish a blood line connection.

104. Document no. 54, *Documenti diplomatici . . . confidenziale*.

105. Salvetti, *Rope and Soap*, 86.

106. Salvetti, 25; see 28ff. on "blood price."

107. Salvetti, 40.

108. Sen. William Dillingham, *Reports of the Immigration Commission: Immigration Legislation*, 61st Congress, 3rd session (Washington, D.C.: Government Printing Office, 1911), 77–78.

109. For example, a "finality clause" inserted into the law never actually went into effect, a result of litigation on behalf of Chinese-born Americans. See Salyer, *Laws Harsh as Tigers*, 27–28.

110. The Supreme Court in 1892 ruled in *Nishimura Ekiu* that using a finality clause to exclude Asian migrants was not a violation of their constitutional right to due process, and further affirmed that the judiciary had no right to interfere in the decision of immigration inspectors. See Salyer, *Laws Harsh as Tigers*, 27–28.

111. Dillingham, *Reports of the Immigration Commission*, 78.

112. Testimony of Senator Morgan, Senate Foreign Relations Committee, Hearing, "Violations of Treaty Rights of Aliens," 52nd Congress, 1st session, 10 May 1892. Published by the Congressional Record; copy held in box 109, pos. 155, RDI.

113. Report, "Ogg: Incidente di New Orleans. Progetto di legge al Senato," 19 March 1892, box 109, RDI.

114. See Report of 4 April 1892 by Fava to the MAE, Fava's letters of 9 and 10 May 1892,

and Imperiali's report of 25 May 1892, no. 192/100, "Bill Dolph per la protezione degli stranieri," all pos. 152, fasc. II quinque, box 109, RDI. The recall of Ambassador Fava and the yearlong official diplomatic rupture had left the chargé d'affaires, the Marquis Imperiali, at the helm in Washington to carry out the business of the royal government. By choosing to leave the undersecretary in place, the government in Rome left channels open, and the American ambassador to Rome also anticipated a return to his post and quickly reassumed official duties the same day as Fava's reappointment on 16 May 1892. See Daniele Fiorentino, "Gli Stati Uniti e L'Italia dal Risorgimento all'immigrazione" in *Gli Stati Uniti e l'Italia alla fine del xix secolo* (Rome: Gangemi Editore, 2010), 56.

115. After Dolph introduced the bill saying he did not think there would be much to debate, a few other senators suggested it needed to go to the Judiciary Committee to deliberate what critics saw in the bill as a major change in legal precedent. Dolph added that the Foreign Relations Committee, offering its unanimous support for the proposed legislation, dropped misdemeanors from the text of the bill so that only felonies could be prosecuted. Even with this change, over two more debates in May and August the Senate eventually decided that federal courts lacked the jurisdiction under the Constitution to hear cases of violations of state criminal law, defeating legislation that would explicitly protect against mob violence fueled by ethnic hatred. Immigrants, if they could pass the bar to gain entry, were on their own. See *Violations of Treaty Rights of Aliens*, Pub. L. No. S.2409, 23rd Congressional Record (9 May 1892), 4093–94.

116. Report of 15 June 1891 cited in Salvetti, *Rope and Soap*, 67.

117. "Rapporto di Bill Dolph," box 109, RDI.

118. Salvetti, *Rope and Soap*, 71. "Italy will forever have the honor of having being [*sic*] the first to force the attention of this government on a defect of the law concerning its relations with foreign nations." Fava to MAE, 25 May 1891, quoted in Salvetti, *Rope and Soap*, 71.

119. Salvetti, *Rope and Soap*, 33. Harrison, a Republican, lost reelection to the same man he defeated in 1888. Grover Cleveland, Democrat, became the first and only president to serve two nonconsecutive terms when he took office in 1893.

120. Political barriers blocked consular attempts to demand punishment for anti-Italian violence and reinforced federal power to limit the rights of migrants. Italians lacked "constituency before the law-creating body—Congress—where the excluded and poor had virtually no influence." Evans, "Likely to Become a Public Charge," 233.

121. "The People Will Not Have to Pay," *Daily Picayune*, 8 April 1894, pacco 2180, box 109, RDI.

122. Report no. 66, "Ogg: Liti Italiane," New Orleans Consulate to MAE, 30 May 1894, pacco 2180, box 109, RDI. This report was bound up around a number of local articles (mentioned in the letter in passing) and other documents.

123. "The Italian Cases," 8 April 1894, clipping found in box 109, pacco 2180, RDI. For more on the circulation of New Orleans's major papers, see Barbata Jackson, *Dixie's Italians*, 14.

124. Gabaccia, *Foreign Relations*, 108.

125. The phrase "to sift" comes from an 1890 joint congressional report that heavily influenced the shape of the 1891 immigration act. U.S. Congress, House, Select Committee on Immigration and Naturalization, *Report*, 51st Congress, 2d session (1891), ii, quoted in Salyer, *Laws Harsh as Tigers*, 26.

126. Saverio Fava, "I linciaggi agli Stati Uniti," *Nuova Antologia*, 16 February 1902, 649. Fava used the phrase "col lavoro delle loro braccia," signifying work of manual labor, of blood, sweat, and tears.

127. U.S. House of Representatives, *Report no. 1628: Amendment to Chinese Exclusion Act* (Washington: Government Printing Office, 1898), box 112, pos. 155, pacco VIII, RDI. Newspaper clipping "Per l'emigrazione" dated 20–21 July 1898 was attached to the document.

128. "Per l'emigrazione." The response of the Italian government through its own emigration law will be discussed in subsequent chapters.

129. "Quiet in New Orleans," *Philadelphia Inquirer*, 16 March 1891.

130. For more on the work of agents among Italians, see chapter 2 in this book.

131. *Report from the House Committee . . . Affairs on Ellis Island*, iv.

132. This commonly traded slur grew out of racial ideas circulating in Italy in the decades after unification in 1871. According to Peter Vellon, this imagery included "illustrations of rural brigands hanging from scaffolds intertwined with stories of barbarous actions[, which] increasingly informed the image of a demonic Mezzogiorno" (Vellon, "Italian Americans and Race," 16).

133. "The Parkerson Outrage," *Times-Democrat* (New Orleans), 24 December 1892. Clipping in box 109, fasc. 2178, RDI.

134. Regio Console Motta to Ambassador Fava, "Rapporto: Minarie contro gli italiani," 25 December 1892, box 109, fasc. 2179, RDI.

135. Russell M. Magnaghi, "Louisiana's Italian Immigrants Prior to 1870," *Louisiana History: Journal of the Louisiana Historical Association* 27, no. 1 (1986): 43–68; see also Barbata Jackson, *Dixie's Italians*, chap. 1; Nystrom, *Creole Italian*, chap. 1.

136. Paolo Giordano, "Italian Immigration in the State of Louisiana: Its Causes, Effects, and Results," *Italian Americana* 5, no. 2 (Spring/Summer 1979): 160–77.

137. Louisiana reported 64,222 Italian-born people versus 22,802 in Texas, 5,508 in Mississippi, and 3,908 in Arkansas. George E. Cunningham, "The Italians: A Hindrance to White Solidarity in Louisiana, 1890–1898," *Journal of Negro History* (January 1965): 22.

138. See chapter 4 on the history of Italians on cotton plantations in the post-emancipation South; for a focused examination of Black and Italian labor on one plantation, see Jeannie Whayne, ed., *Shadows over Sunnyside: An Arkansas Plantation in Transition* (Fayetteville: University of Arkansas Press, 1993); for more on recruited Italian labor in Louisiana, see Jean Ann (Vincenza) Scarpaci, *Italians in Louisiana's Sugar Parishes: Recruitment, Labor Conditions, and Community Relations, 1880–1910* (New York: Arno, 1980), and her article "Labor for Louisiana's Sugar Cane Fields: An Experiment in Immigrant Recruitment," *Italian Americana* 7, no. 1 (Fall/Winter 1981): 19–41.

139. Barbata Jackson, *Dixie's Italians*, citing eleventh and twelfth U.S. Census figures, 31. Italians made up 33 percent of Louisiana's foreign-born population in 1900 and 40 percent by 1910.

140. *Thirteenth Census of the United States Taken in the Year 1910: Statistics for Louisiana* (Washington, D.C.: Government Printing Office, 1913). See Barbata Jackson, *Dixie's Italians*, chap. 1, esp. 30–33.

141. Barbata Jackson, *Dixie's Italians*, 11. See also Nystrom, *Creole Italian*, chap. 1.

142. Grant E. Hamilton, "Where the Blame Lies," *Judge*, 4 April 1891, 458–59. Library of Congress Prints and Photographs Division, https://www.loc.gov/pictures/item/97515495/.

143. See table 6.5, "Italian emigration overseas, 1876–1915," in Maddalena Tirabassi, "Why Italians Left Italy: The Physics and Politics of Migration, 1870–1920," in *The Routledge History of Italian Americans* (New York: Routledge, 2018), 124. Tirabassi's compilation of Italian government statistical data indicates a marked shift in patterns of migration around 1895 and 1896. For the ten years between 1886 and 1895, Argentina and Brazil absorbed more emigrants than the United States, while the United States became the single largest destination for Italian emigrants in the decade from 1896 to 1905, outnumbering the two South American destinations combined by more than 350,000 people.

144. Robert DeCourcy Ward, "Open Letters: An Immigration Restriction League," *Century*, February 1895.

145. "Restriction of Immigration," *Atlantic*, June 1896. On Walker's influence, see Higham, *Strangers in the Land*, 140–42.

146. Roger Waldinger, *The Cross-Border Connection: Immigrants, Emigrants, and Their Homelands* (Cambridge, Mass.: Harvard University Press, 2015), 9.

147. See Young, *Alien Nation*, chap. 4; Torrie Hester, *Deportation: The Origins of U.S. Policy* (Philadelphia: University of Pennsylvania Press, 2018). The two fundamental mechanisms of American gatekeeping power, the "likely to become a public charge" clause and the power of deportation constructed in Chinese exclusion law, when "taken together . . . were indicative of a Congressional intent to create a strong, unified, centralized administration." Evans, "Likely to Become a Public Charge," 114.

148. Mae Ngai, *Impossible Subjects: Illegal Aliens and the Making of Modern America* (Princeton, N.J.: Princeton University Press, 2004).

### Chapter 2. The Italian Government and U.S. Border Enforcement in the 1890s

1. *Chap. 206, An Act to Facilitate the Enforcement of the Immigration and Contract-Labor Laws of the United States*, 52nd Congress, 2nd session, 3 March 1893. By 1896 Dr. J. H. Senner, the commissioner of Ellis Island, would emphasize the 1893 clause with a slight shift in the language. He wrote in the *North American Review*: "It is also true that since about the middle of March there have been detained at this port an unprecedented number of [Italian] immigrants, either for special examination or for deportation, but this condition was not due to any unusual undesirability on the part of these immigrants, but solely to the strict enforcement of the latest law (of March 3, 1893), which made it the duty of the Inspectors of the Immigration Service to detain for special inquiry every immigrant who was not clearly and beyond doubt entitled to admission." J. H. Senner, "Immigration from Italy," *North American Review*, June 1896, 649–50.

2. "The Detained Immigrant," *Harper's Weekly*, 26 August 1893, 821–22, emphasis added. "Section 8 of the 1891 general immigration act stated that all decisions were final and the courts could not review the secretary's decision." See Torrie Hester, "'Protection, not Punishment': Legislative and Judicial Formation of U.S. Deportation Policy, 1882–1904," *Journal of American Ethnic History* 30, no. 1 (Fall 2010): 14–15.

3. "The Detained Immigrant."

4. Ronald H. Bayor, *Encountering Ellis Island: How European Immigrants Entered America* (Baltimore: Johns Hopkins University Press, 2014); Vincent J. Cannato, *American Passage: A History of Ellis Island* (New York: HarperCollins, 2009); Thomas M. Pitkin, *Keepers of the Gate: A History of Ellis Island* (New York: New York University Press, 1975), 23.

5. Katherine Benton-Cohen, *Inventing the Immigration Problem* (Cambridge, Mass.: Harvard University Press, 2018); Mae Ngai, *Impossible Subjects: Illegal Aliens and the Making of Modern America* (Princeton, N.J.: Princeton University Press, 2004), esp. 11, 17–20.

6. Benton-Cohen, *Inventing the Immigration Problem*; Deirdre Moloney, *National Insecurities: Immigrants and U.S. Deportation Policy since 1882* (Chapel Hill: University of North Carolina Press, 2012); Lucy Salyer, *Laws Harsh as Tigers: Chinese Immigrants and the Shaping of Modern Immigration Law* (Chapel Hill: University of North Carolina Press, 1995); Yael Schacher and Julia Rose Kraut, comments at roundtable, "Immigration Advocacy Then and Now," Organization of American Historians Annual Meeting, April 6, 2019, Philadelphia.

7. Rapporto #79, "Emigranti Italiani respinti [Excluded Italian Immigrants]," 22 November 1894, box 113, fasc. 2206, RDI.

8. Photo in Bayor, *Encountering Ellis Island*, 67.

9. Ngai, table A.1: Immigration to the United States, 1820–2000, in *Impossible Subjects*, 273.

10. Figures from the INS cited in Patricia Russell Evans, "'Likely to Become a Public Charge': Immigration in the Backwaters of Administrative Law, 1882–1933" (PhD diss., George Washington University, 1987), 231.

11. Bayor, *Encountering Ellis Island*, 68.

12. "Detained Immigrant." The Board of Special Inquiry was initially created to deal with general immigration deportation proceedings, while an individual judge or justice in the judicial branch heard suspected cases of violation of Chinese exclusion laws. Hester argues that this policy created two separate tracks for the application of deportation prerogatives, one that applied to the Chinese and one that considered all others. General immigration deportations were heard by the Board of Special Inquiry, which was made up of three immigration agents who acted under the aegis of administrative law, not legal procedure. The secretary of the department that housed the Bureau of Immigration heard appeals and had the final say. Hester, "Protection, not Punishment," 14–15.

13. Hidetaka Hirota argues that the finality clause "simply codified what had become the norm in the actual enforcement of immigration exclusion and deportation" in the treatment of European immigrants by the primary receiving states in the decades before the federal takeover of immigration policy. Hidetaka Hirota, *Expelling the Poor: Atlantic Seaboard States and the Nineteenth-Century Origins of American Immigration Policy* (New York: Oxford University Press, 2017), 204.

14. Egisto Rossi, "2.0 Rapporto annuale, dal 30 giugno 1895 al 30 giugno 1896 [2nd Annual Report from the Office of Labor Information and Protection, from 30 June 1895 to 30 June 1896]," 10 September 1896, box 111, pp. 3–4, RDI (hereafter "2nd Annual Report").

15. Hirota, *Expelling the Poor*, 198.

16. Roger Daniels, *Guarding the Golden Door: American Immigration Policy and Immigrants since 1882* (New York: Hill & Wang, 2004), 26.

17. House of Representatives, House Committee on Immigration and Naturalization, *Report from the House Committee on Immigration and Naturalization under the Resolution of Jan. 29, 1892 [Affairs on Ellis Island]*, report no. 2090 (Washington, D.C.: Government Printing Office, 28 July 1892), iv.

18. Salyer, *Laws Harsh as Tigers*.

19. On the strategy of using petitions of habeas corpus, see Salyer, *Laws Harsh as Tigers*, chap. 3; see also Hester, "Protection, not Punishment."

20. *Nishimura Ekiu* ruled that the agents enforcing immigration law had the power to set their own rules and trust their own judgment. See Salyer, *Laws Harsh as Tigers*, chap. 2, "Contesting Exclusion."

21. Chinese-born Fong Yue Ting refused to register as required by the 1892 Geary Act, like tens of thousands of Chinese resident aliens who attempted to fight the restrictive law as a mass strategy. His case challenged the deportation order issued for his refusal to register, even though at the time, the U.S. government refused to spend the estimated $7.3 million it would cost to enforce the law. Salyer, *Laws Harsh as Tigers*, 55.

22. Quoted in Salyer, 52. In his sharply critical dissent Justice Stephen J. Field feared that this ruling allowed the government to exercise what he called "arbitrary and despotic power" in exclusion and deportation cases. See also Salyer, 53–54, 57–58.

23. Hester, "Protection, not Punishment," 31.

24. Donna Gabaccia, "The 'Yellow Peril' and the 'Chinese of Europe': Global Perspectives on Race and Labor, 1815–1930," in *Migration, Migration History, History: Old Paradigms and New Perspectives*, ed. Jan Lucassen and Leo Lucassen (Bern: Peter Lang, 1999), 177–96.

25. This summary of the history of exclusion is attributed to Lauren Braun-Strumfels and Maddalena Marinari, "U.S. Immigration Restriction Reconsidered: The Italian Case," paper delivered at the Organization of American Historians Annual Meeting, April 2018, Sacramento. For more on the construction and application of the LPC clause, see Evans, "Likely to Become a Public Charge."

26. Senner, "Immigration from Italy." Prescott Hall, founding member of the Immigration Restriction League, replied to Senner in the August 1896 issue. See chapter 4 for more on the IRL.

27. For more on Italian law, see chapter 5 of this book; Dolores Freda, *Governare i migranti. La Legge sull'emigrazione del 1901 e la giurisprudenza del tribunale di Napoli* (Rome: Giappichelli, 2017); Mark Choate, *Emigrant Nation: The Making of Italy Abroad* (Cambridge, Mass.: Harvard University Press, 2008), 90–92.

28. The fire that destroyed the island's buildings in June 1897 caused the relocation of all inspection functions back to Manhattan. This move threatened the Office's standing, and despite their advocacy Italian diplomats were unable to secure new quarters when the island reopened in December 1900. See correspondence in box 112, RDI; chapter 5 in this book details the story of the closure.

29. While women worked at the island, only men held the role of inspector in this period.

30. Betty Boyd Caroli, table X, Immigration to the United States 1861–1899, in *Italian Repatriation from the United States, 1900–1914* (New York: Center for Migration Studies, 1973), 33.

31. On the overall impact of the *Fong Yue Ting* case on immigration law, see Ngai, *Impossible Subjects*, 11, 18; Salyer, *Laws Harsh as Tigers*.

32. Oldrini to Fava, report no. 80, "Relazione dell'ufficio Ital. colle autorità Americane e l'emigrazione," 1 December 1894, p. 3, box 113, fasc. 2206, RDI. See also Pitkin, *Keepers of the Gate*, on the history of the Bureau.

33. Oldrini to Fava, report no. 80, p. 3.

34. Stump's title shifted as Congress elevated the name and position of immigration management within the executive branch. Initially, Stump held the title of superintendent of immigration at the Office of the Superintendent of Immigration. By 1895 he would be promoted to commissioner-general of the Bureau of Immigration.

35. Oldrini to Fava, report no. 80, pp. 3–5.

36. Personal to Secretary of State Gresham [re: establishment of Labor Bureau], 19 April 1894, box 113, fasc. 2206, RDI. Fava's and his government's project to help migrants settle away from crowded cities reflected the fear of urbanization, industrialization, and related social problems that was a common trait of the Italian elite at the time, who were still largely a rural landed class. See Giancarlo Jocteau, *L'armonia pertubata. Classi dirigenti e percezione degli scioperi nell'Italia liberale* (Rome-Bari: Laterza, 1988).

37. Telegram, Fava to Blanc, 22 April 1894, box 113, fasc. 2206, RDI. In the telegram Fava mistakenly identified Stump as the secretary of the Treasury.

38. This chain of command resulted from what Hester calls a "secondary track" that isolated much of immigration law from federal judicial oversight. Hester, "Protection, not Punishment," 14.

39. Carlisle to Fava, 13 June 1894, box 113, fasc. 2206, RDI.

40. Carlisle to Fava, 13 June 1894.

41. *Chap. 206.*

42. Carlisle to Fava, 13 June 1894.

43. "Sentenze arbitrali in materia di emigrazione," 1 June 1895, box 111, RDI.

44. Letter of 14 June 1894, box 113, fasc. 2206, RDI.

45. Box 113, fasc. 2206. See also undated page of testimony in support of SR 207, likely published in the *Congressional Record* on 12 June 1894, also in box 113, fasc. 2206, RDI.

46. June 11 and 14, 1894, box 113, RDI.

47. W. E. Chandler, Senate Resolution, Miscellaneous Document no. 207, 53rd Congress, 2nd session (11 June 1894), copy found in box 113, fasc. 2206, RDI. The exploitative labor practice was a frequent target for legislative reform by Congress and state governments that struggled for decades to combat it. For more evidence of Italian views on the problem and the ongoing dialogue between Fava and Chandler in the spring of 1894, see Minister of Foreign Affairs Baron Blanc, Report: "Ogg: Emigrazione agli Stati Uniti" (8 March 1894), box 90, RDI; Baron Saverio Fava to W. E. Chandler, "Re Investigations by U.S. Senate on Abuses in Boston" (8 March 1894), box 109, folder 2190, RDI. See also W. E. Chandler, "S. 3240: A Bill to Facilitate the Enforcement of the Immigration and Contract-Labor Laws of the United States" (52nd Congress, 1st session, 6 June 1892), copy found in box 90, RDI.

48. See correspondence and related documents spanning March 1892 to June 1894 in boxes 90 and 113. In the summer of 1892 Ambassador Fava tracked the progress of a Senate bill designed to strengthen enforcement of the 1885 Alien Contract Labor Law and endow inspectors with more tools to judge a migrant's suitability for entry. Chandler, "S. 3240."

49. Undated, likely 12 June 1894, box 113, fasc. 2206, RDI.

50. "Urgente: Protezione degli emigranti," 14 June 1894, box 113, fasc. 2206, RDI.

51. "This apartment will be open to all nationalities." Carlisle to Fava, 13 June 1894, box 113, fasc. 2206.

52. "Urgente: Protezione degli emigranti," 14 June 1894, box 113, fasc. 2206.

53. "Baron Fava Cares for His Countrymen," *Washington Post*, 16 June 1894, newspaper clipping with notes in the ambassador's hand, box 113, fasc. 2206.

54. Report 386/188, "Urgente: Protezione degli emigranti," 14 June 1894, box 113, fasc. 2206.

55. "In Honor of Garibaldi," *New York Times*, 11 March 1884. The article described Oldrini as "a compatriot of Garibaldi . . . whom he had followed through battles and exile" to New York in the early 1850s. This is doubtful. While no birth or death dates have been found, later references to Oldrini in the same paper describe his relief activity during World War I. An article published in 1918 identified him as the treasurer for a New York Committee of the National Organization for the Benefit of Soldiers Crippled in the War in Milan. The article directs persons wishing to contribute to send checks to Oldrini "in care of the Guaranty Trust Company, 513 Fifth Avenue." If he had fought with Garibaldi, he would have been almost ninety years old by World War I. "Soldiers Approve Red Cross Canteens; For Crippled Italian Soldiers," *New York Times*, 10 February 1918; Prof. Alex Oldrini, "Chapter X: Education in Italy," in *Annual Report of the Commissioner of Education*, vol. 1, *For the Year 1890–91* (Washington, D.C.: Government Printing Office, 1894), 321–39.

56. Unattributed newspaper clipping, c. 14 June 1894, box 113, fasc. 2206.

57. Exclusions grew from 1.70 percent of total Italian emigrants arriving in 1894 to 2.75 percent of arrivals in 1895, before falling again to 1.84 percent of all arrivals in 1896. I am unable to say for sure how effective the Office was in securing releases, but the available statistics and the handful of stories covered in the press seem to support this assertion, at least generally. Rossi, "2nd Annual Report," 3–4.

58. Oldrini, report no. 80. This report contained a number of edits in Fava's hand.

59. Disregarding the intrusiveness of such "control," the editorial reasoned that while "this protection *continues* to be condemned by those who believe in the autonomy of the individual, [it] is instead a necessity for Italians" because they are coming in "*absolute*" poverty. "Che fa il prof. A. Oldrini ad Ellis Island?" (New York, 18 May 1895), signed "g.v.," box 111, RDI. Emphasis in original.

60. "Che fa il prof. A. Oldrini ad Ellis Island?"

61. I. D. Marshall, "Italian Immigrants. Professor Odrini [*sic*] Looks after Them at Ellis Island," Times (n.d., c. 1895), box 111, fasc. 2195, RDI.

62. Report no. 79, 22 November 1894, box 113, fasc. 2206.

63. Calculated from Rossi, "2nd Annual Report," 9–11. Related statistics on 2–4.

64. Italians were excluded at a rate of 1.89 percent out of a total of 66,425 arrivals in the fiscal year 1895–96, while by comparison Chinese migrants entering in 1896 suffered a rejection rate of 11 percent out of a total of 3,925 arrivals. Rossi, "2nd Annual Report," 9–11; Salyer, table 1: Chinese Admitted to the United States, 1894–1901, in *Laws Harsh as Tigers*, 67.

65. Violations of the Contract Labor Law were the second most common reason for exclusion between 1892 and 1910. Bayor, *Encountering Ellis Island*, 40.

66. See discussion in letter from Oldrini to Fava, 13 December 1894, box 113, fasc. 2206, RDI. See also Cannato, *American Passage*, 81.

67. Hirota, *Expelling the Poor*, chap. 7. Hirota views the creation of the flexible LPC clause as an extension of this earlier practice.

68. See, for example, Bulletin of the Department of Foreign Affairs of Italy, no. 48, se-

ries 16 (April 1895), translated from the Italian by Oldrini to share with American officials, box 111, fasc. 2195, RDI.

69. Oldrini to Fava, 13 December 1894, box 113, fasc. 2206, RDI.

70. Fava forwarded to the minister of foreign affairs news of Oldrini's discovery and
a copy of the circular in question (which unfortunately does not appear in his files). He
agreed that the directions, which he characterized as "not new or said to have a special
influence on inspections . . . will certainly increase the proportional number excluded,
especially of Italians who on this side represented a third of the total European emigration excluded last year." "Ogg: Istruzioni restrittive copia l'immigrazione agli S.U.," 13 December 1894, box 113, fasc. 2206.

71. A deep economic depression struck in 1893 when the United States was setting up
qualitative barriers to entry. The overall number of migrants arriving dropped significantly, recovering somewhat by 1900. Oldrini tracked a decline in Italian immigration
through Ellis Island and gestured to this problem in his frequent and detailed reports to
the ambassador. From 1891 to 1894, the United States reported half the number of immigrant arrivals overall compared to the four previous years from 1886 to 1890. (Figures
from Ngai, table A1: Immigration to the United States, 1820–2000, in *Impossible Subjects*,
273.) Particular to the Italian case, Oldrini noted an increase in Italian arrivals to Ellis Island in 1895–96 that reversed what had been a four-year period of decline, demonstrating that the arbitrary application of bureaucratic exclusion did little to affect migration.
While the Office mediated the Ellis Island inspection process, their commentary reveals
an initially intense focus on the LPC tool of gatekeeping.

72. Rossi, "2nd Annual Report," 3–4. See tables 2.1 and 2.2 in this chapter.

73. "Crowded with Immigrants: Plans Made for Improvements at Ellis Island," *New
York Times*, 5 April 1896.

74. Rossi, "2nd Annual Report," 5–6. Rossi wrote, "in the three months of March, April
and May when our emigration reached an unprecedented figure, at 38,450, while in the
same quarter of 1895 had been only 13,750 and in the 12 months ended June 30 of that
year, the whole total did not even reach the 34 thousand emigrants, as we have already
seen [arrive in the first six months of this year]."

75. Rossi, "2nd Annual Report," 6. See also telegram from New York Consul Branchi to
Fava, 21 April 1896, box 111, RDI.

76. Rossi, "2nd Annual Report," 6–7.

77. See the appendix for specific ship-level data on arrivals and exclusions taken from
Rossi's report. The figure Rossi reported is only slightly higher than the average rate of rejection estimated by historian Mae Ngai more broadly for all European immigrants between 1880 and World War I. Ngai estimated that 1 percent of the 25 million European
immigrants processed through Ellis Island were excluded between the years of 1880 and
1914. Ngai, *Impossible Subjects*, 18. Average Italian rates of rejection calculated from data
table of April and May 1896 arrivals in Rossi, "2nd Annual Report," 2–4, 9–12; overall figures for Italian migration from Caroli, table X, in *Italian Repatriation*, 33.

78. Ngai, *Impossible Subjects*, 18.

79. Average figures calculated from data table of April and May 1896 arrivals in Rossi,
"2nd Annual Report," 2–4, 9–12.

80. Rossi, "2nd Annual Report," 6–7.

81. Laura Pilotti, *L'Ufficio di informazioni e protezione dell'emigrazione italiana di Ellis*

*Island,* vol. 15, *Fonti per la storia dell'emigrazione* (Rome: Ministero degli Affari Esteri / Istituto poligrafico e Zecca dello stato, 1993), 141.

82. "Annual Report of the Executive Committee of the Immigration Restriction League for 1895," cited in Cannato, *American Passage,* 104.

83. Oldrini to Fava, 13 December 1894, box 113, fasc. 2206, RDI.

84. "In the fiscal year 1894–5 there were 731 Italian emigrants rejected out of 33,902 who had reached Ellis Island." Luigi Bodio, "On the Protection of the Italian Emigrant in America," *Chautauquan,* April 1896, 42–46. Based on my own textual analysis I determined the English version is a mostly accurate but not line-for-line translation of Bodio's article "Della protezione degli emigranti italiani in America," *Nuova Antologia,* 16 December 1895. Bodio would go on to become the first Italian commissioner general of emigration in 1901.

85. Senner, "Immigration from Italy," 649–50, 655.

86. Initially described in report of 12 June 1894, box 113; see also reports in box 111, RDI, which describe strategies emigration agents near the port of Naples had begun to deploy to outfox American inspectors.

87. "Four Men Escape from Ellis Island," *New York Times,* 8 May 1895.

88. Rossi, "2nd Annual Report," 3–4.

89. Box 111, pos. 155, pacco IV, RDI.

90. Cannato argues that the island became more corrupt under the leadership of Assistant Superintendent McSweeney after 1897, until a congressional investigation intervened and shook up the leadership of the island. See *American Passage,* chap. 6 and 7.

91. "Giuseppe Mintello Happy. Order for His Deportation Rescinded Just in Time," *New York Times,* 10 March 1897.

92. "Freed by Brother's Death," *Ferris Wheel* (Ferris, Tex.), 17 March 1897. https://texas history.unt.edu/ark:/67531/metapth18841/m1/7/ (accessed March 7, 2019).

93. Senner had jurisdiction over operation on the island, a result of what Torrie Hester has called the "parallel track" development of administrative, not judicial, oversight over immigration. See Hester, "Protection, not Punishment."

94. Two presentations at the Organization of American Historians Annual Meeting in Philadelphia, 4–6 April 2019, indicated notable work in progress: Jane Hong, "Roundtable: Immigration Advocacy Then and Now," and Julian Lim, on the panel "Looking Outside the Nation: The Exercise of U.S. Migration Policy Abroad." Julian Lim subsequently published "Mormons and Mohammedans: Race, Religion, and the Anti-Polygamy Bar in U.S. Immigration Law," *Journal of American Ethnic History* 41, no. 1 (Fall 2021): 5–49. While Lim's article begins with the 1891 immigration act and spends some time examining nineteenth-century antecedents, both historians focus on the twentieth century.

95. Phrase found in letter of 1 December 1894, box 113, RDI.

96. See Vincenzo Grossi, "L'emigrazione italiana in America," *Nuova Antologia,* 16 February 1895, 740–57. Grossi, a Roman Catholic priest who was canonized in 2015, extensively cited speeches to Parliament by Senator Giuseppe Mintello, who served from 1882 to 1895 until he was appointed consul general to Canada.

97. Bodio, "On the Protection of the Italian Emigrant in America," 46.

98. Letter dated 2 August 1897 in box 112, pos. 155, pacco VIII, folder 2199, RDI. On the problems at Castle Garden, see Cannato, *American Passage,* chap. 2.

99. Letter dated 2 August 1897.

100. See Cannato, *American Passage*, chap. 2.

101. Supplement to the Annual Report, November 1899, box 113, fasc. 2204, RDI.

102. See Cannato, *American Passage*, 108.

103. Letter dated 7 June 1898, box 112, fasc. 2199, pos. 155, pacco VIII, RDI.

104. As reported in Sherman to Vinci, 31 March 1898, box 112, fasc. 2202, RDI.

105. Pilotti, *L'Ufficio di informazioni e protezione*, 159.

106. "Italian Agency to Close," *New York Times*, 26 November 1899.

107. See report from Count Vinci to Rome that asks for a new subagent to be named to the post at Ellis Island. This position apparently remained unfilled. "Ogg: Nomine del sotto agente ad Ellis Island," 28 February 1899, box 112. See also Rossi's final annual report, November 1899, box 113, fasc. 2204, RDI.

108. Count Vinci to Fava, 13 April 1898, box 112, pos. 155 a, RDI.

109. Oldrini to Fava, 28 August 1894, box 109, pos. 155, RDI.

110. Confidential message from Fava to Secretary of State and Prime Minister Baron Blanc, "Suggerimenti per frenare il rinvio non giustificato degli emigranti (confidenziale riservato to Baron Blanc)," 29 November 1894, box 113, fasc. 2206, RDI.

111. Julie Greene, "Movable Empire: Labor, Migration, and U.S. Global Power during the Gilded Age and Progressive Era," *Journal of the Gilded Age and Progressive Era* 15, no. 1 (January 2016): 6.

112. In this period of Italian history the prime minister also served as the minister of the interior, a fact that amplified the ambassador's concerns in the highest level of government and gave the prime minister's domestic policies transatlantic impact.

113. Choate, *Emigrant Nation*, 91.

114. Telegram, 20 August 1894, box 109, RDI.

115. Grossi, "L'emigrazione italiana in America," 744.

116. Letter, 16 December 1895, box 109, pos. 155, pacco 1 bis. no. 1, RDI.

117. Carlisle to Fava, 12 April 1895, box 111, RDI. The Office represented the sum total of Italy's "immigration officials" in the United States in the 1890s.

118. Strikeouts and awkward phrasing in English language original. Likely Fava's own translation. 16 December 1895, box 109, pos. 155, pacco 1 bis. no. 1, RDI.

119. Rossi, "2nd Annual Report," 7.

120. See Bayor, *Encountering Ellis Island*, chap. 3; Douglas Baynton, *Defectives in the Land: Disability and Immigration in the Age of Eugenics* (Chicago: University of Chicago Press, 2016); Torrie Hester, *Deportation: The Origins of U.S. Policy* (Philadelphia: University of Pennsylvania Press, 2018).

121. Elliott Young argues that "'remote control' was not ancillary to immigration restriction; it was the main mechanism for exclusion." Young also offers a new periodization of policy history that shows racism was central to migration policy both before and after the Quota Act of 1924. See "Beyond Borders: 'Remote Control' and the Continuing Legacy of Racism in Immigration Legislation," in *A Nation of Immigrants Reconsidered: U.S. Society in an Age of Restriction, 1924–1965*, ed. Maddalena Marinari, Madeline Y. Hsu, and Maria Cristina Garcia (Champaign: University of Illinois Press, 2019), 38.

122. Noel King and Monica Ortiz Uribe, "El Paso, Texas, Is at the Forefront of the Immigration Crisis," *Morning Edition*, NPR (originally aired July 9, 2019). Ortiz Uribe defined "Remain in Mexico"—officially called the Migration Protection Protocol—as a "program that forces migrants to wait out their day in U.S. immigration court across the

border in Mexico, in cities like Juárez and Tijuana. The Trump administration claims that doing so helps root out migrants who are trying to game the system. So far, roughly fifteen thousand people have been sent back since the policy began earlier this year."

### Chapter 3. From Ellis Island to Sunnyside Plantation, Arkansas

1. Report, 14 June 1894, box 113, RDI.

2. Jeannie M. Whayne, ed., *Shadows over Sunnyside: An Arkansas Plantation in Transition, 1830–1945* (Fayetteville: University of Arkansas Press, 1993).

3. King Umberto I, *Regio decreto 10 gennaio 1889, n. 5892, che l'approva l'annesso regolamento per l'esecuzione della legge 30 dicembre 1888, numero 5866 sull'emigrazione,* 5892 serie 3a § (1889). https://www.normattiva.it/uri-res/N2Ls?urn:nir:stato:regio.decreto:1889 -01-10;5892 (accessed June 19, 2020).

4. Vincenzo Grossi, "L'emigrazione italiana in America," *Nuova Antologia,* 16 February 1895, 740–57.

5. "A Nation of Murderers," *Washington Post,* 18 April 1891.

6. "Mr. Corbin's Decoration," *New York Herald,* n.d. (estimated June 1896), box 110, RDI.

7. Roger Waldinger and Nancy Green, eds., *A Century of Transnationalism* (Champaign: University of Illinois Press, 2015).

8. Daniele Fiorentino, *Gli Stati Uniti e il Risorgimento d'Italia 1848–1901* (Rome: Gangemi Editore, 2013).

9. Report, 14 June 1894, box 113, RDI.

10. Fava cites it as Article 9 of the law of 3 August 1882. See report of 14 June 1894.

11. In May 1885 John Calhoun and his brother Patrick defaulted on $133,305 in bonds that the Corbin Banking Company had underwritten for the brothers' Florence Planting Company. Through an order of the U.S. Circuit Court, the title to Sunnyside transferred to the bank trustees, and in October 1886 Corbin assumed full control of the plantation. Willard B. Gatewood, "Sunnyside: The Evolution of an Arkansas Plantation, 1840–1945," in Whayne, *Shadows over Sunnyside,* 15.

12. By 2003 the "dilapidated" building risked demolition to make room for a new MTA transit station at Fulton Street. Instead, it was saved, restored, and repurposed as part of the station. David W. Dunlap, "Spared Demolition, an 1889 Building Gets a New Life," *New York Times,* 2 June 2013.

13. Visit to and discussion with the Angel family, owners of Sunnyside Plantation, Lake Village, Arkansas, September 2005.

14. Gatewood, "Sunnyside," 16.

15. Testimony of Ed Trice, in "Shadows over Sunnyside," Federal Writers' Project, Works Progress Administration manuscript 1, Arkansas History Commission, Little Rock, quoted in Gatewood, "Sunnyside," 16.

16. Gatewood, "Sunnyside," 16–17. He writes that the contract existed in 1895 and 1896, but I doubt that was the case considering the lack of evidence for this claim in other sources.

17. *National Cyclopedia of American Biography,* vol. 31 (New York: James T. White, 1944), 279; see also Sidney Schaer, "Riding the LIRR Together," Long Island Newsday.com, available at https://web.archive.org/web/20040928125310/http://www.newsday.com /community/guide/lihistory/ny-history_motion_rail1,0,7579885,print.story?coll=ny

-lihistory-navigation (accessed 10 January 2023). Notably, these same traits were also ascribed to Ambassador Fava.

18. Fabrizio Rossi, "Ruspoli, Emanuele, principe di Poggio Suasa," *Dizionario biografico degli italiani*, vol. 89 (Treccani, 2017), https://www.treccani.it/enciclopedia/ruspoli -emanuele-principe-di-poggio-suasa_%28Dizionario-Biografico%29/ (accessed 10 January 2023).

19. This connection is the best I can intuit from *New York Times* society columns, obituaries, and the sketchy record of the ASDMAE on the initial connection of Corbin to Sunnyside. I have uncovered absolutely no evidence of how precisely the two met. This theory seems most plausible given what I know about these two men.

20. Partial newspaper clipping (n.p., n.d), box 110, pacco 2193, RDI.

21. Alessandro Oldrini, "To Fava Re: Southern Colonization Convention," 26 August 1894, box 110, pos. 155, pacco 2193, RDI.

22. Mark Choate, *Emigrant Nation: The Making of Italy Abroad* (Cambridge, Mass.: Harvard University Press, 2008), 32.

23. Crispi and his Democratic Party ruled from 1887 to 1891, and again from 1893 to 1896.

24. Oldrini to Fava, report no. 590, 8 February 1894, box 110, pacco 2193, RDI.

25. Fava to unnamed recipient, 8 February 1894, box 110, pacco 2193. For more on Crispi's reforms, see Dolores Freda, *Governare i Migranti. La legge sull'emigrazione del 1901 e la giurisprudenza del Tribunale di Napoli* (Rome: Giappichelli, 2017), 40; Corrado Bonifazi, *L'Italia delle migrazioni* (Bologna: il Mulino, 2013), 92.

26. Alessandro Oldrini to Ambassador Saverio Fava, 7 September 1894, box 110, pacco 2193. See also Ambassador Saverio Fava, Rapporto con oggetto: "Ufficio di Ellis Island / proposte del Sig. Corbin. Urgente," 22 October 1894, box 110, pacco 2193.

27. "Plan for Italian Colonization," *New York Times*, 11 January 1895.

28. Reported in "Come from Italy to Find Homes," *Atlanta Constitution*, n.d. (estimated January 1897), box 110, pacco 2193, pos. 155, pacco 1 sex, RDI.

29. James C. Cobb, *The Most Southern Place on Earth: The Mississippi Delta and the Roots of Regional Identity* (New York: Oxford University Press, 1992), 52; see also John C. Willis, *Forgotten Time: The Yazoo-Mississippi Delta after the Civil War* (Charlottesville: University of Virginia Press, 2000), and Kenneth R. Hubbell, "Always a Simple Feast: Social Life in the Delta," in *The Arkansas Delta: Land of Paradox*, ed. Jeannie Whayne and Willard B. Gatewood (Fayetteville: University of Arkansas Press, 1993), 184–207.

30. Roberta Miller, interview with Mrs. Flowers Pierini, 15 August 1977, Washington County Oral History Project, Washington County Library System, Mississippi Department of Archives and History, https://www.mdah.ms.gov/arrec/digital_archives/vault /projects/OHtranscripts/AU413_099290.pdf.

31. James Cobb argued that some Deltans coped with the unpredictability of agriculture by diversifying their sources of income. By pursuing a career as a lawyer, politician, and planter, LeRoy Percy insulated himself from the vagaries of weather and the world cotton market and secured a steadier income. Interestingly, Cobb theorized, "Percy was less tempted to squeeze his tenants for debts or cheat on their settlements. Consequently, he had less trouble retaining labor than did many of his contemporaries." *Most Southern Place on Earth*, 93.

32. Report to Fava, 12 September/27 November 1894, box 110, RDI.

33. See report no. 234, 11 October 1896, pacco 2193, RDI. For more on the Alien Contract Labor Law and its implications, see Mae Ngai, *Impossible Subjects: Illegal Aliens and the Making of Modern America* (Princeton, N.J.: Princeton University Press, 2004); Erika Lee, *At America's Gates: Chinese Immigration during the Exclusion Era, 1882–1943* (Chapel Hill: University of North Carolina Press, 2003); Gunther Peck, *Reinventing Free Labor: Padrones and Immigrant Workers in the North American West, 1880–1930* (New York: Cambridge University Press, 2000); Daniel J. Tichenor, *Dividing Lines: The Politics of Immigration Control in America* (Princeton, N.J.: Princeton University Press, 2002).

34. Reflected in 1896–97 season records and contract materials, "Conti sull'Sunnyside," box 110, RDI.

35. Soon after their arrival, in January 1896, the first seven hundred Italians on the plantation welcomed Father Pietro Bandini to their colony. He would serve as the plantation's primary conduit for information, both relaying his reports on conditions out to the ambassador and dispersing the consulate's directives among the colonists. See the extensive record of their communications in RDI, box 110, pacco 2193, including multiple series of telegrams exchanged between Bandini, Consul Vinci (stationed in New Orleans), and Ambassador Fava.

36. Box 110, pacco 2193.

37. Fava to MAE, report 291/86, 17 April 1896, box 110, pacco 2193. MAE records indicate that at least two high-ranking officers received the letter and responded directly to Fava in regard to his report.

38. Report, "[Re: Arrival of 79 Families to Sunnyside]," 8 January 1897; Oldrini to Fava, "Re: Kaiser Wilhelm Arrival," 8 January 1897, both items in box 110, pacco 2193, pos. 155, pacco 1 sex, RDI.

39. This promise is corroborated by the ASDMAE records. "It would be truly desirable that a good example is made of the late Mr. Corbin and of Prince Ruspoli coming to establish among the other American capitalists, Italians," *Il Corriere Italiano* encouraged its readers. "La Colonia Italiana dell'Arkansas," *Il Corriere Italiano* (Texas), 19 February 1897. See also "Colonizzazione?" *L'Araldo Italiano* (New York), 23 November 1895, which reported on the arrival and significance of the initial group of settlers. All newspaper clippings in box 110, pacco 2193, pos. 155, pacco 1 sex, RDI.

40. Fava to MAE, report 291/86, box 110, RDI.

41. See Willis, *Forgotten Time.*

42. Report, Bandini to Fava, 17 April 1896, box 110, RDI.

43. Report, Bandini to Fava, 17 April 1896.

44. Letter, Edgell to Fava, 15 July 1896, "re: water supply and new colonists," box 110, RDI.

45. Letter, Oldrini to Fava, 18 August 1896, box 110, RDI.

46. See Gavin Wright, *Old South New South: Revolutions in the Southern Economy after the Civil War* (Baton Rouge: Louisiana State University Press, 1989); Willis, *Forgotten Time*; Harold D. Woodman, *King Cotton and His Retainers* (Lexington: University Press of Kentucky, 1968; Columbia: University of South Carolina Press, 1990).

47. Oldrini to Fava, 18 August 1896.

48. The fiction writing of Mary Bucci Bush, a descendant of the original Sunnyside settlers, dramatizes the hardships of life on the plantation. See, for example, "Planting," in *The Voices We Carry: Recent Italian-American Women's Fiction*, ed. Mary Jo Bona (Toronto: Guernica, 2007), 31–52.

49. Ten years later, this remained the only transportation option across the river. See report by Mary Grace Quackenbos, Department of Justice Special Investigator, folder 100937, Record Group 60, National Archives and Records Administration, College Park, Maryland (hereafter RG 60, NARA).

50. For Corbin's plans for a railroad on Sunnyside, see Oldrini, "Intervista Corbin," spring 1894, box 110, folder 2193, RDI; also pictures of railroad in folder 100937, RG 60, NARA.

51. Adamoli to Fava, report no. 112, "Ogg: Ricorsi d'emgiranti alle Commissioni Arbitrali," 13 April 1895, box 111. Fava's hand recorded this was sent first to Oldrini on 28 April in report no. 335; next to the consul in New York on 28 April in report no. 336; and finally to Rome on 28 April in report no. 337/136.

52. "Italians Show Their Vengeance. Friends of Deported Immigrants Attack Ellis Island Officials," *New York Times*, 21 May 1894.

53. G. Adamoli, "Ogg: I emigranti alle commissioni arbitrali," n.d. [spring 1895], box 111, RDI.

54. Report no. 60, Copies of Instructions to Rejected Emigrants, Oldrini to Fava, 1 June 1895, box 111, RDI.

55. Report no. 79, 22 November 1894, box 113, fasc. 2206, RDI.

56. Report no. 79, emphasis in original. Oldrini continued: "As a practical conclusion of this Report, I believe it is useful to suggest in a confidential manner that the complaints of migrants rejected as a recurrence of damages and expenses at the end of art. 17 above, observing that the legal responsibility should fall not only on the Emigration Agents, if there were inducements to emigrate, but more on the Navigation Commissioners who know better than the first the Immigration Laws of the U.S., and therefore should not accept with their eyes closed the emigrants sent to them by the agents."

57. Fava to MAE, "Ogg: Viaggi ferroviari oltre New York," Washington, 14 June 1895, box 111, RDI.

58. G. Adamoli, "Ogg: I emigranti alle commissioni arbitrali," n.d. [spring 1895], box 111. See RDI, boxes 90 and 112 on the period before 1898, and Ambasciata Washington 1901–1909, boxes 143 and 144 for the period 1901–1907, all ASDMAE.

59. Fava to Stump, regarding immigrants refused entry, 18 June 1895, box 111, RDI.

60. Grazia Dore, "Some Social and Historical Aspects of Italian Emigration to America," *Journal of Social History* 2, no. 2 (Winter 1968), 95–122. Historian Mark Choate, who wrote about the more comprehensive Italian emigration law of 1901 as a watershed that transformed Italian policy toward emigration, paid very little attention to the 1888 law in his book *Emigrant Nation*, 90–92.

61. Maddalena Marinari, *Unwanted: Italian and Jewish Mobilization against Restrictive Immigration Laws, 1882–1965* (Chapel Hill: University of North Carolina Press, 2019), 23. In Italian see in particular Dolores Freda, "La Legislazione sulle migrazioni italiane fino al 1901," *Studi Emigrazione* 215 (2019): 379–92.

62. On Behalf of Blanc, Minister of Foreign Affairs, to Fava, 27 May 1895, box 111, pos. 155, pacco IV, RDI.

63. Letter of 27 May 1895. A letter of 27 April had warned that De Martini and Bertini may be actively working in violation of the 1888 act, but this letter garnered no response.

64. Report, "Sentenze arbitrali in materia di emigrazione," Undersecretary of State to Fava, 1 June 1895, box 111, fasc. 2195, RDI.

65. Letter from Fava to Commissioner Stump regarding emigrants refused entry, 18 June 1895, box 111, RDI. Act of 2 March 1895 promoted Stump to the commissioner general of the Immigration Bureau.

66. Alessandro Oldrini, "Relations of the Office for Italians with the American Immigration Authorities," 1 December 1894, box 113, p. 3, RDI.

67. "Orders for Railroad Transportation to Points beyond N. York," translation of the Bulletin of the Ministry of Foreign Affairs (April 1895) enclosed in a letter from Oldrini to Stump dated 7 June 1895, box 111, pos. 155, pacco IV, RDI.

68. Oldrini to Stump, 7 June 1895.

69. 27 April 1895, box 111, RDI.

70. Oldrini sent a packet to Commissioner Stump on 7 June 1895 that contained a copy of a guide published by the MAE. In a cover letter Oldrini told Stump: "Herewith I beg to enclose a translation of the article concerning the 'orders for R.R. Transportation for Points Beyond N. York,' as it appeared in the Bulletin of the Ministry of Foreign Affairs of Italy April 1895." Bulletin of the Department of Foreign Affairs of Italy, no. 48, series 16, April 1895, box 111, pos. 155, pacco IV, RDI.

71. Oldrini, "Ogg: Agente d'emigrazione De Martini ecc," Office of Information and Protection for Italian Emigrants, 10 June 1895, box 111, pos. 155, pacco IV, RDI.

72. "Emigrante Respinto: AVVISO," n.d. (c. 1895), box 111, pos. 155, RDI.

73. Oldrini, "Ufficio dell'immigrazione italiana ad Ellis Island. Consigli agli immigranti," 6 May 1895, box 111, pos. 155.

74. Telegram, 11 June 1895, box 111, RDI.

75. Fava to Stump regarding emigrants refused entry, 18 June 1895, box 111, RDI.

76. Letter, McSweeney to Fava, 20 June 1895, box 111, RDI.

77. Sen. William Dillingham, *Reports of the Immigration Commission*: vol. 4, *Immigration Conditions in Europe* (Washington, D.C.: Government Printing Office, 1911), 149.

78. Undersecretary of the Interior to Fava, 5 September 1896, box 111, fasc. 2198, pos. 155, pacco vii, RDI.

79. Dore, "Some Social and Historical Aspects," 108.

80. Freda, *Governare i migranti*, 4.

81. Matteo Pretelli, "L'era dell'immigrazione di massa," in Matteo Petrelli and Stefano Luconi, *L'immigrazione negli Stati Uniti* (Bologna: il Mulino, 2008), 90.

82. Adam Goodman, *The Deportation Machine* (Princeton, N.J.: Princeton University Press, 2020).

83. Egisto Rossi, "2.o Rapporto annuale, dal 30 giugno 1895 al 30 giugno 1896 [2nd Annual Report from the Office of Labor Information and Protection, from 30 June 1895 to 30 June 1896]," 10 September 1896, box 111, p. 3, RDI.

84. Charles Scott, "Italian Farmers for Southern Agriculture," *Manufacturers' Record*, 9 November 1905, 424. Emphasis in original.

85. Lee Langley, "Italians as Southern Farmers, Striking Characteristics of Their Success," *Manufacturer's Record*, 30 June 1904, 535.

86. Egisto Rossi, annual report, November 1899, box 113, fasc. 2204, p. 16, RDI.

### Chapter 4. Colonization, the Literacy Test, and the Evolution of Gatekeeping

1. Egisto Rossi, "2.o Rapporto annuale, dal 30 giugno 1895 al 30 giugno 1896 [2nd Annual Report from the Office of Labor Information and Protection, from 30 June 1895 to 30 June 1896]," 10 September 1896, box 111, p. 8, RDI (hereafter "2nd Annual Report").

2. Rossi, "2nd Annual Report," 7.

3. Rossi compared the volume of Italian arrivals in a series of charts. From June 1894 to June 1895, the Office counted 33,902 total persons. In March, April, and May 1896, in part as a result of the cheap tickets sold aboard the "tramp steamers," Rossi counted 38,450 persons landed at Ellis Island in those three months alone. See Rossi's figures on 4 and 6. See also the appendix in this book.

4. Rossi, "2nd Annual Report," 7, 8.

5. Maria Rosaria Ostuni, "Leggi e politiche di governo nell'Italia liberale e fascista," in *Storia dell'emigrazione italiana: Partenze* ed. Piero Bevilacqua, Andreina De Clementi, and Emilio Franzina (Rome: Donzelli Editore, 2001), 314. She notes that "the most frequent damages suffered by emigrants regarded the rejection by the United States, the loss of baggage and delays boarding the ship." As Ostuni explains, and will be discussed at length in chapter 5, these challenges greatly influenced the eventual shape of the 1901 emigration law.

6. Erin Elizabeth Clune has written about southern efforts to recruit European migrants in order to rebalance the region's racial makeup and limit Black southerners' access to land and rights. See "Emancipation to Empire: Race, Labor, and Ideology in the New South" (PhD diss., New York University, 2002); Clune, "Black Workers, White Immigrants, and the Postemancipation Problem of Labor: The New South in Transnational Perspective," in *Global Perspectives on Industrial Transformation in the American South*, ed. Susanna Delfino and Michele Gillespie (Columbia: University of Missouri Press, 2005). See also J. Vincent Lowery, "'Another Species of Race Discord': Race, Desirability, and the North Carolina Immigration Movement of the Early Twentieth Century," *Journal of American Ethnic History* 35, no. 2 (2016): 32–59.

7. John Griffin Carlisle and Herman Stump, "Mission to Italian Government," Senate Document (Washington, D.C.: U.S. Senate, 54th Congress, 2d session, 3 December 1896), 2. Carlisle was the secretary of the Treasury at that time, the department overseeing the Bureau of Immigration.

8. Appended to the report is a translation of a directive sent out to the prefects in the kingdom responsible for issuing documents needed to emigrate, clarifying how Italy should interpret U.S. law on contract labor and excluded persons in specific cases. "It is impossible to give fixed and unchanging rules on this subject," the directive stated. Translated and reproduced in Carlisle and Stump, "Mission to Italian Government," 6–8. Copy of the original directive held in box 111, RDI, as published by Ministero dell'Interno, Direzione generale di pubblica sicurezza, 8 November 1896. On 27 August 1896 the undersecretary of state in Rome had written to Ambassador Fava with an urgent request. "Mr. Ambassador, As a result of new attentions made to me by my esteemed colleague the Minister of the Interior, who wishes to have a standard to give the Prefects of the Kingdom convenient instructions and to prevent the difficulties that emigrants now meet at every step when a passport is required for the United States, I pray your Excellency seek to obtain, from this federal government, the greatest possible clarifications about the interpretation to be given to the restrictive provisions of the American law on emigration, which was mentioned last by you in your report No. 506 / I69 of July 28 p.p. — It is of utmost importance to have on this an unofficial interpretation from the United States, as the V.E. [vostra excellenza, yourself, the Ambassador wants the] same, after having questioned the government agent of Ellis Island on the same subject, he affirms, with the response indicated above, that the scope and the meaning of the said provisions are not very evident. I think, moreover, that it is

in the very interest of this federal government that its legislative provisions on emigration are understood in their precise meaning. Waiting for its response to resolutions. I renew, Mr. Ambassador, the acts of my highest consideration. For the Minister, the Undersecretary of State [signed] Bonino." Bonino to Fava, "Interpretazione della legga degli Stati Uniti sull'immigrazione. Urgente," 27 August 1896, box 111, pos. 155, pacco VII, RDI.

9. Roger Daniels, *Not Like Us* (Chicago: Ivan R. Dee), 43. See Erika Lee, *America for Americans: A History of Xenophobia in the United States* (New York: Basic Books, 2019), chap. 4 on the IRL as the first group to lobby Congress effectively and employ lobbyist tactics in its campaign for a literacy test.

10. Gustavo Tosti, "The Agricultural Possibilities of Italian Immigration," *Charities,* 7 May 1904.

11. See Moon-Ho Jung, *Coolies and Cane* (Baltimore: Johns Hopkins University Press, 2006); Julie Greene, *The Canal Builders: Making America's Empire at the Panama Canal* (New York: Penguin, 2009); Cindy Hahamovitch, *No Man's Land: Jamaican Guestworkers in America and the Global History of Deportable Labor* (Princeton, N.J.: Princeton University Press, 2011). On Brazil, see Thomas Holloway, *Immigrants on the Land: Coffee and Society in São Paulo, 1886–1934,* e-book ed. (1980; Chapel Hill: University of North Carolina Press, 2017), chap. 3.

12. This article and several subsequent reports written over the next year describe the second influx of settlers to arrive at Sunnyside in winter 1895/96. "Waiting for the Chateau Yquem. Italian Farmers Expected in New Orleans To-Morrow on Their Way to Their New Homes," *The World* (November 29, 1895), box 110, and reports in box 111, fasc. 2193, pos. 155, pacco 1 sex, RDI.

13. Borrowing from the concept of "circuits of mobility" in Julie Greene, "Movable Empire: Labor, Migration, and U.S. Global Power during the Gilded Age and Progressive Era," *Journal of the Gilded Age and Progressive Era* 15, no. 1 (January 2016): 4–20.

14. Hidetaka Hirota, "Alien Contract Labor Law and the Problem of Imported Labor in Gilded Age America," paper delivered at the American Historical Association Annual Meeting (New York), January 3, 2020.

15. On the history of the contract in Western thought, see Robert J. Steinfeld, *The Invention of Free Labor: The Employment Relation in English and American Law and Culture, 1350–1870* (Chapel Hill: University of North Carolina Press, 1991). On the significance and meaning of the contract in the post-emancipation South, see Amy Dru Stanley, *From Bondage to Contract: Wage Labor, Marriage and the Market in the Age of Slave Emancipation* (Cambridge: Cambridge University Press, 1998).

16. "Waiting for the Chateau Yquem."

17. The result can be ascertained from several items that describe two waves of settlement, in box 110, pacco 2193, pos. 155, pacco 1 sex, RDI. The second major wave of settlers generated a new set of reports in the winter of 1897. Report, "[Re: Arrival of 79 Families to Sunnyside]," 9 January 1897; "La Colonia italiana dell'Arkansas," *Il Corriere Italiano,* 19 February 1897; Oldrini to Fava, "Firsthand Report of Conditions at Sunnyside," 15 March 1897, box 110, pacco 2193, pos. 155, pacco 1 sex, RDI.

18. Dolores Freda, *Governare i migranti. La Legge sull'emigrazione del 1901 e la giurisprudenza del Tribunale Di Napoli* (Rome: Giappichelli, 2017), 147. See also chapter by Lauren Braun-Strumfels and Clara Zaccagnini on regulating Italian migration to New Orleans in *Managing Migration in Italian and U.S. History,* ed. Lauren Braun-Strumfels, Maddalena Marinari, and Daniele Fiorentino (forthcoming, DeGruyter).

19. See Henry Marshall Booker, "Efforts of the South to Attract Immigrants" (PhD diss., University of Virginia, 1965); Mary Emily Colegate, "The Efforts to Promote White Immigration to the South after the Civil War" (MA thesis, University of Texas, 1936); Carol Mary Tobin, "The South and Immigration, 1865–1910" (MA thesis, Duke University, 1967); Rowland T. Berthoff, "Southern Attitudes toward Immigration, 1865–1914," *Journal of Southern History* 17, no. 3 (1951): 328–60; Paul M. Gaston, *The New South Creed: A Study in Southern Mythmaking* (New York: Knopf, 1970; Vintage, 1973); C. Vann Woodward, *Origins of the New South, 1877–1913*, 2nd ed. (Baton Rouge: Louisiana State University Press, 1971).

20. Gavin Wright, *Old South New South: Revolutions in the Southern Economy since the Civil War*, 2nd ed. (Baton Rouge: Louisiana State University Press, 1997).

21. Wright, *Old South New South*; Gilbert Fite, *Cotton Fields No More: Southern Agriculture, 1865–1980* (Lexington: University Press of Kentucky, 1984).

22. Lee Langley, "Italians as Southern Farmers, Striking Characteristics of Their Success," *Manufacturer's Record*, 30 June 1904, 535.

23. See Jean Ann (Vincenza) Scarpaci, *Italians in Louisiana's Sugar Parishes: Recruitment, Labor Conditions, and Community Relations, 1880–1910* (New York: Arno, 1980).

24. Colegate, "Efforts to Promote White Immigration," 25–26a.

25. Colegate, 25–27, 28.

26. Walter Lynwood Fleming, "Immigration to the Southern States," *Political Science Quarterly* 20, no. 2 (June 1905): 276.

27. Berthoff, "Southern Attitudes toward Immigration"; Robert L. Brandfon, "The End of Immigration to the Cotton Fields," *Mississippi Valley Historical Review* 50, no. 4 (1964): 591–611.

28. Lauren H. Braun, "Italians, the Labor Problem, and the Project of Agricultural Colonization in the New South, 1884–1934" (PhD diss., University of Illinois at Chicago, 2010); J. Vincent Lowery, "The Transatlantic Dreams of the Port City Prophet: The Rural Reform Campaign of Hugh MacRae," *North Carolina Historical Review* 90, no. 3 (2013): 288–324; J. Vincent Lowery, "'Another Species of Race Discord': Race, Desirability, and the North Carolina Immigration Movement of the Early Twentieth Century," *Journal of American Ethnic History* 35, no. 2 (2016): 32–59; Hugh MacRae, "Bringing Immigrants to the South: Address Delivered before the North Carolina Society of New York, December 7, 1908" (n.p., 1908); Walter Lynwood Fleming, "Immigration to the Southern States," *Political Science Quarterly* 20 (June 1905): 276–97; J. A. Harrell, ed., *The South: An Immigration Journal* (Weldon, N.C.: n.p., 1888).

29. Biographical information from Charles F. Brooks, "Obituary: Robert DeCourcy Ward," *Geographical Review*, January 1932, 161. Brooks wrote: "Altogether some 330 articles and perhaps 2000 notes and reviews in 100 publications at home and abroad are to be credited to his pen. A large number of these contributions dealt with immigration restriction, a subject in which he was an acknowledged leader." He also held the academic title professor of climatology at Harvard.

30. Rossi wrote about the "so-called tramp steamers" in his 1896 "2nd Annual Report," 8.

31. Robert DeCourcy Ward, "Immigration and the South," *Atlantic Monthly*, November 1905, 615.

32. Vincent J. Cannato, *American Passage: A History of Ellis Island* (New York: HarperCollins, 2009), 92.

33. Zebulon B. Vance to A. J. McWhirter and the Southern Immigration Association, reprinted in *Proceedings of the Southern Interstate Immigration Convention, Convened in Montgomery, Alabama, December 12–13, 1888, and of the Southern Interstate Immigration Executive Committee, Convened in Montgomery, Alabama, December 14, 1888, and the Address of F. B. Chilton, General Manager, December 20, 1888* (Dallas: Wilmans Brothers, 1888), 312. Vance was governor of North Carolina during the Civil War. Notably, Vance was a Unionist from Asheville who led through the decision by the legislature to secede.

34. Ward, "Immigration and the South," 615.

35. Lee Langley, "Italians as Southern Farmers, Striking Characteristics of Their Success," *Manufacturer's Record*, 30 June 1904, 535.

36. Charles Scott, "Italian Farmers for Southern Agriculture," *Manufacturers' Record*, 9 November 1905.

37. Langley, "Italians as Southern Farmers," 535. See also J. Russell Borzilleri, *Italian Immigration in the South* (Rochester, N.Y.: n.p., 1910–1919[?]).

38. Immigration Restriction League, *The Present Italian Influx, Its Striking Illiteracy; Comparison of Educational Test and Consular Certificate Plans*, Publications of the Immigration Restriction League No. 14 (Boston: Immigration Restriction League, 1896), Widener Library, Harvard. Immigration Collection of Prescott Farnsworth Hall, https://curiosity.lib.harvard.edu/immigration-to-the-united-states-1789-1930/catalog/39-990100030790203941; Immigration Restriction League, *Distribution of Illiterate Immigrants* (Boston: Immigration Restriction League, 1896), https://curiosity.lib.harvard.edu/immigration-to-the-united-states-1789-1930/catalog/39-990100034970203941.

39. See Luigi Bodio, "The Protection of Italian Immigrants in America," *Chatauquan*, 1896, 45, which emphasized that the Office was intended as a clearinghouse for all of the disparate information flowing to the ambassador and to migrants: for "the dissemination of information regarding the different states and their inducements to immigrants, the railways, corporations, and individuals who might offer work." See also Saverio Fava, "Le colonie agricole italiane nell'America del Nord," *Nuova Antologia*, 1 October 1904.

40. Alessandro Oldrini, "Lettera circolare con cui si informa dall'apertura del nuovo ufficio," 1 August 1894, reproduced in appendix in Laura Pilotti, *L'Ufficio di informazioni e protezione dell'emigrazione italiana di Ellis Island*, vol. 15, *Fonti per la storia dell'emigrazione* (Rome: Ministero degli Affari Esteri / Istituto poligrafico e Zecca dello Stato, 1993), 255–56.

41. "Maps, plans, circulars, and advertisements, adding proper information as to location and climate; nature of labor; present conditions of lands; wages; terms and conditions of payments; means of transportation; cost of victuals; dwelling houses; agricultural implements," before concluding "and, generally, all those local and surrounding indications, such as may lead willing Italian immigrants to enter into reliable and durable agreements." 1 August 1894, quoted in Pilotti, *L'Ufficio di informazioni*, 255–56.

42. Oldrini, "Lettera circolare"; see also interview with Oldrini in "Come from Italy to Find Homes," *Atlanta Constitution*, [1897], box 110, pacco 2193, pos. 155, pacco 1 sex, RDI.

43. On the founding of the Virginia Board of Immigration, see the Act of the General Assembly of 3 March 1866, "to promote and encourage immigration into the State of Virginia." See also Colegate, "Efforts to Promote White Immigration," 32–34.

44. Chronology of South Carolina derived from records of the Kohn-Hennig Collection of the South Caroliniana Library, University of South Carolina, Columbia.

45. The London office existed according to their official stationery, at least. See "South Carolina: Her Resources Epitomized," "Handbook of the State of South Carolina," and "Catalog of Displays on Permanent Exhibition for the State of South Carolina," variously published by the South Carolina Department of Agriculture between 1904 and 1909; R. Beverley Herbert, "Immigration to South Carolina," undated typescript c. 1910, describes undertaking a recruiting trip to Europe in 1904 on behalf of Watson, Kohn-Hennig Collection.

46. "Handbook of the State of South Carolina."

47. See J. T. Henderson from John Denis Keiley, 7 April 1888, Keiley Family Papers, Virginia Historical Society, Richmond, Virginia (hereafter VHS).

48. Records of the James River Valley Immigration Society (hereafter JRVIS), folder 5: Minutes of Stockholders, VHS.

49. Letter from C. S. Thomas, 6 February 1889, folder 7, correspondence files, JRVIS records, VHS. Required by its constitution to have a large number of voting stockholders, the need to coordinate the schedules and opinions of so many men sapped the energy of the active officers. A person could become a stockholder for only ten dollars by purchasing 10 percent of a $100 share. The low point of entry created an unmanageable number who owned a piece of the company.

50. Bondurant to Grant, 4 February 1889, box 1, JRVIS, VHS.

51. Holloway, *Immigrants on the Land*, chap. 3.

52. "The government of São Paulo was itself the *instrument* of the coffee planters. Immigration policy must be understood in this context. The Paulista elite did not see the Sociedade Promotora as a private interest group using state subsidies for the exclusive benefit of a restricted segment of the body politic. Rather, it was an extension of the executive branch, a special administrative apparatus established in critical circumstances [transition to free labor] to serve an extraordinary purpose." Holloway, chap. 3.

53. "From 1889 to the turn of the century nearly three-quarters of a million more foreigners arrived in São Paulo, of which 80 percent were subsidized by the government." Holloway, chap. 3.

54. Holloway, chap. 3.

55. *Proceedings . . . at Nashville*; *Proceedings . . . in Montgomery*.

56. *Proceedings . . . in Montgomery*, 10.

57. *Proceedings . . . at Nashville*, 15, 91–92.

58. *Proceedings . . . at Nashville*, 4. Charles Hooker attended both the Montgomery and Nashville meetings where he represented the state of Mississippi. In Montgomery Hooker emphasized the content and impact of their promotional work "mak[ing] public the interesting points concerning the fertility of our soils, agricultural and mineral products." *Proceedings . . . in Montgomery*, 12–13.

59. "Resolution," *Proceedings . . . in Montgomery*, 26.

60. Langley, "Italians as Southern Farmers," 535.

61. *Railway World*, 1904, 32.

62. The Southern Land Advertising Agency and Real Estate Exchange, "Number 2. Lands Bought, Sold, and Exchanged in All Parts of the Country" (n.d., c. 1890s), South Caroliniana Library. Emphasis in original.

63. "Address of A. J. McWhirter, President Southern Immigration association of America, at Vicksburg, Mississippi, November 21, 1883," repr. in *Proceedings . . . at Nashville*, 345.

64. *Proceedings . . . at Nashville*, 160–61. Hooker was listed as the SIA director for his home state in the opening page of the *Proceedings*.

65. "Address of A. J. McWhirter, President Southern Immigration association of America, at Vicksburg, Mississippi, November 21, 1883," repr. in *Proceedings . . . at Nashville*, 344–45.

66. See *Railway World*; pamphlets about Daphne; letters to ambassador in box 113, RDI.

67. Elliott Young, "Beyond Borders: Remote Control and the Continuing Legacy of Racism in Immigration Legislation," in *A Nation of Immigrants Reconsidered: U.S. Society in an Age of Restriction, 1924–1965*, ed. Maddalena Marinari, Madeline Y. Hsu, and Maria Cristina Garcia (Champaign: University of Illinois Press, 2019), 30–33.

68. Report no. 234, 11 October 1896, box 110, pacco 2193, RDI.

69. Undersecretary of State Bonino to Fava, 12 June 1896, box 111, RDI. Bonino wrote, "I beg you, may I insist that when you can you press Mr. Corbin on the question of potable water for the colonists to bring them a permanent remedy, and that with this pecuniary sacrifice [made], the best will be possible."

70. On the issues of treatment and clean water, see Bonino to Fava, 31 October 1896; Fava to MAE, report, 3 July 1896, box 111, RDI; on the recruitment of seventy-two families, see Ernesto Milani, "Peonage at Sunnyside and the Italian Government," in *Shadows over Sunnyside: An Arkansas Plantation in Transition, 1830–1945* (Fayetteville: University of Arkansas Press, 1993), 41.

71. Oldrini to Fava, letter, 18 August 1896, box 111, RDI.

72. After the concept of "new circuits of global migration" in Greene, "Movable Empire," 8.

73. Egisto Polmonari and Giovanni Vivarelli to Consul at New Orleans, "delle quattro fattori di Sunny Side il 22 November '97," attached to letter from Consul Magenta to Conte G. C. Vinci, Incaricato d'Affari, 27 December 1897, box 110, pacco 2193, pos. 155, pacco 1 sex, RDI.

74. Polmonari and Vivarelli, 22 November 1897; "in una parola siamo ridotti quali schiavi in una squalida miseria" [in a word, we have been reduced to living like slaves in a miserable poverty]. Polmonari and Vivarelli to Consul at New Orleans, 4 December 1897, box 110, pacco 2193, pos. 155, pacco 1 sex, RDI.

75. Luigi Bruni, "Questo è l'elenco di tutti i dannegiati sunnyside Il 10 febbraio 1898," 10 February 1898, box 110, pacco 2193, pos. 155, pacco 1 sex; Alfonso Mazocchi to Consul Vinci, telegram, 8 March 1898, box 112, RDI.

76. Fava (assumed) to Egisto Polmonari, no. 791, 28 December 1897, box 110, pacco 2194, RDI.

77. For detail about Fava's absence, see Milani, "Peonage at Sunnyside," 42. Milani argued that this was part of a larger campaign to minimize the reports of poor conditions that had begun to emanate from the plantation, but I see no direct evidence of that.

78. F. Romano to Vinci, 31 December 1897, box 110, pacco 2194, RDI.

79. An outbreak of yellow fever in 1897 killed twenty-eight adults and forty-four children. Milani, "Peonage at Sunnyside," 43.

80. Ambassador Fava to Company President George Edgell, 2 January 1898, box 110, pacco 2194, pos. 155, pacco 1 sex bis, RDI.

81. Edgell to Vinci, letter no. 230, 24 March 1898, box 110, RDI.

82. Milani, "Peonage at Sunnyside," 44.

83. Edgell to Vinci, letter no. 332, 22 April 1898, box 110, RDI.

84. Vinci to Edgell, no. 266, 27 March 1898, box 110.

85. Magenta to Vinci, 4 April 1898, box 110.

86. Edgell to Vinci, 22 April 1898.

87. Fava to MAE, 3 January 1898, box 110.

88. Report to Fava, 12 September/27 November 1894, box 110.

89. *Bollettino dell'emigrazione* no. 14 (1905), 22.

90. The IRL included this phrase at the conclusion of each of its pamphlets published in 1896. See also Lee, *America for Americans*, 115; Maddalena Marinari, *Unwanted: Italian and Jewish Mobilization against Restrictive Immigration Laws, 1882–1965* (Chapel Hill: University of North Carolina Press, 2019), 9–12.

91. Lee, *America for Americans*: "weaponized statistics," 124; membership, 115–16.

92. Rossi, "2nd Annual Report," 7.

93. The introduction to Publications of the Immigration Restriction League no. 14 reads: "The recent extraordinary influx of Italians seemed a favorable time for further investigation, and through the courtesy of Dr. J. H. Senner who placed the records of the Ellis Island station completely at the disposal of the League, it is now enabled to present an analysis of the recent Italian immigration based on an examination of the official manifests." IRL, *Present Italian Influx*.

94. IRL, *Present Italian Influx*.

95. U.S. Bureau of the Census, "Series H 664–668. Percent Illiterate in the Population by Race and Nativity: 1870 to 1969," in *The Statistical History of the United States to 1970* (New York: Basic Books, 1976), 382.

96. Hirota, "Alien Contract Labor Law."

97. Young, *Alien Nation*; Kathleen López, "Gatekeeping in the Tropics: U.S. Immigration Policy and the Cuban Connection," in Marinari et al., *Nation of Immigrants Reconsidered*, 48; Grace Delgado, *Making the Chinese Mexican: Global Migration, Localism, and Exclusion in United States–Mexico Borderlands* (Stanford, Calif.: Stanford University Press, 2013).

98. Hirota, "Alien Contract Labor Law."

99. IRL, *Present Italian Influx*, 3.

100. See Cannato, *American Passage*, 81, for whole story of Beirne and rule, no specific cite given but guessing from his testimony. See also 77 on Chandler's investigation in March 1892.

101. IRL, *Present Italian Influx*, 3.

102. Cannato, *American Passage*, 104.

103. Lee, *America for Americans*.

104. See table 7.1, Immigration Restriction Chronology: Votes on the Literacy Test, in Claudia Goldin, "The Political Economy of Immigration Restriction in the United States, 1890–1921," in *The Regulated Economy: A Historical Approach to Political Economy* (National Bureau of Economic Research, Chicago: University of Chicago Press, 1994), 227. https://www.nber.org/chapters/c6577.pdf.

105. In the House, on 9 February 1897. *Congressional Record* 29, p. 1675.

106. When the literacy test failed to block enough immigrants from entry, due in part to the law coinciding with rising literacy rates in Europe, Congress turned to a system of quotas in 1921 and 1924. This cemented the move from qualitative to quantitative restriction, making the literacy test an almost superfluous tool of exclusion in the face of strict national quotas and bans. According to Goldin, "The forces that prompted these more

restrictive measures [in 1921 and 1924] were the same as those that led to the passage of the literacy test." However, she argues that any form of restriction outside of the literacy test was not "of great qualitative significance," and she highlighted in a footnote that Asian exclusion was exempted from her study. Goldin, "Political Economy of Immigration Restriction," 226.

107. Lee, *America for Americans*, 115; see also 127 on Lodge.

108. See box 112 in RDI for how this played out in the Italian language and American press.

109. See chapter 1; Henry Cabot Lodge, "Lynch Law and Unrestricted Immigration," *North American Review*, May 1891.

110. "The worst thing is this italophobia mania that cannot be stopped because the embassy in Washington is deserted and the Italian government's special officer at Ellis Island, Cavalier Egisto Rossi, has been limited in his defense of our co-nationals facing the preconceived ideas of the federal authorities." "Ridicolo zelo delle autorità di Ellis Island," *L'Araldo Italiano*, c. 29 January 1897, box 112, pos. 155, pacco VIII, RDI.

111. See box 112, pos. 155, pacco VIII, RDI.

112. Thomas Bailey Aldrich, *Unguarded Gates, and Other Stories* (New York: Houghton Mifflin, 1895).

113. The 1924 act established consular relationship; Young, "Beyond Borders" has documented how shipping companies carried out this work.

114. George Pozzetta, "Italian Migration: From Sunnyside to the World," in *Shadows over Sunnyside: An Arkansas Plantation in Transition, 1830–1945*, ed. Jeannie Whayne (Fayetteville: University of Arkansas, 1993), 98.

115. Concept of "managing mobility" from Greene, "Movable Empire," 4–20.

116. See Daniele Fiorentino, *Gli Stati Uniti e il Risorgimento d'Italia 1848–1901* (Rome: Gangemi Editore, 2013); Giampaolo Ferraioli, *L'Italia e l'ascesa degli Stati Uniti a rango di potenza mondiale* (Naples: Edizioni Scientifiche Italiane, 2013); Ferdinando Fasce, *Tra due sponde: Lavoro, affari e cultura fra Italia e Stati Uniti nell'eta della grande migrazione* (Genova: Graphos, 1993).

117. See, for example, the roundtable in *Labor: Studies in Working Class History* 16, no. 3 (September 2019), especially Sarah McNamara, "A Not-so-*Nuevo* Past: Latina Histories in the U.S. South," 73–78; Julie Weise, *Corazon de Dixie: Mexicanos in the U.S. South since 1910* (Chapel Hill: University of North Carolina Press, 2015); Mary Odem and Elaine Lacy, eds., *Latino Immigrants and the Transformation of the U.S. South* (Athens: University of Georgia Press, 2009).

118. Whayne, *Shadows over Sunnyside*, a collection of essays produced originally as conference papers, examines Italian colonization within the context of Arkansas history. Pilotti, *L'Ufficio di informazioni e protezione dell'emigrazione italiana di Ellis Island*, a comprehensive guide to the ASDMAE collections on its eponymous subject, gives colonization a broad and insightful treatment in the process and as part of series on institutional history intended for researchers. Unfortunately copies are not widely available.

### Chapter 5. Partners in Gatekeeping

1. "Italians Show Their Vengeance. Friends of Deported Immigrants Attack Ellis Island Officials," *New York Times*, 21 May 1894.

2. Aristide Zolberg, *A Nation by Design: Immigration Policy in the Fashioning of America* (Cambridge, Mass.: Harvard University Press, 2006), 8.

3. Maddalena Marinari, Madeline Y. Hsu, and Maria Cristina Garcia, eds., *A Nation of Immigrants Reconsidered: U.S. Society in an Age of Restriction, 1924–1965* (Champaign: University of Illinois Press, 2019), 13.

4. Dolores Freda, *Governare i migranti. La legge sull'emigrazione del 1901 e la giurisprudenza del tribunale di Napoli* (Torino: Giappichelli), 28–29.

5. Corrado Bonifazi, *L'Italia delle migrazioni* (Bologna: il Mulino, 2013), 78.

6. Dolores Freda, "La legislazione sulle migrazioni italiane fino al 1901," *Studi Emigrazione* 215 (2019): 379–92.

7. Freda, *Governare i migranti*, 24ff., 27–28.

8. Bonifazi, *L'Italia delle migrazioni*, 78.

9. See Freda, *Governare i migranti*, chap. 2. For more on the complicated role of emigration agents, see Tara Zahra, *The Great Departure: Mass Migration from Eastern Europe and the Making of the Free World* (New York: W. W. Norton, 2016), esp. 38–39. Hungary's 1903 emigration law had a protectionist goal that also targeted emigration agents. Zahra cited one of the law's architects, Baron de Levay, in a 1906 article where he blamed agents' deceptive practices. But Zahra argues this was a ruse—the mostly Jewish agents were used as scapegoats. The 1903 law became the basis for further restrictive legislation to control emigration after 1914 in the Austro-Hungarian Empire's successor states. See also Zahra, "Travel Agents on Trial: Policing Mobility in East Central Europe, 1889–1989," *Past and Present* 223, no. 1 (2014): 161–93.

10. Rossi used this phrase in his 1896 annual report; on *il burrascoso* or "stormy marriage," see Freda, *Governare i migranti*, chap. 2.

11. For more on passport law in Italy, see John Torpey, *The Invention of the Passport: Surveillance, Citizenship, and the State*, 2nd ed. (New York: Cambridge University Press, 2018), 126–30.

12. Issued by Riascoli, Minister of the Interior, circular no. 81, 1 November 1861, quoted in Bonifazi, *L'Italia delle migrazioni*, 78.

13. Circular, 7 December 1867, quoted in Bonifazi, 79.

14. Circular, 28 January 1868, quoted in Bonifazi, 79.

15. Bonifazi, 79. Circulars are used to bypass the difficult and lengthy process needed to pass legislation in Italy.

16. Bonifazi, 79–80.

17. Giovanni Battista Scalabrini, "*Il Disegno di legge sull'emigrazione italiana. Osservazioni e proposte*" (Piacenza: Tipografia dell'amico del popolo, 1888).

18. Silvano Tomasi and Gianfausto Rosoli, eds., *Scalabrini e le migrazioni moderne: Scritti e carteggi* (Torino: Società Editrice Internazionale, 1997), 50.

19. Freda, *Governare i migranti*, 40ff.

20. On "emigration is free," see Freda, *Governare i migranti*, 28–29; Daniele Fiorentino, *Gli Stati Uniti e il Risorgimento d'Italia, 1848–1901* (Rome: Gangemi Editore, 2013), 250.

21. King Umberto I, Regio decreto 10 gennaio 1889, n. 5892, che l'approva l'annesso regolamento per l'esecuzione della legge 30 dicembre 1888, numero 5866 sull'emigrazione, 5892 serie 3a § (1889), articles 16 and 20. *https://www.gazzettaufficiale.it/eli/gu/1889/01/10/8/sg/pdf* (accessed 10 January 2023).

22. Robert F. Foerster, "A Statistical Survey of Italian Emigration," *Quarterly Journal of Economics* 23, no. 1 (1908): 74–75.

23. Torpey, *Invention of the Passport*, 127. For more on Italian politics in the late nineteenth century, see Alexander De Grand, *The Hunchback's Tailor: Giovanni Giolitti and*

*Liberal Italy from the Challenge of Mass Politics to the Rise of Fascism, 1882–1922* (Westport, Conn.: Praeger, 2001).

24. Royal decree no. 36 on passports and Law no. 23 on emigration, both 31 January 1901. See Torpey, *Invention of the Passport*, 126–27 and notes.

25. Torpey, 126.

26. Quoted in Torpey, 127–28, from Atti del Parlamento Italiano, Camera dei Deputati, sessione 1900, 1, della XXI legislatura, vol. 1 (Rome: Tipografia della Camera dei Deputati, 1900), 604.

27. Torpey, *Invention of the Passport*, 127–28.

28. Aliza Wong, *Race and the Nation in Liberal Italy, 1861–1911: Meridionalism, Empire, and Diaspora* (New York: Palgrave Macmillan, 2006), 116.

29. Claudia Baldoli, *A History of Italy* (Basingstoke, U.K.: Palgrave Macmillan, 2009), 226.

30. See Baldoli, 218. See also Wong, *Race and the Nation*, 116; Nicholas Doumanis, *Italy: Inventing the Nation* (London: Arnold / Oxford University Press, 2001), 117. The number of Socialist deputies increased from six at the founding of the National Socialist Party in 1892 to thirty-two in 1900.

31. Torpey, *Invention of the Passport*, 128–29.

32. Wong, *Race and the Nation*, 116.

33. Torpey, *Invention of the Passport*, 128–29.

34. See Fiorentino, *Gli Stati Uniti e il Risorgimento d'Italia*; Giampaolo Ferraioli, *L'Italia e l'ascesa degli Stati Uniti a rango di potenza mondiale* (Naples: Edizioni Scientifiche Italiane, 2013).

35. Marcello Curti, ed., "Lo statistico e l'industriale: Carteggio tra Luigi Bodio e Alessandro Rossi (1869–97)," *Annali di statistica* anno 128, serie X, no. 19 (1999): 53. Bodio had asked Egisto Rossi to provide extensive notes on his drafts of the report for 1880 and 1881 based on Rossi's direct knowledge of conditions for Italian emigrants in the United States. Before his appointment to the commissariat, Bodio had most recently served as the director of the Italian Bureau of Statistics during a difficult time when Parliament made painful cuts to the agency's budget. Those cuts contributed to the failure of the 1891 census, which devastated him. Curti, "Lo statistico e l'industriale," 219.

36. Political resistance from shipowners and transport industry also interfered. See Curti, 220.

37. Curti, 220, citing Z. Ciuffoletti, *Luigi Luzzatti e l'emigrazione*, in *Luigi Luzzatti e il suo tempo*, ed. P. Pecorari and P. L. Ballini (Venice: Ist. Ven., 1994), 479–98.

38. Curti, "Lo statistico e l'industriale," 220, quoting Bodio, "Dell'emigrazione italiana e dell'applicazione della legge 31 gennaio 1901," *Bollettino dell'emigrazione* 8 (1902): 3–30.

39. Eliot Lord, John J. D. Trenor, and Samuel June Barrows, *The Italian in America* (New York: B. F. Buck, 1905), 56.

40. For more on the label "social law," see Dolores Freda, "La Legislazione sulle migrazioni italiane fino al 1901," *Studi Emigrazione* 215 (2019): 379–92; on the precedents set, see Maria Rosaria Ostuni, "Leggi e politiche di governo nell'Italia liberale e fascista," in *Storia dell'emigrazione italiana: Partenze*, ed. Piero Bevilacqua, Andreina De Clementi, and Emilio Franzina (Rome: Donzelli Editore, 2001), 314; see Fiorentino, *Gli Stati Uniti e il Risorgimento d'Italia*, on the character of the negotiation.

41. Ostuni, "Leggi e politiche," 314.

42. Donna Gabaccia, *Foreign Relations: American Immigration in Global Perspective* (Princeton, N.J.: Princeton University Press, 2012), chap. 3.

43. Mark Choate, *Emigrant Nation: The Making of Italy Abroad* (Cambridge, Mass.: Harvard University Press, 2008), 90–92.

44. This body was weak relative to the commissariat of 1901 as it lacked enforcement powers, and its scope was limited to actions in Italy since it was housed in the Ministry of the Interior.

45. Foerster, "Statistical Survey of Italian Emigration," 74.

46. Choate, *Emigrant Nation*, 90–92.

47. Betty Boyd Caroli, *Italian Repatriation from the United States* (New York: Center for Migration Studies, 1973), 53.

48. Unfortunately for historians' understanding of the function of the commissariat and the views of these early leaders, the records from the first two years (1901–3) have been lost. According to the official finding aid, the correspondence measured "50,000 letters and around 2,000 telegrams, of which practically nothing remains." For more background and detail on the commissariat in its later years, including what can be researched at the ASDMAE, see Stefania Ruggeri, *Il Fondo archivistico Commissariato generale dell'emigrazione 1901–1927*, vol. 8, *Fonti per la storia dell'emigrazione* (Rome: Istituto poligrafico e Zecca Dello Stato, 1991), quotation on 77.

49. Curti, "Lo statistico e l'industriale," 220.

50. On this episode see Marco Soresina, *Luigi Bodio: Carriera e relazioni personali*, in *Colletti bianchi. Ricerche su impiegati funzionari e tecnici in Italia fra '800 e '900*, ed. Marco Soresina (Milan: Franco Angeli, 1998), 284–98.

51. Caroli, *Italian Repatriation*, 57.

52. The commissariat was eliminated in 1927 in the Fascist reorganization of the government. The early records of the Commissariato generale dell'emigrazione (1901–27) at ASDMAE are not extensive and are quite practical in nature. I have examined boxes 9 and 13, which focus largely on logistics for the planning and construction of a large new emigration port building at Naples.

53. See also Maddalena Marinari, *Unwanted: Italian and Jewish Mobilization against Restrictive Immigration Laws, 1882–1965* (Chapel Hill: University of North Carolina Press, 2019), 23.

54. Oldrini's "Avviso" letter tried to fix this problem. See image 3.1. Alessandro Oldrini, "Emigrante respinto. [Form and Advisory on Process to Claim Refund of Ticket Costs If a Migrant Is Rejected at Ellis Island.]," Office of Information and Protection for Italian Emigrants (1895), box 111, fasc. 2195, p. 1). See also Egisto Rossi, "2.0 Rapporto annuale, dal 30 giugno 1895 al 30 giugno 1896 [2nd Annual Report from the Office of Labor Information and Protection, from 30 June 1895 to 30 June 1896]," 10 September 1896, box 111, p. 8, RDI (hereafter "2nd Annual Report").

55. Rossi, "2nd Annual Report," 35–36.

56. See letter 66 between Bodio and Alessandro Rossi published in Curti, "Lo statistico e l'industriale."

57. These tickets were not equivalent to first, second, and third class but instead referred to the age of the passenger: 8 lire for *posto intero*, 6 lire for a half seat, 2 lire for a quarter of a seat. Children under one year old traveled for free, 1–4 years old pay for a quarter of a seat; 5–10 years old pay half of a seat; 10 years and up pay full seat. See Seba-

stiano Marco Cicciò, *Il porto di imbarco di Messina: L'ispettorato e i servizi di emigrazione (1904–1929)* (Milan: Franco Angeli Edizioni, 2016).

58. Curti, "Lo statistico e l'industriale," 220.

59. Elliott Young, "Beyond Borders: Remote Control and the Continuing Legacy of Racism in Immigration Legislation," in Marinari et al, *Nation of Immigrants Reconsidered*, 33.

60. John Griffin Carlisle and Herman Stump, "Mission to the Italian Government," Senate Report no. 9 (Washington, D.C.: U.S. Senate, 54th Congress, 2d session, December 3, 1896).

61. Letter, Fava to Department of Treasury, reproduced in "Mission to the Italian Government," 3.

62. "Mission to the Italian Government," 3–4.

63. "Mission to the Italian Government," 1. See also Laura Pilotti, *L'Ufficio di informazioni e protezione dell'emigrazione italiana di Ellis Island*, vol. 15, *Fonti per la storia dell'emigrazione* (Rome: Ministero degli Affari Esteri/Istituto poligrafico e Zecca dello stato, 1993), 112–14. The cost of deportation was a major topic of conversation at the two-day summit.

64. Pilotti, *L'Ufficio di informazioni*.

65. Young, "Beyond Borders"; Aristide Zolberg, "The Archaeology of Remote Control," in *Migration Control in the North Atlantic World: The Evolution of State Practices in Europe and the United States from the French Revolution to the Inter-War Period*, ed. Andreas Fahrmeir, Olivier Faron, and Patrick Weil (New York: Berghahn, 2003).

66. "Mission to the Italian Government," 2.

67. See in particular Daniele Fiorentino, *Gli Stati Uniti e il Risorgimento d'Italia 1848–1901* (Rome: Gangemi Editore, 2013); Giampaolo Ferraioli, *L'Italia e l'ascesa degli Stati Uniti a rango di potenza mondiale* (Naples: Edizioni Scientifiche Italiane, 2013); Ferdinando Fasce, *Tra due sponde: Lavoro, affari e cultura fra Italia e Stati Uniti nell'età della grande migrazione* (Genova: Graphos, 1993); Freda, *Governare I migranti*.

68. Letter to Fava describing his mission to Italy in a personal tone, 6 October 1896, box 111, pos. 155, pacco VII, RDI.

69. Fava, "Interpretazione delle leggi americani d'emigrazioni," 10 September 1896, box 111, pos. 155, pacco VII, RDI.

70. "Mission to the Italian Government," 2, 6–8.

71. Egisto Rossi, "Annual Report of the Office at Ellis Island," November 1899, page 16, box 113, fasicolo 2204, RDI.

72. Circular of 8 November 1896, cited in Pilotti, *L'Ufficio di informazioni*, 162.

73. Circular of 8 November 1896 requiring the proof of criminal record, cited in Pilotti, *L'Ufficio di informazioni*, 162.

74. Letter dated 2 August 1897 in box 112, pos. 155, pacco VIII, folder 2199, RDI.

75. See Vincent J. Cannato, *American Passage: A History of Ellis Island* (New York: HarperCollins, 2009), 108.

76. Rossi to Vinci, 13 April 1898, box 112, RDI.

77. Telegram from Rossi to Fava, c. 3 April 1898, box 112, pos. 155a, RDI.

78. Teresa Fava Thomas, "Arresting the Padroni Problem and Rescuing the White Slaves in America: Italian Diplomats, Immigration Restrictionists and the Italian Bureau 1881–1901," *Altreitalie* 40 (June 2010): 71n23.

79. Pilotti, *L'Ufficio di informazioni*, 159.

80. Fitchie to Powderly, 14 July 1898, Terence Powderly Papers, Catholic University of America, quoted in Fava Thomas, "Arresting the Padroni Problem," 71.

81. Fava Thomas, "Arresting the Padroni Problem," 72.

82. Pilotti, *L'Ufficio di informazioni*, 162.

83. Pilotti, 162.

84. Pilotti, 159, quoting Powderly.

85. Pilotti, 159.

86. Vinci to MAE, 5 April 1898, b. 112, fasc. 2202, quoted in Pilotti, *L'Ufficio di informazioni*, 160.

87. Pilotti, 161.

88. Testimony of Hon. T. V. Powderly, Commissioner-General of Immigration, 10 February 1899, *Reports of the Industrial Commission on Immigration, including Testimony . . . and Special Reports*, 15 (Washington, D.C.: Government Printing Office, 1901) 32–46., quoted in Fava Thomas, "Arresting the Padroni Problem," 69.

89. Fava Thomas, "Arresting the Padroni Problem," 69.

90. Fava Thomas argued that Celso Moreno suffered from "status anxiety," which made him chase a diplomatic title. "Perhaps his intense dislike for the Italian embassy staff was linked to its titled diplomats who had once served the Bourbons [whom he appeared to hate], and now filled the foreign ministry's ranks: Baron Fava, Count Oldrini, Marquis Romano, Chevalier Rossi, etc." (61). On Moreno's attacks, see 63; his article was reproduced in Moreno's 1896 self-published treatise, *History of a Great Wrong*. For more on Moreno, see Rudolph Vecoli and Francesco Durante, *Oh Capitano! Celso Cesare Moreno—Adventurer, Cheater, and Scoundrel on Four Continents*, trans. Elizabeth Venditto (New York: Fordham University Press, 2018).

91. Fava Thomas, "Arresting the Padroni Problem," 63–64, 69.

92. Fava Thomas, 70.

93. Cited in Fava Thomas as *Testimony of Dr. Egisto Rossi*, July 26, 1899, *Reports of the Industrial Commission on Immigration*, 15 (Washington, D.C.: Government Printing Office, 1901), 154–60. Prescott Hall and Herman Stump were also called to testify before the commission.

94. Count Vinci to Fava, 13 April 1898, box 112, pos. 155a, RDI.

95. *New York Times*, 26 November 1899.

96. Rossi, 2nd Annual Report, box 113, page 13, emphasis added.

97. Bodio to Blanc, 28 July 1894, b. 113, f. 2206, RDI. The Office was officially chartered by Senate decree on 11 June 1894.

98. Freda, *Governare i migranti*, 56.

99. Marinari, *Unwanted*, 23.

### Epilogue. The Arc of Immigration Restriction in the United States

1. Democratic and Republican administrations have advanced markedly similar policies, and the years under Bill Clinton stand out. In late December 2021, historian Yael Schacher asked on Twitter (pleaded, really) for historians of immigration to examine the 1990s to explain why today the policy debate seems trapped, unable to move beyond frameworks that introduced militarization of the border alongside stirrup pants, oversized flannel, and grunge music. Yael Schacher, Twitter post, 28 December 2021, 9:54 a.m., https://twitter.com/YaelSchacher/status/1475842682245337092.

2. See table A2 in Mae Ngai, *Impossible Subjects: Illegal Aliens and the Making of Modern America* (Princeton, N.J.: Princeton University Press, 2004), 274.

3. Julia Rose Kraut, *Threat of Dissent: A History of Ideological Exclusion and Deportation in the United States* (Cambridge, Mass.: Harvard University Press, 2020). Kraut argues that immigration law has been used as a tool for political repression since 1798.

4. According to figures historian Patricia Russell Evans culled from the records of the former Immigration and Naturalization Service, 67 percent of all aliens excluded from entry to the United States happened under the LPC clause in the period 1892–1900. In these years 22,515 total people were excluded. Cited in Patricia Russell Evans, "'Likely to Become a Public Charge': Immigration in the Backwaters of Administrative Law, 1882–1933" (PhD diss., George Washington University, 1987), 231. Figures are calculated in ten-year increments.

5. House of Representatives, House Committee on Immigration and Naturalization, *Report from the House Committee on Immigration and Naturalization under the Resolution of Jan. 29, 1892 [Affairs on Ellis Island]*, Report no. 2090 (Washington, D.C.: Government Printing Office, 28 July 1892), iv.

6. Figures from Stump's report to Congress; Senner in 1896 identified Italians as the "largest percentage of the detained" at Ellis Island. J. H. Senner, "Immigration from Italy," *North American Review*, June 1896, 650. Roger Daniels estimates that Ellis Island had a rejection rate of around 1 percent. Daniels, *Guarding the Golden Door: American Immigration Policy and Immigrants since 1882* (New York: Hill & Wang, 2004), 35. See also undated newspaper clipping (c. 14 June 1894), box 113, fasc. 220, RDI.

7. Thomas Bailey Aldrich, *Unguarded Gates, and Other Poems* (New York: Houghton Mifflin, 1895), 13–17.

8. Senner, "Immigration from Italy," 496.

9. House of Representatives, House Committee on Immigration and Naturalization, *Report from the House Committee on Immigration and Naturalization under the Resolution of Jan. 29, 1892 [Affairs on Ellis Island]*, Report no. 2090 (Washington, D.C.: Government Printing Office, 28 July 1892), iii–iv.

10. Erika Lee, *America for Americans: A History of Xenophobia in the United States* (New York: Basic Books, 2019); Kraut, *Threat of Dissent*.

11. Jane Hong, comments at roundtable, "Immigration Advocacy Then and Now," 6 April 2019; Julian Lim, Jana Lipman, and Ana Minian, discussion of current research at panel, "Looking Outside the Nation: The Exercise of U.S. Migration Policy and Law Abroad," 5 April 2019, both at Organization of American Historians Annual Meeting, Philadelphia.

12. I. D. Marshall, "Italian Immigrants. Professor Odrini [*sic*] Looks after Them at Ellis Island," *Times* (n.d., c. 1895), box 111, fasc. 2195, RDI.

13. Egisto Rossi, "Annual Report of the Office at Ellis Island," November 1899, box 113, fasc. 2204, 8–9.

14. Rossi, "Annual Report," 16.

15. Cited in Rossi, 20.

16. Daniele Fiorentino, "Gli Stati Uniti e l'Italia dal Risorgimento all'immigrazione," in *Gli Stati Uniti e l'Italia alla fine del xix secolo* (Rome: Gangemi Editore, 2010), 58.

17. Rossi, "Annual Report," 20–21.

18. See Deborah S. Kang, *The INS on the Line: Making Immigration Law on the U.S.-*

*Mexico Border, 1917–1954* (London: Oxford University Press, 2017); David Fitzgerald, *A Nation of Emigrants: How Mexico Manages Its Migration* (Berkeley: University of California Press, 2009).

19. Maddalena Marinari, *Unwanted: Italian and Jewish Mobilization against Restrictive Immigration Laws, 1882–1965* (Chapel Hill: University of North Carolina Press, 2019), 187.

20. Ngai, *Impossible Subjects*, 76.

21. Ngai argued that "immigration policy not only speaks to the nation's vision of itself, it also signals a position in the world and its relationships with other nation-states. At one level this means that foreign policy invariably becomes implicated in the formulation of immigration policy." *Impossible Subjects*, 9.

22. See Joseph Nevins, *Operation Gatekeeper: The Rise of the "Illegal Alien" and the Making of the U.S.-Mexico Boundary* (London: Routledge, 2002). For a comprehensive history of the border patrol, see Kelly Lytle Hernandez, *Migra!: A History of the U.S. Border Patrol* (Berkeley: University of California Press, 2010).

23. This was part of a National Endowment for the Humanities Summer Seminar on "The Cross-Border Connection," led by sociologist Roger Waldinger at the University of California at Los Angeles.

24. Salvador Rivera, "Border Report: More Northbound Lanes Coming to California Port of Entry," KRQE (Albuquerque), 18 September 2020, https://www.krqe.com/news/border-report/more-northbound-lanes-coming-to-california-port-of-entry/. Rivera reported the construction funded by the Mexican government would wrap up in November 2020, following a U.S.-funded $741 million multiphased expansion project completed between 2011 and 2019, according to the Government Services Administration. U.S. General Services Administration, "San Ysidro Land Port of Entry," last reviewed 27 May 2022, https://www.gsa.gov/about-us/regions/welcome-to-the-pacific-rim-region-9/land-ports-of-entry/san-ysidro-land-port-of-entry.

25. On the "unintended consequences" of Operation Gatekeeper, see Douglas S. Massey and Karen A. Pren, "Unintended Consequences of U.S. Immigration Policy: Explaining the Post-1965 Surge from Latin America," *Population and Development Review* 38, no. 1 (March 2012): 1–29.

26. See the 1994 gubernatorial reelection campaign ad of California Republican Pete Wilson, known as "They Keep Coming," https://www.youtube.com/watch?v=oofiPE8Kzng (accessed 19 December 2022), and a 1996 campaign ad for Republican presidential candidate Bob Dole that attempts to make a case for why the nation should care about California's "two million illegal aliens" who, the ad claims, are costing billions of federal tax dollars and pose a risk to the health, safety, and educational opportunities for native-born Americans, https://www.youtube.com/watch?v=pUspqabjZPs (accessed 12 October 2020). For an interesting short take on the language of the "brown tide," see Leslie Berenstein Rojas, "They Keep Coming in a Wave," KPCC, 28 October 2010, https://www.scpr.org/blogs/multiamerican/2010/10/28/8272/they-keep-coming-in-a-wave/.

27. Ira Glass, "Act 2: Kitchen Sink," in episode 656: "Let Me Count the Ways," *This American Life*, WBEZ Chicago Public Radio, original air date 15 September 2018.

# INDEX

Gage, Lyman J., 63
gatekeeping, definition, 8. *See also* emigration policy, Italian; immigration policy, U.S.
gatekeeping partnership, Italy-U.S.: development, 3–4, 6–15, 37–39, 115–16, 160n38; effects of, 145–46; informal diplomacy, 60–62; necessity of collaboration, 161n49; overview, 48–49, 64–67. *See also* diplomatic relations, Italy-U.S.; emigration policy, Italian; immigration policy, U.S.; Sunnyside Plantation, Ark.
Grant, William, 16
Grisanti, Nicholas, 146–47
Grossi, Vincenzo, 69, 180n96
Guglielmo, Thomas, 25

habeas corpus, writs of, 35, 46
*Harper's Weekly* (magazine), 13, 44–46, 174n2
Harrison, Benjamin, 33, 172n119
health inspections, 2–4, 29, 45, 103, 121–22, 124
Hennessy, David, murder of, 11–12, 27, 39, 43, 167n45. *See also* lynching in New Orleans

*Il Corriere Italiano*, 76–77
*Il Progresso Italo-Americano*, 32
illegal emigration (*emigrazione clandestina*), 60
*Illustrated American* (magazine), 23, 24, 25–26
Immigration Act (1891, U.S.): Finality Clause, 18, 38, 46, 171n109; impacts of, 2, 4, 44–45, 174nn1–2; passage into law, 17, 18; proposed amendments, 29–31; Superintendent of Immigration, 18, 24, 46. *See also* Department of Treasury, U.S.; LPC Clause, Immigration Act
Immigration Act (1893, U.S.): Boards of Special Inquiry, 7, 30, 45–46, 143, 175n12; effects, 48, 59, 110, 126–27
Immigration and Naturalization Service (INS), 142
Immigration Bureau, U.S., 4, 46–47, 50
Immigration Commission (Dillingham Commission, U.S. Congress), 10–11, 165n29
Immigration Investigation (U.S. Congress), 146
Immigration Investigation Committee (U.S. Department of Treasury), 52
immigration officers: as border control agents, 142; Code of Conduct, 61; discretionary power, 29–30, 38–39, 52, 61–62, 64, 144–45; inspection protocols, 44–45; LPC clause application, 57–59; uniforms, 46. *See also* Boards of Special Inquiry

immigration patterns: arrivals and exclusions, numbers of, 55–56, 154–56, 179nn70–75; arrivals at Ellis Island, 48, 159n20; colonization efforts, 13–14, 50–51, 68, 92–96, 107–8; destinations, 5, 102, 174n143; Italians versus Chinese, 158n15, 178n64; LPC effects on, 58, 60, 90–91, 178n57; railroad companies' influence, 83, 95, 102–3; recruitment efforts, 95–103, 190–91nn41–45; tramp steamers, 90–91, 96, 118, 187n3. *See also* agricultural colonization; immigration policy, U.S.; Italians in United States
immigration policy, U.S.: control, federal, 6–7, 18, 21, 37–39, 46–49; control shift, regional to federal, 42, 109, 111–13; development, 28–40, 141–45; enforcement, 29–31, 45, 46–48, 55–56; foreign influences, 48, 70–71, 144; Italian response to, 49, 51–52, 68–69, 79–80, 87–88; Italian-U.S. cooperation, 145–46; legal precedents (*see* Supreme Court, U.S.); modern policy, 67, 141–42, 146–49, 182n122, 199n1; national sovereignty, 47, 143–44; plenary power doctrine, 38, 144; recruitment efforts, 95–103, 190–91nn41–45; society, impacts on, 21, 47–48; vague nature of, 4–5, 86, 114, 130–32, 142–43. *See also* asymmetric partnership, Italy-U.S.; Department of Treasury, U.S.; exclusion; gatekeeping partnership, Italy-U.S.; immigration patterns; qualitative restriction
Imperiali, Marquis (Guglielmo), 28, 31, 36, 172n114
IRL (Immigration Restriction League): concerns, 108, 143, 144, 145, 169n74; creation, 42; Ellis Island, investigation of, 14, 109–10, 193n93; literacy test, 13, 92, 96–97, 108–12
Italians in United States: industrial work, 5, 40; labor recruitment, 94–97; in Louisiana, 39–41; protection of, 20, 117–18, 138–39; race politics, 26–27, 47, 164n20, 168n64; San Francisco murders, 34–35; status, 19, 41, 70, 94–97, 101–2. *See also* agricultural colonization; immigration patterns; lynching in New Orleans
Italy: citizenship laws, 171n103; economic conditions, 73; emigration regulation debate, 38, 59, 80; protection of emigrants, 19, 62–63, 82, 88, 107–8; Southern Question, 10, 11, 25–26, 163n1; U.S. immigration policy and, 4–5. *See also* emigration policy, Italian; Ministry of

*North American Review* (journal), 17, 47–48, 60, 143, 174n1

North Carolina, 98

*Nuova Antologia* (magazine), 32, 37, 59–60, 69, 173n26

Office of Immigration, U.S., 7, 29, 31, 142

Office of Labor Information and Protection for Italians, Ellis Island ("the Office"), 49–54; Barge Office, 63, 134, 138, 176n28; closure of, 50, 63–64, 133–38; creation of, 8, 12–13, 50–53, 71; emigrant education, 57–58, 83–86, 85; LPC and, 53–54, 57–61, 84, 178n59; mission, 86; padrone system, 51–52, 64, 66, 137; role, 48–49, 51–52, 63, 146, 190n39

Oldrini, Alessandro: bulletin for consuls, 83–86, 85; career, 53, 54, 178n55; colonization efforts, 97–98, 104; libel against, 136–37; protection of immigrants, 13, 58–61, 79–84, 127, 145; rapport with U.S. officials, 49–50, 54, 65–67, 84; Sunnyside and, 72–73, 74, 93–94, 95, 107

Operation Gatekeeper (1994, U.S.), 147–49

padrone system, 51–52, 64, 66, 136, 137, 159n19

Papini, Giuseppe, 37, 163n9

Parkerson, William S., 22, 39

Parlange (judge), 36

passports: emigration restriction, 84, 117, 118, 120–23, 125; immigration requirements, 3–4, 187n8

Polizzi, Emanuele, 23, 163n7

Polmonari, Egisto, 105, 192n73

Powderly, Terence, 14, 63, 134–37, 139

public charge. *See* LPC Clause, Immigration Act

*Puck* (magazine), 23–24

qualitative restriction: Alien Contract Labor Law, 51, 75–76; class-based decisions, 5, 18, 29–30, 45–47, 64, 68; colonization and, 91–92; foundations of, 9, 47–48, 143–44, 146; immigration patterns and, 179nn70–71; literacy tests, 92, 108–13, 162n53, 193n106; medical inspections, 2–4, 29, 45, 103, 121–22, 124; undesirable immigrants and, 3, 9–10, 14, 25, 37, 68

quantitative restriction, 9, 45, 142, 193n106

race politics: color versus race privilege, 25–27; criminality and gatekeeping, 10–11; Italians and African Americans, 26–27, 168n64; postwar labor recruitment, 94–96, 101–2

Remain in Mexico policy (U.S.), 148, 158n10

remote control: beginnings of, 30, 48, 69; colonization as, 88–89, 113–14; De Martini and Bertini case, 81–83; definition, 2–3; gatekeeping and, 6–11, 144–46, 147; limitations, 66, 83; 1901 emigration law, 9, 131; overlap of U.S.-Italian laws, 54. *See also* Emigration Law (1888, Italy); Emigration Law (1891, Italy); emigration policy, Italian

Romano, C. F., 105–6

Roosevelt, Theodore, 32–33, 134–35, 170n96

Rossi, Egisto: on exclusionary practices, 61, 66, 90–91, 145; relationship with U.S. authorities, 54, 61–62; role, 57–58, 107

Rudinì. *See* di Rudinì, Marquis

Ruspoli, Emanuele (prince), 72, 76, 104

Scala, Luigi, 27, 168n75

Scalabrini, Giovanni Battista, 119–20

Scalabrini, Giuseppe, 11, 123

Scott, Charles, 88–89

Senate, U.S.: Committee on Immigration and Naturalization, 24–25, 142, 143–44; Immigration Committee, 110; Resolution (No. 207), 51, 52, 177n47

Senner, Joseph: Ellis Island role, 52, 57, 60–62, 112, 143, 180n93; on gatekeeping policy, 47–48; IRL and, 193n93; publications, 47–48, 60, 143, 174n1

Shakespeare (mayor), 22

shipping companies, 80, 93–94, 103, 116, 154–56, 194n113

Sicilian versus Italian identity, 25–26, 163n1

Social Law. *See* Emigration Law (1901, Italy)

society, immigration's effects on, 21, 25, 47–48

Southern Question (Italy), 10, 11, 25–26

sovereign power, 47, 143–44

Starabba, Antonio. *See* di Rudinì, Marquis

steamship companies. *See* shipping companies

Stump, Herman: career, 46, 177n34; immigration concerns, 29–31, 39, 46, 64, 142–44; Italians' relationship with, 50–51, 65–66; Italy visit, 14, 91, 130–33; reports to Congress, 24–25, 142–44, 146

Sunnyside Company (Corbin Company), 71–72, 104–6

Sunnyside Plantation, Ark., 71–78; contract terms, 74, 75–76, 104, 107; contracts, Italians' release from, 106–7; gatekeeping partnership, 13–14, 68, 79, 89, 103–8; living conditions, 74,

Sunnyside Plantation, Ark. (*continued*)
76–78, 103–6, 107; organization plan, 72–74;
recruitment for, 70–71; settlers, 74, 76, 92–93,
104; in southern context, 92–93
Superintendent of Immigration, 18, 24, 46. *See
also* Department of Treasury, U.S.; Immigration Act (1891, U.S.); immigration officers
Supreme Court, U.S.: *Chae Chan Ping* case,
47; constitutionality of exclusion, 29; federal immigration regulation, 7, 45; *Fong Yue
Ting* case, 47, 49, 143–44, 147, 176nn21–22;
*Nishimura Ekiu* case, 47, 171n110

*Times-Democrat* (New Orleans), 37, 39, 95
Tontitown, Ark., 106
tramp steamers, 90–91, 96, 118, 187n3
Treasury. *See* Department of Treasury, U.S.
Treaty Rights of Foreigners, 36
Trump, Donald, 148

United States: Bureau of Immigration, 4, 46–47,
50; gatekeeping nation, development as, 2–3;
immigration's effects on society, 21, 25, 47–
48. *See also* Congress, U.S.; Department of
Treasury, U.S.; immigration policy, U.S.; Italians in United States; Senate, U.S.

Virginia, 98–99
Vittorio Emmanuele II (king), 1, 157n1
Vivarelli, Giovanni, 105, 192n73
*Voce del Popolo* (San Francisco), 34

Watkins, George, 74

xenophobia, 29, 112, 144

YMDA (Young Men's Democratic Association),
23, 27

## POLITICS AND CULTURE IN THE TWENTIETH-CENTURY SOUTH

*A Common Thread:*
*Labor, Politics, and Capital Mobility in the Textile Industry*
BY BETH ENGLISH

*"Everybody Was Black Down There":*
*Race and Industrial Change in the Alabama Coalfields*
BY ROBERT H. WOODRUM

*Race, Reason, and Massive Resistance:*
*The Diary of David J. Mays, 1954–1959*
EDITED BY JAMES R. SWEENEY

*The Unemployed People's Movement:*
*Leftists, Liberals, and Labor in Georgia, 1929–1941*
BY JAMES J. LORENCE

*Liberalism, Black Power, and the*
*Making of American Politics, 1965–1980*
BY DEVIN FERGUS

*Guten Tag, Y'all:*
*Globalization and the South Carolina Piedmont, 1950–2000*
BY MARKO MAUNULA

*The Culture of Property:*
*Race, Class, and Housing Landscapes in Atlanta, 1880–1950*
BY LEEANN LANDS

*Marching in Step:*
*Masculinity, Citizenship, and The Citadel in Post–World War II America*
BY ALEXANDER MACAULAY

*Rabble Rousers:*
*The American Far Right in the Civil Rights Era*
BY CLIVE WEBB

*Who Gets a Childhood?:*
*Race and Juvenile Justice in Twentieth-Century Texas*
BY WILLIAM S. BUSH

*Alabama Getaway:*
*The Political Imaginary and the Heart of Dixie*
BY ALLEN TULLOS

*The Problem South:*
*Region, Empire, and the New Liberal State, 1880–1930*
BY NATALIE J. RING

*The Nashville Way:*
*Racial Etiquette and the Struggle for Social Justice in a Southern City*
BY BENJAMIN HOUSTON

*Cold War Dixie:*
*Militarization and Modernization in the American South*
BY KARI FREDERICKSON

Printed in the United States
by Baker & Taylor Publisher Services